BORDERLINES AND
BORDERLANDS

BORDERLINES AND BORDERLANDS
Political Oddities at the Edge of the Nation-State

Edited by Alexander C. Diener and Joshua Hagen

ROWMAN & LITTLEFIELD PUBLISHERS, INC.
Lanham • Boulder • New York • Toronto • Plymouth, UK

Published by Rowman & Littlefield Publishers, Inc.
A wholly owned subsidiary of The Rowman & Littlefield Publishing Group, Inc.
4501 Forbes Boulevard, Suite 200, Lanham, Maryland 20706
http://www.rowmanlittlefield.com

Estover Road, Plymouth PL6 7PY, United Kingdom

British Library Cataloguing in Publication Information Available

Library of Congress Cataloging-in-Publication Data

Borderlines and borderlands : political oddities at the edge of the nation-state / edited by Alexander C. Diener and Joshua Hagen.
  p. cm.
 Includes bibliographical references and index.
 ISBN 978-0-7425-5635-5 (cloth : alk. paper) — ISBN 978-0-7425-5636-2 (pbk. : alk. paper)
 1. Boundaries. 2. Boundary disputes. 3. Human territoriality—Political aspects. 4. Geopolitics. I. Diener, Alexander C. II. Hagen, Joshua, 1974–
 JC323.B6665 2010
 320.1'2—dc22
                                2009039997

∞ ™ The paper used in this publication meets the minimum requirements of American National Standard for Information Sciences—Permanence of Paper for Printed Library Materials, ANSI/NISO Z39.48-1992.

Printed in the United States of America

Contents

Figures and Table

Figures

Table

Acknowledgments

First and foremost, we would like to thank the chapter authors. This volume would not have been possible without their expertise, dedication, and hard work. We would also like to thank two institutions that provided vital financial assistance for this volume: Pepperdine University, which helped fund the cartographic work; and the Alexander von Humboldt Foundation, which supported research for chapter 8. We would be remiss if we did not acknowledge the efforts of Susan McEachern and her colleagues at Rowman & Littlefield in formatting, proofing, and designing this volume, Cory Johnson of XNR for his cartographic work, and the two anonymous reviewers for their helpful comments. Finally, we would like to thank our families: John and Bethany Diener, and Rachel, Sabina, and Oliver Hagen.

1

Introduction

Borders, Identity, and Geopolitics

Alexander C. Diener and Joshua Hagen

FORMING A NARROW GATEWAY between the Mediterranean Sea and the Atlantic Ocean, the Strait of Gibraltar and its adjoining territories have been the scene of international competition and conflict for centuries. Combatants have included Romans and Visigoths, Moors and Christians, English and French, to name but a few. Indeed, territorial disputes along this strategic waterway linger as sources of international contention into the twenty-first century. A quick examination of a contemporary map of the region reveals the odd border arrangements that have resulted from the shifting fortunes of this centuries-long struggle for political and military control of the territories flanking the strait (figure 1.1).

Although Spanish territory dominates the northern shores of the strait today, the striking coastal promontory known as Gibraltar is in fact a British overseas possession. Following its seizure from Spain in 1704, Gibraltar served as an important military hub for the expanding British Empire. While most British colonies achieved independence after World War II (1939–1945), Gibraltar and its small, but largely pro-British, population remained under British control. For more than three centuries, successive Spanish governments have claimed that full legal sovereignty should lie with them, leading to numerous unsuccessful attempts to overturn British rule. The acrimony eventually led the Spanish government to close all the border crossings with Gibraltar in 1969, but this "siege" actually strengthened anti-Spanish sentiment among Gibraltar's inhabitants. Fortunately, representatives from Gibraltar, Britain, and Spain have recently agreed on a series of measures to relax border restrictions and facilitate connections between Gibraltar and Spain. Despite

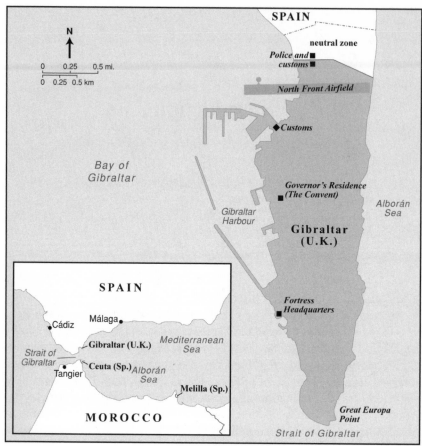

FIGURE 1.1
The British and Spanish Exclaves along the Strait of Gibraltar. Cory Johnson of XNR.

these steps, Spain continues to assert its claim to "rightful" ownership of Gibraltar. Indeed, Spain's willingness to reopen the border could be interpreted as a new strategy to improve Spain's image and political influence within the territory through greater economic integration and cooperation.[1]

Ironically, while struggling to push this small British presence from what it regards as Spanish territory, Spain has been embroiled in similar border disputes with Morocco on the other side of the strait. Like Britain, Spain gradually relinquished its remaining possessions in Africa after 1945. Yet Spain was able to maintain control over Ceuta and Melilla, two relatively small Spanish-majority cities along the northern coast of Africa. After being under Muslim control for several centuries, the cities fell captive to Spanish forces by the sixteenth century. Although Moroccans insist that Spain vacate what they regard as occupied and colonized territories, the Spanish government has remained steadfast. Indeed, recent visits to the cities by Spain's prime minister and king were intended to demonstrate Spanish resolve and triggered strong denouncements from the Moroccan side. While the status of these cities obviously continues to be a source of discord between the two countries, the apparent oddity of Spanish territorial outposts in Africa has not gone unnoticed beyond the region. Leaders of the Al Qaeda terrorist organization, for example, have exhorted followers to destroy the Spanish presence in North Africa. On the other hand, thousands of poverty-stricken migrants, primarily from western Africa, have recently tried to enter Ceuta and Melilla as way stations toward better economic prospects in Europe. While some manage to make the crossing, expanded border barricades and policing by both Spanish and Moroccan forces have resulted in the deaths of several migrants.[2] In contrast to the recent relaxation of border controls between Spain and Gibraltar, it appears that the Spanish-Moroccan borders are likely to experience the opposite trend in the near future.[3]

While the apparent oddity of the international borders along the Strait of Gibraltar may appear without precedent, anyone who peruses a world atlas will soon notice other borders or portions of borders with seemingly odd or discontiguous shapes. Indeed, these borders are often the subject of conflicting territorial claims and international tension. The continued division of the islands of Cyprus and Ireland, the Nagorno-Karabakh region disputed by Armenia and Azerbaijan, and Angola's Cabinda exclave are just a few examples. Yet people rarely reflect on the historical development or contemporary significance of international borders, regardless of their shape. For many people, the lines that divide the world's landmasses possess an air of unquestionable sanctity, as though they were based on some higher logic.

This is simply not the case. Indeed, professional geographers have long discounted the notion of "natural" borders. All borders, whether they appear oddly contrived and artificial, as in some of the examples mentioned above, or appear to be based on objective criteria, such as rivers or lines of latitude, are and have always been constructions of human beings. As such, any border's delineation is subjective, contrived, negotiated, and contested. While this is true of virtually any scale of place, from the personal, to the municipal, to the provincial, to the international, the modern political map of the world has been largely shaped by disputes over land and the division of resources between states (i.e., countries). Even today, more than a hundred active border disputes (not counting disputed islands) exist among the 194 independent states worldwide.[4] This means that of the roughly 301 contiguous international land borders, some 33 percent are sites of contestation.

Obviously, examples of contested international boundaries and border-related issues abound, but ironically they exist today amid a growing sense that borders are diminishing in importance. Reflecting on the development of the European Union, the North American Free Trade Agreement, and other supranational institutions, some scholars have posited a general de-territorialization of national economies, state sovereignty, and human identity leading to the emergence of a borderless world. If projected uncritically into the future, such trends would seem to signal the end of the state's role as the primary organizational unit of global political space. This volume demonstrates that even though the role of borders may be changing and scholars may be gaining new insights into the processes of bordering and the institutions related to borders, a borderless world is not an imminent possibility. Rather, processes of transnationalism and transmigration, as well as terms such as transborder and transstate, are significant only to the extent that something remains to "trans" (i.e., cross, breach, or span). In short, borders still matter.

This volume focuses on select international borders and the visually odd territorial shapes they demarcate in an effort to challenge the general perception of borders as immutable, natural, or sacred features of the geopolitical landscape. The individual chapters examine some of the world's most glaring border oddities, the historical context in which these borders came into existence, and the effect these borders have had and continue to have on the people and states they bound. By focusing on some of the most visually striking borders, the volume aims to demonstrate that *all* borders and territories, even those that appear "normal" or "natural," are social constructions. In an era where the continued relevance of the state is being questioned and where transnationalism is altering the degree to which borders effectively demarcate spaces of belonging, such a point is of great importance.

Frontiers, Borders, and Border Studies

Although modern maps of the ancient world often give the impression that these earliest civilizations were highly integrated political entities bounded by clearly defined borders, the reality was often much more complicated. Although their rulers may have desired sharp international borders, ancient empires, like that of the Romans spanning the Mediterranean basin or the Han Dynasty covering much of modern-day China, tended to have relatively vague political borders in practice. Unlike the clearly demarcated border lines that characterize much of the modern world, these empires were generally bounded by frontier zones. Such zones suggested a more gradual transition of political control containing a mixture of imperial forces, various allied or tributary states, and possible opponents.

Despite their appearance to modern viewers, the Roman defensive *limes*, which ringed much of the empire, or the Great Wall of China, built over several centuries through the borderlands between ancient China and the Mongolian steppe, did not in practice mark the end of imperial territory, power, or activity. Instead of "precisely demarcated borders," one scholar noted, "the history of Chinese wall-building gives no clear sense of a bricks-and-mortar frontier maintaining Chinese within and barbarian northerners without."[5] Despite the Great Wall's depiction of China as "unified and bounded by clearly demarcated borders since time immemorial, a strong case can be made for a more nuanced and dynamic view of China's imperial boundaries as being mobile and indeterminate."[6] For ancient Romans as well as modern visitors, the monumental nature of Hadrian's Wall, a system of forts, towers, and walls stretching across northern England, gives the impression of marking the exact limits of imperial rule. Yet as one historian noted: "Rather than thinking of Hadrian's Wall as a fence, it might be more accurately seen as a spine around which Roman control of the north of Britannia toughened and stabilized."[7] The various Roman successor states, including the early Byzantine Empire in the east and the Germanic kingdoms in the west, as well as the Ottoman Empire, premodern Japan, and Iran, also possessed relatively fluid and ill-defined frontiers.[8]

Much of the modern state system, including contemporary notions of borders, territory, and sovereignty, can be traced to political developments beginning in Europe around the sixteenth century. This does not imply that societies outside of Europe did not possess their own conceptions of political and territorial organization,[9] but rather that the extension of European colonial and imperial control over much of the world entailed wide-ranging political and territorial reorganizations of these lands, societies, and economies according to European norms. It was largely the political and geographical notions championed by Europeans that provided the basis for the state system that dominates the modern world.

Yet the emergence of Europe's political space as a collection of sovereign, centralized states evolved over several centuries. Politics, law, and governance in medieval Europe were structured around what is popularly known as the feudal system. Feudalism involved a complex and varied system of contractual privileges and responsibilities where subservient vassals were granted the right to control land and its income in exchange for pledging service and loyalty to a lord. This seems to suggest a clear hierarchy of territorial control, with Europe's kings, emperors, and popes at the top. Yet the hereditary nature of feudal land title eventually produced a complicated web of decentralized decision making, discontiguous territorial holdings, and overlapping (and at times, divided) loyalties. While the dukes of Burgundy, for example, possessed large land holdings within the Kingdom of France, they also held considerable territories in the Holy Roman Empire. The dukes technically owed simultaneous allegiance to the French kings and the German emperors. As a result, borders between feudal territories generally remained vaguely defined. Instead of clear linear demarcations of sovereign territorial control, Europe's political frontiers were marked by "indeterminacy and permeability."[10]

This began to change gradually as Europe's feudal system gave way to what scholars commonly refer to today as the modern state system. The reasons for this shift are incredibly complex and can be dealt with only briefly here. In the simplest terms, the emergence of the modern state system in Europe was marked by the increasing exercise of political and economic control by a central government, first embodied by a monarch but later usually vested in democratically elected institutions. This was a highly contingent and interactive transformation involving a range of factors including the rise of capitalism and industrialization, the development of a professional civil service, growing demands for popular representation, and especially the emergence of nationalism as a mass phenomenon. Indeed, many of the new states were strongly identified with and controlled by one dominant national group. The idea of the nation-state, where the political borders of the state would coincide with the cultural boundaries of the nation, had become the ideal, although not the norm, by the beginning of the twentieth century.[11]

As political power became centralized, the ability of governments to control territory effectively increased dramatically. States could now devote greater attention to the clear demarcation of their borders. Whereas broad, ill-defined frontiers were once satisfactory, the development of modern states helped stimulate the delineation of precise borders marking which territories, populations, and economies were included in the state's jurisdiction and which were excluded. Implicit here was also a new understanding of sovereignty. Unlike the European feudal system, which entailed somewhat flexible and overlapping conceptions of sovereignty, the new state system posited the world as a mosaic of centralized governments, each possessing absolute political sovereignty over some clearly defined territory and the undivided allegiance of its inhabitants. While nearly impossible to achieve in practice, this reorganization did necessitate a new function for international borders.

The desire by European governments to move from vague frontiers to more precise borders, both for their national homelands in Europe as well as their extensive overseas possessions, obviously raised the question of what criteria should be used to determine these borders. Various proposals for border delineation emerged beginning around 1500, and by the end of the eighteenth century, the idea that borders should coincide with "natural" features had become widely accepted. It was believed that these natural borders, as opposed to artificial borders, would be more stable and less likely to generate conflict. The assumption was that nature had already predetermined "correct" international borders. States simply had to seek them out and adjust their borders accordingly.

Although seemingly offering an objective basis for delineating international boundaries and arbitrating border disputes, individuals tended to interpret the term *natural* in ways that supported their particular geopolitical agendas. Many French writers, for example, argued that borders should follow physiographical features, such as rivers or mountain ranges, a view that provided a convenient justification for annexing new territories.[12] Reflecting rising nationalist sentiment, others contended that it was "natural" for the state's borders to encompass all the members of one nationality. Numerous German nationalists believed that the borders of their state should expand to include all German speakers, regardless of physiographical features. Often labeled the founder of political geography, the German professor Friedrich Ratzel argued that Darwinian ideas from the biological sciences also governed the spatial characteristics of state formation, growth, and decline. Ratzel likened states to organic entities that required "living space" to survive. As the leading edge of this territorial competition between states, international borders were seen as the fluid and dynamic outcomes of this "natural" struggle for living space.[13] Although the idea of natural borders seemed logical, it did not lead to objective criteria for determining the territorial limits of states. Rather, border theorists, heavily influenced by nationalist perspectives, invariably put forth criteria for natural borders that supported their own particular territorial aspirations.

The dramatic territorial realignment initiated by World War I (1914–1918) triggered a surge of interest in border studies in Europe. A variety of practical approaches to setting borders was put forth in an effort to reduce the likelihood of military conflict, but many of those approaches still maintained the dichotomy between natural and artificial borders. As one author noted: "Where no natural feature exists to mark the place at which the territory of one state ends and another begins it is necessary to establish some artificial boundary mark."[14] While authors varied in the relative weight they placed on physiographic features, geopolitical strategy, or ethnographical characteristics when positioning international borders, they generally viewed natural borders, however defined, as good and artificial borders as bad. Given the continued importance of natural borders, it is not surprising that these studies tended to be highly subjective, often reflecting their authors' national origins.

Partially in response to these inherent biases and the difficulties in defining and locating objective natural borders, professional geographers soon concluded that all borders were arbitrary, subjective, and the result of human decisions, not forces of nature. "All political boundaries are man-made, that is, artificial; obviously, they are not phenomena of nature," Richard Hartshorne argued. "Consequently, man, not nature, determines their location; we must eliminate, therefore, any distinction between 'natural' and 'artificial' political boundaries."[15] As a result, most border research during the 1930s and 1940s focused on empirical descriptions of border locations, before-and-after case studies of border realignments, and new systems of border classification.[16] While no standard system of classification or methodology emerged, scholars widely agreed that the natural-artificial distinction was pointless.

While much of the general public continued to think of borders as either natural or artificial, geographers during the 1950s began to reject attempts to develop systems of classification or generalization as useless since each border was regarded as unique. As one scholar noted: "Geographers have spent too much time in devising classifications and generalizations about boundaries and frontiers which have led to little or no progress."[17] Partially as a result, geographers focused on descriptive, nontheoretical case studies aimed at understanding the practical impact of individual borders on international phenomena such as trade and migration.

This new focus was, however, relatively short lived as geographers, for a variety of reasons, nearly abandoned border research altogether during the 1960s and 1970s. At a time when the rest of the social sciences sought to develop overarching theoretical or methodological frameworks, political geographers were concluding that this was not possible regarding international borders. As a result, many geographers shifted their research toward understanding the impact of central governments on internal processes of economic and social modernization. "The phenomenon called the 'state,'" one geographer concluded, "has been accepted by geographers generally as the formal or central subject matter of political geography."[18] The study of borders was viewed as somewhat irrelevant in this line of inquiry since borders were seen as merely separating the modernization process of one state from that of neighboring states without having any real impact on the processes themselves.

The broader geopolitical context of the Cold War also seemed to lessen the importance of international borders. Communist ideologues envisioned a confederation of the world's working classes leading to the collapse of the state system and the dissolution of international borders, while economic integration among capitalist states also suggested a diminishing role for international borders. Reflecting this context of intense geopolitical rivalry, geographers focused on describing each state's "determinants of power" (i.e., population, resources, economy) to gauge its relative power in international relations.[19] Borders were assumed to be rather passive territorial markers. "Whether we like it or not, boundary disputes, so dominant in international politics a generation ago, are fading away from diplomatic agenda," one geographer claimed. "They are replaced in both urgency and importance by problems of a new kind of frontiers—frontiers of ideological worlds."[20]

Surprisingly, renewed interest among geographers in border research began in the 1980s, partially in reaction to predictions of an emerging "borderless world." In response to general trends toward greater economic, cultural, and political integration and cooperation, some scholars, especially economists, predicted that the modern state system that had long dominated world politics was collapsing. These complex processes of transnational integration and interdependence, popularly lumped together under the term *globalization*, were seen as undermining states' sovereignty and leading to their increasing irrelevance. Indeed, economist Kenichi Ohmae asserted in 1995 that "nation states have *already* lost their role as meaningful units of participation in the global economy of today's borderless world."[21] Although one can find similar pronouncements following World War II, growing awareness of the emergence of multinational corporations, global financial markets, and supranational organizations, among other things, fueled declarations of the "end of geography" and the "end of the nation-state."[22]

Despite these bold predictions, numerous geographers, political scientists, and other scholars have demonstrated the continued power of state borders and the centrality of territorial concerns for the political, economic, environmental, and cultural discourses of the early twenty-first century. While the apparent "disappearance" of borders across much of Western Europe is often presented as irrefutable evidence supporting the borderless world thesis, these developments do not appear to be the global norm. It is difficult to argue that a similar "de-bordering" is imminent in, for example, Africa, the Middle East, or Central Asia.

This does not suggest that borders, their functions, or their meanings remain static. Rather, the rich interdisciplinary body of research that has emerged since the 1990s conceives of borders as social constructions possessing both material and symbolic aspects, rather than preordained, rigid lines marking the absolute limits of the state.[23] As such, geographers have endeavored to understand the processes involved in border construction and how the dynamics of contemporary globalization, nationalism, migration, or environmental change, for example, may impact these processes. Given the breadth of this field, as well as the highly unique and variable character of state borders around the globe, it may be impossible to develop a single border theory applicable and explanatory of all borders at all times. Nor is it possible to review the entire field in the space available here. Yet there are some general questions, concerns, and themes that characterize much of contemporary border research that can be mentioned succinctly.[24]

Reflecting the persistence of the "borderless" world claims, one obvious point of departure has been to ask whether international borders are indeed becoming more permeable, becoming more rigid, or staying the same. Or, put another way, to what extent are borders "opening" versus "closing"? At present, the answers are ambiguous and at times contradictory. While barriers to international trade have generally declined, for example, security concerns following the September 11, 2001, terrorist attacks have led to increased border enforcement measures in the United States and many other countries. Indeed, in a certain sense, the same border may be in the process of becoming more open to the flow of trade goods, investment, or information via the Internet but simultaneously less open to the flow of people. Indeed, David Newman noted globalization's influence on international borders "is as geographically and socially differentiated as most other social phenomena—in some places, it results in the opening of borders and the associated creation of transition zone borderlands, while in others, the borderland remains a frontier in which mutual suspicions, mistrust of the other and a desire to maintain group or national exclusivity remain in place."[25]

Related to this, some scholars have reconceptualized borders as areas of transition and meeting. Whereas state borders have generally been seen as rather sharp dividing lines, recent research has emphasized borders or borderlands as sites of cultural interaction, exchange, and possibly hybridity. This approach emphasizes how borders "became not sites for the division of people into separate spheres and opposing identities and groups, but sites for interaction between individuals from many backgrounds, hydribization, creolization, and negotiation."[26] While certainly offering opportunities for cultural exchange, it is important to acknowledge that border regions all too often constitute sites of cultural animosity and, unfortunately, military conflict.[27]

Another important avenue in border research examines the growing importance of regional or supranational organizations and their implications for member states. While often cited as evidence of the coming "borderless" world, current research reveals a more complicated and contingent picture. The incremental strengthening of the European Union, undoubtedly the best studied of these organizations, has certainly facilitated cross-border interaction and movement among member states, but it has also entailed greater attention to the borders between EU and non-EU members. As Sami Moisio noted, it remains unclear "whether European integration is producing landscapes of hope and respect or rather re-dividing Europe into two and thus creating distrust and hatred in Eastern Europe."[28]

Finally, although the role of central governments remains an important topic, scholars are increasingly interested in understanding borders on a more local scale. Although not dismissing the importance of governmental institutions or international agreements on borders, the local focus facilitates deeper understanding of how borders may affect and be affected by the everyday, individual experiences of local residents. This approach has produced detailed studies of local interaction between communities facing each other across state borders, but again, the results have proven highly variable. In some instances, local communities have cooperated effectively with their counterparts across the border to achieve common goals, while in other instances, local groups have resisted cross-border cooperation, even when they likely stand to gain from the effort or it has been encouraged by their central governments.[29]

Given the complexities involved, these results are understandable. But rather than diminishing the importance of future border studies, they highlight the need for continued efforts to understand the forces shaping international borders. Indeed, despite the differences in focus, scale, and location, recent research has clearly demonstrated that the world's borders and the processes involved in their construction, maintenance, and evolution continue to play an important role in ordering the world's economies, societies, and geopolitics. "Instead of becoming redundant in a 'borderless' world," James Anderson and Liam O'Dowd argued, "the increasing differentiation, complexity and contradictions of political borders make border research more important and more revealing of wider social change."[30]

Chapter Summaries

All borders have histories, and these histories affect current realities of border regions and the states they bound. In the chapters that follow, scholars examine some oddly shaped international borders and territories in an effort to outline the processes by which they came into existence and the impact they continue to have. Obviously, there are more odd borders than could be reasonably included in this modest volume. Instead of an exhaustive catalog, this volume offers a sampling of some of these borders from around the globe. In the end, the chapters serve to highlight that all borders, regardless of how odd or logical they may appear, are the result of human activity. Yet despite their rather arbitrary origins, these borders have very real consequences for the peoples, places, and things they divide.

In chapter 2, Reece Jones analyzes the complex Indian-Bangladeshi border region. In what could be termed a political archipelago, the partition of British India in 1947 resulted in the creation of ninety-two Bangladeshi (formerly East Pakistan) enclaves in India and 106 Indian enclaves in Bangladesh. This chapter explores the evolution of this extraordinary border region and delves into the complex sociopolitical, cultural, and economic ramifications of such an intermingling of sovereignties.

Nick Megoran examines the Ferghana Valley in chapter 3. The convoluted division of the area between Uzbekistan, Tajikistan, and Kyrgyzstan stemmed from Stalin's desire to designate ethnic republics within the Soviet Union. In practice, these internal divisions had little meaning during the Soviet period. Yet once the Soviet Union dissolved, these formerly internal boundaries became the borders of the newly independent states of Central Asia. The consequences of these Soviet-era policies continue to reverberate throughout the region in complex and troublesome ways.

In chapter 4, William Rowe explores the Wakhan Corridor. To create a buffer territory between their respective empires, the British and Russians agreed to establish a semiautonomous Afghanistan. To ensure a complete separation, this new Afghan state was given an odd eastern appendage known as the Wakhan Corridor. Wedged between Tajikistan, Pakistan, and China, this mountainous corridor region was further isolated as Soviet and Chinese communist regimes closed their respective borders during the Cold War. Its remote location contributes to its continued marginality in the democratization and development of post-Taliban Afghanistan.

Robert Lloyd provides a detailed discussion of the Caprivi Strip that forms the northeastern border of Namibia in chapter 5. Originally carved out to serve Germany's colonial interests, the Caprivi Strip became embroiled in several regional conflicts in the wake of decolonization in southern Africa. The area's extreme poverty and remote location relative to the rest of the country have helped fuel demands among some residents for independence from Namibia.

In chapter 6, David Newman explores the controversial process of fortifying the border between Israel and the West Bank territories. The wall currently under construction along the Green Line dividing the two nations' territories is having and will continue to have profound consequences for people living on both sides. It is, at this point, unclear whether the wall will eventually serve to facilitate the formation of a Palestinian state in the West Bank territories or make such an outcome practically impossible.

Karen Culcasi examines the creation and evolution of the international borders that divide ethnic Kurds in chapter 7. Despite Kurdish demands for the creation of an independent state after World War I, the postwar settlement eventually led to the division of the Kurdish population among Turkish, Syrian, Iraqi, and Iranian territories. Yet following the Gulf War and the invasion of Iraq, Kurds in northern Iraq have achieved a level of de facto independence, although the future prospects of a unified Kurdistan remain ambiguous at best.

In chapter 8, Alexander Diener and Joshua Hagen examine developments leading to the emergence of Russia's Kaliningrad exclave. Before World War II, the area was actually a German exclave. Following Germany's defeat, the Soviet Union annexed the territory and renamed it Kaliningrad. During the Cold War, Kaliningrad was firmly integrated and territorially contiguous with the rest of the Soviet Union. Yet following the collapse of the Soviet Union, Kaliningrad became a Russian exclave situated between Lithuania and Poland.

Chapter 9 features Robert Ostergren's examination of the Principality of Liechtenstein. Nestled between Austria and Switzerland, Liechtenstein is one of the world's smallest sovereign entities. As a result, the principality's territorial integrity has been closely tied to its larger neighbors. Liechtenstein's affiliation and deepening integration with Switzerland since the end of World War II has helped the principality play a disproportionate role in international finance, especially as a reputed tax shelter for wealthy foreigners.

In chapter 10, Eric Carter focuses on Argentina's province of Misiones, the noticeable northerly protrusion between Brazil and Paraguay. Originally home to the Guaraní Indians, the area was dramatically altered by the initial arrival of Jesuit missionaries and later migrants from Europe as well as by contested territorial claims. Although Argentinean sovereignty was eventually secured, a unique Misiones identity has developed, shaped by the region's remoteness, its tropical landscapes, and the constant circulation of people across the adjacent borders.

Finally, Julian Minghi explores the American exclave of Point Roberts in chapter 11. Resulting from the 1846 Oregon Treaty that established the forty-ninth parallel as the boundary between the United States and Canada in the Pacific Northwest, Point Roberts occupies the southernmost tip of the Tsawassen Peninsula, Washington. This chapter examines the exclave's creation, development, and finally its contemporary sociopolitical and economic evolution following the implementation of the post-9/11 border security measures.

The book's brief conclusion reviews recent writings on the nature and role of borders within an increasingly globalized world. While some have predicted the emergence of a borderless world where traditional states are irrelevant, this conclusion and the preceding chapters demonstrate that borders are and likely will remain important factors in contemporary economic, political, and cultural affairs. Although borders retain significance, the conclusion does not indicate that their function and meaning remain constant. Rather, it discusses how borders are evolving in the changing global context of the twenty-first century.

2

The Border Enclaves of India and Bangladesh

The Forgotten Lands

Reece Jones

THE 198 ENCLAVES ALONG the northern border between India and Bangladesh are enigmas even within each country. While preparing to travel to the area in northern Bangladesh where many of the enclaves are located, conversations with Bangladeshi colleagues revealed that most were only vaguely aware that there are more than one hundred islands of Indian territory inside their country. Are there border guards at the enclaves? No one knew. Are there fences around the enclaves like the one India was building along the rest of the border? Maybe. The uncertainty extended to the location of the enclaves. I had some rough maps found on the Internet, but they were only sketches because official maps are unavailable. With the exception of Dahagram, a large enclave over which Bangladesh has maintained sovereignty, the rest of the enclaves are not depicted on any maps in Bangladesh. It is as if they do not exist (figure 2.1).

As my research assistant and I walked down a dirt path toward a stand of bamboo trees, where a man on the main road had told us an Indian enclave was located, we did not know what to expect. We cautiously passed the bamboo, and we saw that the path continued through some fallow rice paddies toward a field of turmeric. An old woman was coming toward us along the path, so we asked her where the enclave was. "The enclave?" She responded, "You are in it now. When you crossed that embankment and entered this field you came into the enclave." "So this is India?" we asked her. She thought for a moment and said, "I don't know, it's an enclave." She kept going down the path and crossed into Bangladesh to gather some firewood.

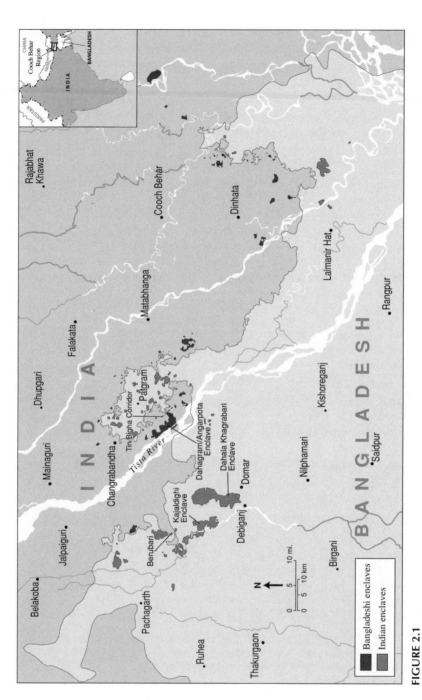

FIGURE 2.1

The Northern Border between India and Bangladesh Showing the Enclaves on Both Sides. Cory Johnson of XNR.

Just as the enclaves are invisible on most maps, they are also largely invisible on the ground. There are a few remaining concrete pillars from a British survey in the 1930s, but many have been knocked down or simply buried over the past seventy years. On the Bangladeshi side are rice paddies; in the enclave are rice paddies. On the Bangladeshi side are mud paths leading to tin and bamboo houses; in the enclave are mud paths leading to tin and bamboo houses. Indeed, without someone to tell you, it would be easy to pass through an enclave without even realizing it.

However, first impressions are sometimes misleading. The Indian enclaves inside Bangladesh are *not* part of Bangladesh, and their continued existence does have devastating consequences for the people who live in them. Because most are small and located several kilometers inside Bangladesh, they have completely lost contact with India. India does not treat the residents as Indian citizens and provides no services to these areas. However, because the enclaves are not officially Bangladeshi territory either, the Bangladeshi government does not administer them. This leaves the residents in a space without an official authority to set rules and establish order. The roads are made of mud by the residents of the enclaves. There are no bridges or culverts. Electricity, water, and telephone services are not available. There are no markets. There are no schools. There are no health facilities. Nongovernmental organizations (NGOs) are not able to operate in the enclaves. There are no official ways to register land. There are no laws, and there are no police or judges to settle disputes. A forty-four-year-old male resident of an enclave sums it up:

> Although the land in the enclave is Indian, the people here have no contact with India, there is not any administration by India and the people do not get any facilities from India. So we are not Bangladeshi but not Indian either. We are *chitmahal bashi* [enclave people].[1]

This chapter examines the creation of these enclaves and their impact on the everyday lives of the people who continue to live in these stateless spaces. The first half of the chapter provides historical context to the series of decisions that culminated in the creation of the enclaves after the 1947 partition of British India. It also explains the circumstances that have prevented the situation from being resolved over the past six decades. The second half of the chapter, by drawing on interviews with current enclave residents, describes the everyday hardships faced by the estimated one hundred thousand to two hundred thousand people who continue to reside in the enclaves.[2] The conclusion argues that the continued existence of the enclaves sixty years after their creation demonstrates the problems that arise from territorializing basic human rights and linking them to state sovereignty. It concludes that it is the moral obligation of the governments of India and Bangladesh to move beyond rigid claims of sovereignty to resolve the situation by expeditiously exchanging the enclaves.

The Origins of the Enclaves

Although there are many legends about the origins of the enclaves that describe tracts of land being gambled away by drunken maharajas, the actual reason for the creation of the enclaves was the incompatibility of the feudal political schemes that prevailed in South Asia during the Mogul era and the territorial organization of the sovereign state system that was introduced by the British.[3] Before the arrival of the British in South Asia in the late eighteenth century, the northern areas of Bengal were ruled by maharajas and local emissaries of the Mogul empire.[4] These officials often lived in distant administrative centers but collected taxes on the land. The system was not based on territorially de-fined sovereignty, but rather patronage that could vary from village to village.[5] The areas where the enclaves would be formed were particularly remote and roughly in the middle of four different administrative centers: Cooch Behar, Dinajpur, Jalpaiguri, and Rangpur (figure 2.2).

The treaty that eventually resulted in the creation of the enclaves was signed in 1713 at the end of a long war between the maharaja of Cooch Behar and the Mogul rulers who controlled the land to the west. In order for both rulers to save face, the agreement simply stated that hostilities would end and the land controlled by each army would belong to that army's ruler.[6] Without the concepts of territorial sovereignty and political borders, the only important aspect was that the taxes from those areas went to that particular ruler. The agreement had no other consequences at the time because the residents of lands that belonged to the Maharaja of Cooch Behar but were surrounded by land owned by the Mogul rulers of Rangpur could simply pass through the Rangpur-controlled estates to reach Cooch Behar. It was similar to the boundaries of counties inside the United States today; although they have consequences in terms of school districts and taxes, they remain largely un-noticed in the routines of everyday life.

The British, who arrived in South Asia in the middle of the eighteenth century, slowly defeated the Mogul rulers in southern Bengal and claimed their land.[7] As they expanded their territory, the British made the decision to ally with many of the local maharajas in order to avoid excessive military engagements.[8] Although governing a small, remote kingdom, the maharajas of Cooch Behar found themselves in a strategic location close to trade routes

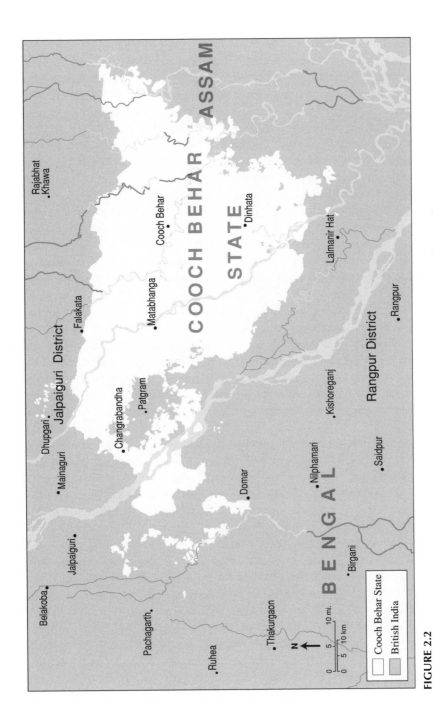

FIGURE 2.2
The Princely State of Cooch Behar during the British Period (late 1700s–1947). Cory Johnson of XNR.

with Tibet.[9] The location of Cooch Behar in the foothills of the Himalayas
prevented the British from bringing a massive army to challenge the maharajas but also meant a friendly ally was desirable there.[10] The maharajas
of Cooch Behar were also modern in their outlook and got along well with
the British.[11] The British tried to honor previous treaties in their diplomatic
relations with the maharajas and adopted the boundaries laid out in the 1713
accord as the limits between their land and the princely state of Cooch Behar.
Consequently, all of the land owned by the maharajas of Cooch Behar remained theirs; including the various estates surrounded by Mogul- and now
British-controlled land.

The British also brought a modern understanding of territoriality and state
sovereignty to South Asia. In order to implement that system, they surveyed
the land, drew maps, and placed boundary markers.[12] The process of survey-
ing the boundaries of the princely state of Cooch Behar was not carried out
until the early twentieth century, and the boundaries of the scattered estates
were finally marked in 1937 with small concrete pillars.[13] The British immediately realized the difficulties these enclaves of land would present for administration, and they promptly exchanged all of the enclaves that were between
other districts they controlled, such as Dinajpur, Jalpaiguri, and Rangpur,
in order to maintain their territorial integrity. However, the residents of the
estates remained loyal to the maharaja of Cooch Behar and did not want to be
exchanged. The British continued to respect the sovereignty of the maharaja,
and the scattered estates were mapped, the boundaries were marked with concrete pillars, but then they were left as they were.[14] During the British period,
this system still had no significant consequences because there were no barriers to movement between the princely state of Cooch Behar and British India.
The arrangement was important only in terms of taxation and land registration. The residents of the Cooch Behar estates went to Cooch Behar for these
services while their neighbors went to the slightly closer British-administered
towns of Dinajpur, Jalpaiguri, or Rangpur.

The critical event that created the enclaves was the partition of British India
in 1947. After much debate, the decision was made to divide British colonial
holdings into two countries, Pakistan for areas with Muslim majorities, and
India for the rest.[15] The two areas with majority Muslim populations were the
western districts, which are contemporary Pakistan, and the eastern half of
the province of Bengal, which is contemporary Bangladesh.[16] The northern
sections of the province of Bengal were a transition area where the populations were almost evenly split between Hindus and Muslims at the time of
the partition. In the 1941 census of India, Rangpur, the farthest to the southeast of the four districts affected by the enclaves, was 71.3 percent Muslim;

Dinajpur, which is in the middle, was 50.7 percent Muslim; Cooch Behar, which is north of Rangpur, was 37.8 percent Muslim; and Jalpaiguri, which is further northwest, was only 23 percent Muslim.[17] Consequently, the partition line was drawn through this area. The district of Rangpur went completely to East Pakistan, while both the Dinajpur and Jalpaiguri districts were divided between the two countries with some subdistricts falling on each side.

The princely states were not officially governed by the British and were not directly addressed in the partition award. Most of the princely states that were completely surrounded by one of the new countries were encouraged to join that country. The maharajas of the princely states that were contiguous with both new countries were given the option of joining either. The accession of the princely state of Kashmir to India, despite its majority Muslim population, has provided a lasting controversy.[18] The princely state of Cooch Behar, however, was 61.6 percent Hindu and had a Hindu maharaja. At the time of the partition it seemed likely that it would opt to join India, which it eventually did two years later, in 1949. Since the land in the scattered estates belonged to the maharaja, he was considered to have sovereignty over them as well, and they also went to India. The land inside Cooch Behar that had been part of the districts of Rangpur and Dinajpur went to East Pakistan, and the enclaves were born (table 2.1).

TABLE 2.1
Number and Area of Indian and Bangladeshi Enclaves

	Bangladesh	India	Total
Enclaves	71	102	173
Counterenclaves	21	3	24
Counter-counterenclaves	1	1	1
Totals	92	106	198
Total area	49.7 km² (19.2 miles²)	69.6 km² (26.9 miles²)	119.3 km² (46.1 miles²)
Exchangeable area	29.0 km² (11.2 miles²)	69.5 km² (26.8 miles²)	98.5 km² (38 miles²)
Berubari union	22.6 km² (8.7 miles²)		
Total area in 1974 agreement	51.6 km² (19.9 miles²)	69.5 km² (26.8 miles²)	121.1 km² (46.8 miles²)

Sources: Whyte 2002; Van Schendel 2002; Vinokurov 2007.
Note: The exchangeable area differs dramatically because the large Bangladeshi enclave of Dahagram will not be exchanged and because Bangladesh has more counterenclaves, which also will not be exchanged.

Disputes between India and Pakistan/Bangladesh

Even after the 1947 partition established an international political border in the area, the creation of the enclaves still did not drastically alter the lives of the residents. In the first few years after the independence of India and Pakistan, the new border was just being surveyed and demarcated, border security forces had not been established, and neither passports nor visas were necessary to travel between the two countries.[19] The residents of the enclaves of Cooch Behar inside East Pakistan could still travel to Cooch Behar unimpeded, just as they had before. The situation had changed for the residents of the enclaves, but the consequences were not immediately clear.

In the years after the partition, relations between India and Pakistan, which British officials had expected to be cordial, deteriorated rapidly. A war had broken out in 1947 over Kashmir, and there was distrust on both sides generated by the appalling violence that marked the migration of refugees across the border.[20] In 1952 Pakistan decided to implement a passport and visa system and begin to securitize the border. The problem posed by the enclaves was recognized at the time, and the residents were promised passports with visas that would allow multiple entries.[21] However, it was unclear how the residents were to apply for and receive them because there were no government offices in the enclaves.

Discussions about exchanging the enclaves also began in the 1950s but were complicated by several factors. First, both countries were writing new constitutions, and it was unclear whether the president, prime minister, or parliament had the authority to make territorial concessions to the other country. Second, the land area of the enclaves on each side was not equivalent. The Indian enclaves inside Pakistan were about 50 percent larger than the Pakistani enclaves inside India. Consequently, any Indian politician that agreed to an exchange would be seen as conceding extra land to an increasingly hostile country. Third, the large Pakistani enclave of Dahagram/Angarpota was only 175 meters (574 feet) from the mainland of East Pakistan. The residents of that enclave wanted to remain with Pakistan, and the government of Pakistan insisted on this arrangement. Fourth, an error by the boundary commission, unrelated to the enclaves but in the same general area, had resulted in a dispute over the union of Berubari.[22] The text of the partition award stated that the union was to go to India, but the published map showed it in Pakistan.[23] Because it was in the same area as the enclaves, it was added to the enclave negotiations. Finally, there was disagreement over whether the residents of the enclaves should be allowed to return to their home country or simply be transferred to the host country with the land.[24]

Despite these impediments and several coups in Pakistan that disrupted the negotiations, an agreement to resolve the situation was reached in 1958. The agreement stated that the enclaves would be exchanged, with the exception of the Dahagram/Angarpota enclave, which would remain with Pakistan, and that the Berubari union would be divided in half, with the northern section going to India and the southern half to Pakistan. This solution was not popular in India and was stalled by repeated court challenges. The final judgment removing all legal obstacles on the authority of the prime minister of India to make the exchange was handed down by the Supreme Court of India on March 29, 1971.[25] The exchange of the enclaves, based on the 1958 agreement between India and Pakistan, could be carried out. Unfortunately, Bangladesh had declared its independence from Pakistan three days earlier, and a civil war was beginning in East Pakistan. Bangladesh eventually gained its independence, with the help of the Indian army, in December 1971.[26] Consequently, agreements between India and Pakistan were no longer valid, and any treaties had to be renegotiated with the newly independent government of Bangladesh.

The government of independent Bangladesh had substantially stronger ties to India, and in 1974 a new agreement on the enclaves was signed. It was identical to the 1958 agreement except that India was given all of Berubari union, which India had maintained possession of since 1947, to make up for the uneven land area of the enclaves.[27] This change generated protests in Bangladesh and led to several court challenges. Unlike the Indian cases, which had dragged on for thirteen years, the challenges in Bangladesh were resolved quickly. In late 1974 the parliament of Bangladesh ratified the treaty and officially transferred sovereignty of Berubari union to India. However, India has still not ratified the treaty, despite the concessions made by Bangladesh. The fate of the enclaves remains stalled in the Indian parliament thirty-five years after the India-Bangladesh agreement was signed, largely because there is persistent resistance to ceding more territory to Bangladesh than will be received in return. Additionally, because the enclaves are small and remote, it is easier to simply put off a decision rather than resolve the situation.

Dahagram/Angarpota and the Tin Bigha Corridor

Despite the intransigence on the broader issue of exchanging the enclaves, some progress has been made in resolving the problems posed by the large Bangladeshi enclave of Dahagram/Angarpota. While many of the smaller enclaves on both sides of the border quickly lost contact with their home countries, the

Dahagram/Angarpota enclave created unique challenges due to its large size, its close proximity to its home country of East Pakistan/Bangladesh, and the desire of its roughly 10,000 residents to maintain their connections with their home country. The enclave, actually two enclaves that are side by side, creating the joint name, is separated from Bangladesh by the Tista River to the west and by a stretch of only 175 meters (574 feet) of Indian territory to the east.[28] Building a bridge over the wide and meandering Tista River was not economically feasible, which forced both sides to work out an agreement for a corridor through the 175 × 85 meter (574 × 279 foot) stretch of Indian territory to the east that separates the enclave from Bangladesh (figure 2.3).

The 1974 Indira-Mujib treaty, which established the framework for exchanging all of the enclaves, included a provision that allowed Bangladesh to retain the Dahagram/Angarpota enclave and granted Bangladesh access to it through the Tin Bigha corridor that would be rented by the Bangladesh government in perpetuity.[29] The proposal to create a corridor through Indian territory was unpopular in India, particularly among nationalist Indian politicians, because it was seen as another instance of ceding sovereignty to Bangladesh.[30] To allay these fears, the agreement was revised in 1982 to make clear that India would maintain sovereignty over the corridor even as it was rented by Bangladesh in perpetuity.

The second argument against the new corridor was that, while allowing Bangladesh access to the Dahagram/Angarpota enclave, it would simultaneously cut off the Indian village of Kuchlibari from the rest of India, making it a new enclave. Kuchlibari, with a population of roughly 60,000 people, is surrounded by Bangladesh on three sides and is just south of the proposed corridor.[31] This was a serious issue because every time the corridor was in use by Bangladeshi residents, it would be closed to Indian Kuchlibari residents who wanted to travel to other parts of India. Despite these objections, the governments of India and Bangladesh reached a final agreement to implement the planned corridor in June 1992. The decision was controversial, and the Bharatiya Janata Party (BJP), an opposition party at the time, used the cause of the Kuchlibari residents as a central part of its political agenda. L. K. Advani, a BJP leader, visited the area and assured the residents of Kuchlibari that they would be protected through violence if necessary.[32] Although the days leading up to the transfer saw protests and violent conflicts with the police, the new corridor was created as planned.

At first, the Bangladeshi residents of the enclave were allowed to pass through the corridor only during three one-hour periods. Over the years, this has been expanded to allow more frequent access, but there are still many times when the enclave residents are not able to travel to mainland Bangladesh.[33] Despite their initial support for the corridor plan, the residents

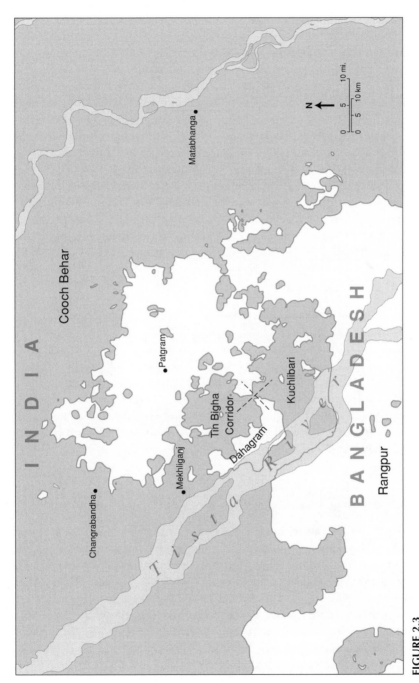

FIGURE 2.3
The Dahagram/Angarpota Enclave and the Tin Bigha Corridor. Cory Johnson of XNR.

of the enclave have found it has made their everyday lives more difficult. Before the corridor was in place, the residents were able to freely cross into India to visit local market towns.[34] Now India has built a fence around the enclave as part of the main border fence completed in 2007 and argues that the residents no longer need access to Indian markets because they can now go to Bangladesh. However, the corridor is subject to many unpredictable and indefinite closings whenever relations between the governments of Bangladesh and India freeze. Consequently, there are ongoing talks between the governments about creating an overpass that would allow unregulated access to the enclave.[35]

In the years since the 1992 agreement on the Tin Bigha corridor, there has been no additional progress on the enclave situation. It is often mentioned in news reports as an agenda item at meetings between Indian and Bangladeshi officials, but the issue is always put off, and the expeditious exchange of the rest of the enclaves appears as unlikely today as during any time of their existence.[36]

Life in the Enclaves

Everyday life in the enclaves is harsh even compared to the poor rural areas of India and Bangladesh that surround them. The lack of administration in the enclaves results in a constant feeling of insecurity, in terms of both the daily threat of violence and persistent concerns about land tenure, food security, and health. Although the residents of the enclaves desperately want their situation to be resolved, after decades of waiting, they have established daily routines and basic support systems that provide some normalcy to their lives.

Reasons for Living in the Enclaves

One of the most surprising characteristics of the enclaves is the fact that very few of the families who were the original inhabitants of the Indian enclaves in Bangladesh remain there today. The majority of the current residents came there through land exchanges in the late 1960s and early 1970s. After the 1947 partition, India and Pakistan established a system through which Hindus whose land was in East Pakistan and Muslims whose land was in the Indian state of West Bengal could swap the land by moving into each other's houses on the opposite side of the border. This system was successful and continued until war between the countries in 1965 led to its permanent suspension. There was consequently no official way for minority populations to immigrate across the border. The enclaves, however, provided an alternative for families who still wanted to move after the official system was ended.

The history of this resettlement in the late 1960s and early 1970s is disputed and, although the enclave residents describe it as a peaceful exchange process, the surrounding Bangladeshi communities remember it as a turbulent period in which Muslim families migrating from India violently evicted the mostly Hindu population living in the enclaves. At that time, there were several violent riots in the Jalpaiguri district of India that targeted Muslim families who had decided to remain there. Because the official exchange program had ended a few years earlier, the only option for moving across the border was to exchange with Hindu families living in Indian enclaves. The land was still officially part of India, which allowed these families to get around the ban on exchanges between the two countries, and it was widely assumed that the land in the Indian enclaves would eventually join Pakistan. Indeed, in the late 1960s the two governments had agreed in principle to trade the enclaves and were waiting only for the Indian courts to finish ruling on the legality of the process. By exchanging into the enclaves or violently occupying them, these Muslim families succeeded in escaping the persecution they were facing in mainland India, and they all assumed they would be quickly joining the predominantly Islamic country of Pakistan (after 1971, Bangladesh).

In addition to the families who came from India, there are some enclave residents who moved into the enclaves from surrounding communities in Bangladesh. These Bangladeshis moved in because property in the enclaves is much cheaper than land in Bangladesh. They are also betting that the enclaves will eventually be exchanged and their landholding will be normalized. Finally, there is a very small percentage of remaining Hindus in the Indian enclaves who are poor and were unable to leave when the rest of their neighbors migrated to India decades ago. These families often did not own land and were not able to participate in the exchanges or were too poor to afford the expenses of traveling to mainland India.

These factors result in the surprising demographics of the Indian enclaves in Bangladesh, which have a population that is almost exclusively Muslim and in percentages that are far higher than even the surrounding areas of Bangladesh proper.[37] This population distribution and the circumstances that brought the majority of the residents to the enclaves undermines the argument that exchanging the enclaves would result in a large population that would want to migrate back to the home country rather than join the host. Indeed, as a forty-five-year-old farmer explains, enclave residents are unanimous that

> [i]t would be best if they exchanged the lands. The areas that India has in Bangladesh would become part of Bangladesh and those areas of Bangladesh that are

inside India would go to India. We would like it to happen tomorrow. . . . But no one hears our cries.

Even if a system that allowed enclave residents the choice of remaining in Bangladesh or repatriating to India was available, it appears that the vast majority of the residents of the Indian enclaves in Bangladesh would not choose repatriation.

Violent and Lawless

By most accounts, the 1980s and early 1990s were a period of substantial violence and instability in the enclaves. As the border between India and Bangladesh was securitized, the last remaining connections with administrators in Cooch Behar were lost, and any semblance of a governing authority disappeared from the enclaves. Insurgent groups such as the Kamtapur Liberation Organization and the Sanwar Group were reported to have taken advantage of the lack of authority to establish training camps in the Dahala Khagrabari and Basunianpara enclaves.[38] In the 1980s the enclaves were also used by thieves as safe zones, where Bangladeshi police could not apprehend them.

In the Kajaldighi enclave the lawlessness culminated with the murder of a prominent politician and two of his brothers in the late 1990s. The politician, the chairperson of a Bangladeshi union council, was asked to arbitrate a dispute over the felling of some trees at the edge of the enclave. As soon as the chairperson and his brothers stepped into the enclave they were captured, held hostage for several days, and later killed. The Bangladeshi residents of the neighboring communities were enraged by the brazen killing of the chairperson, the impunity of the killers in the enclave, and the inability of the Bangladeshi authorities to arrest the perpetrators. They took matters into their own hands and burned down all the houses in that enclave and drove out the residents. It remained abandoned for several months until an understanding was achieved between the two sides and some families slowly moved back.

Although today relations with the surrounding communities have improved, vigilante justice is still the only option because the Bangladeshi police do not have jurisdiction in the enclaves. This has caused many of the enclave residents to enforce order in ways that would be seen as barbaric under most circumstances. A thirty-five-year-old farmer explains:

> In this area, if we catch a thief, then we beat them. Now there are fewer thieves because if we catch them there is no escape for them and they will be finished. There are probably one or two hundred thieves buried under the ground here.

We made them into ashes in a short time. There is not any legal justice here and because of this there is less crime now. The thieves know that if they are caught in the enclaves they will not be left alive.

Through these tactics, many of the enclave residents who had caused problems in previous decades have been killed or forced out of the area. The remaining families appear, under the circumstances, to live a fragile but relatively peaceful existence.

Reliance on Neighboring Communities

Relations with neighboring communities in Bangladesh have also improved partly because the residents of the enclaves have come to realize that they are completely dependent on the good will of their Bangladeshi neighbors to survive. The small size of most of the Indian enclaves means that the enclaves are not able to be self-sufficient in food production. A seventy-five-year-old Bangladeshi man who owns large tracts of land in the enclave explains:

The biggest trouble is that there is not any administration. Because of that we are like parasites on Bangladesh. We have to live by taking help from Domar on one side and Debiganj on the other. If we want to sell our goods at the market, we have to go to Domar or Debiganj. If we want our children to study, they have to do so in Bangladesh. The everyday lives of the enclave residents are absolutely dependent on Bangladesh.

In practice, the residents of the Indian enclaves are completely integrated into the Bangladeshi economy. The enclaves cannot support a market of their own because businesses from Bangladesh are not willing to bring their goods inside the enclave without any laws or police to protect their investments. Consequently, the enclave residents buy all of their supplies in market towns in Bangladesh and sell their crops there during the harvest season. The residents feel they are treated fairly for the most part in these transactions, with the only difference being that they are not eligible for any agricultural subsidies from the Bangladeshi government. The only currency in use is the Bangladeshi taka.

All of the schools that were in the enclaves have been closed because there is not a government to maintain the facilities or pay the wages of teachers. The residents are forced either to not educate their children or to establish residency in Bangladesh, often through illegal means. This is done by using the address of a friend's or relative's house in Bangladesh as their official residence or by buying a small piece of land in Bangladesh, just outside of the enclave, to use in order to be eligible for Bangladeshi services. The residents of the enclaves have repeatedly tried to establish schools but have been unable to secure enough funds for teachers or buildings. A thirty-five-year-old farmer describes the difficulties:

> We had a plan to [build a school] and there is still an acre of land for it. But Bangladesh will not give the salaries for the teachers. Neither will India. We stopped for that reason. There are many people living in the enclave, there is a big need for things like schools and colleges.

Health issues are another problem facing the enclave residents. Because the enclaves are not officially part of the host countries, they are excluded from public health initiatives in the area. Bangladeshi officials question how they can be expected to provide for people who are officially Indian when they do not have enough resources for even their own citizens. At the same time, Indian public health officials are unable to access the enclaves. Beyond the consequences for the everyday health of the residents, the enclaves pose a problem for global disease eradication drives, such as the recent effort to eliminate polio. The enclaves are not properly covered by either country, which leaves gaps that allow diseases to fester. A fifty-year-old farmer and enclave chairperson explains:

> Q: Do you have electricity?
> Electricity is the furthest thing from our minds, people here die from diseases like Cholera. We get very little help. In the whole world there are efforts to eradicate diseases. . . . As hard as they are trying if they do not pay attention to the enclaves it will continue. Will it be able to eradicate it? Never.

Enclave Councils

As it became clear to the residents of the enclaves that their situations would not be resolved expeditiously, the larger enclaves established councils to provide some form of order. Beyond the feelings of insecurity that result from the violent and lawless conditions, the most important issue for many of the enclave residents is land tenure. They face a constant threat from people who seize land in the enclaves by force, and there is no governing authority to legitimate property transactions.

In the years after the partition, the residents would travel to Cooch Behar to buy and sell land. However, as the main political border between the two countries was normalized, securitized, and, more recently, fenced, this process became increasingly arduous. By the 1990s the residents were no longer able to make the trip and began to manage land transactions on their own.

This necessitated the creation of enclave councils to administer transactions, settle minor disputes, and create new deeds for the land. Many enclave councils are composed of unelected elders in the area, but some have even established electoral systems to determine the leaders. These enclaves have campaigns and hold elections every five years. The elections are similar to neighboring communities in Bangladesh except that women are denied a vote. This exclusion is justified on the patriarchal argument that without police to ensure peace during the elections, women could be violently targeted in retaliation for their votes. The fifty-year-old elected chairperson explains the process:

> There are four enclaves that are beside each other. We made a union and have held an election together. Just like Bangladesh has unions, we have a union. At least twelve thousand people live in these four enclaves. We made a system that land transactions are signed in front of the council.
> Q: But where do you register it?
> That is part of my job as the chairman. There is no process for going to India. We are keeping the records for whichever government will come. At the time we will tell the government that we could not go to Haldibari [in Cooch Behar] and we could not register it in Bangladesh. We did it this way and now you need to approve this.

While the enclave residents still hope that their situation will eventually be resolved, many are resigned to the fact that the enclaves have already existed for almost sixty years and the exchange process could very well drag on for many more.

Conclusion

The 198 enclaves along the northern border between India and Bangladesh are stateless spaces that are not integrated into the modern political system of sovereign states. The one hundred thousand to two hundred thousand enclave residents have found themselves living in deplorable conditions simply due to an accident of history and the continued respect each country has shown the other's tenuous claims of sovereignty over the land. Although the residents have worked together to achieve some semblance of order in their daily lives, there is a pervasive feeling of helplessness in the enclaves. The lack of articulate enclave leaders to lobby the governments of India and Bangladesh, the difficulty of organizing across the dispersed enclaves, and the relatively small total population has allowed politicians in both countries to proceed without any urgency as the situation in the remote enclaves has little impact on the affairs of the state. The easiest path for both countries is to continue to put off the issue, as has been done for the past sixty years.

Although some territorial disputes are complicated and require delicate negotiations to find a solution that is suitable to all parties involved, this is not one of them. The enclaves on both sides of the border have functioned as part of their host country since their creation. The home countries have not been able to maintain control over the territories and have at no time provided services to these areas beyond initial land registration. The residents of the enclaves simply want to officially join the host countries, which would normalize what has been the de facto situation since their creation. Indeed, the two countries agreed to such an exchange thirty-five years ago, and Bangladesh long ago ratified the agreement. If India is unwilling to abide by this treaty, then Bangladesh needs to make the hard decision that it should have made decades ago. It should unilaterally provide services to the Indian enclaves by constructing roads, building schools, improving health conditions, allowing NGOs to operate, and enforcing Bangladeshi laws. Put simply, it is the obligation of the governments of India and Bangladesh to exchange the enclaves immediately and to begin to treat these human beings, who have lived in abject conditions for generations, with the humanity and compassion they have been denied for sixty years.

3

The Uzbekistan-Kyrgyzstan Boundary

Stalin's Cartography, Post-Soviet Geography

Nick Megoran

THE VILLAGE OF BARAK IS like many others in Central Asia's Ferghana Valley (figure 3.1). Most of its seven hundred inhabitants are cotton farmers, using water from the Syr Darya river's snowmelt to irrigate a cash crop that has been a mainstay of the valley's economy since the late nineteenth century. However, what sets Barak apart from hundreds of other such villages nearby is that it falls within an undemarcated section of the Kyrgyzstan-Uzbekistan boundary and constitutes a de facto Kyrgyz exclave in Uzbekistan. Although its citizens possess Kyrgyzstani passports, Barak has become disconnected from the rest of Kyrgyzstan, and it is unclear to which state it belongs.

Although a bilateral boundary commission continues its work, the consequences of this uncertainty are enormous for its inhabitants, whose access to vital agricultural markets in Kyrgyzstan is impeded by Uzbekistani border guards. Many people were forced to give up occupations in offices or as drivers in Kyrgyzstan following the solidification of an interim boundary control regime in 1999–2000. The social impact is also considerable, as the whim of border guards can decide whether everyday or extraordinary journeys are possible. A bereaved sibling recounted to the author how, when border guards held up the return of the deceased's corpse, he and his friends smuggled it home through the fields so that a burial could occur the same day, in accordance with Islamic tradition. On a happier note, another young man recounted that, after his future father-in-law forbade his daughter from marrying him because he lived in the enclave, the young lovers eloped. Tradition

FIGURE 3.1
Central Asia's Ferghana Valley. Cory Johnson of XNR.

dictated that this be done in a car. However, as the border guards would not allow the car to pass through, he and his friends drove a short distance and literally carried the car over a ditch dug by the Uzbekistani authorities and through the fields back to his home![1]

The Ferghana Valley is home to numerous such anomalous boundary sections. It contains seven internationally recognized enclaves (apart from Barak), including the world's two largest enclaves of Uzbekistan's Sokh at 238 square kilometers and Tajikistan's Vorukh at 97 square kilometers.[2]

The boundary cuts many villages in two, and in some places it literally divides the adjacent homes of parents and children. Although nominally dividing Uzbekistan ("land of the Uzbeks"), Kyrgyzstan ("land of the Kyrgyz") and Tajikistan ("land of the Tajiks"), significant numbers of ethnic minorities dwell in each country, often living in towns and villages close to the border. Since the late 1990s, the boundary has been the focus of state efforts to regulate and control the movement of goods and people, but at the same time it has become the site of an unprecedented flow of illegal drugs. As this chapter will show, debates about the boundary have been crucial to domestic political contestation. In fact, they contributed to the dramatic overthrow of Kyrgyzstani President Askar Akaev, when demonstrators stormed the presidential administration offices in 2005. "The border" is more than a line on a map. It is crucial to the struggles over the power to identify, claim, and rule post-Soviet Ferghana Valley space. This chapter explores the political geographical history of the intriguing boundary between Uzbekistan and Kyrgyzstan, described by Legvold as "the creative whim of Stalin."[3]

The Origins of the Uzbek-Kyrgyz Boundary

Pre-Soviet Political Geography

Joseph Stalin, as Lenin's commissar for nationalities before the latter's death in 1924, played a key role in the formation of the present boundaries of Uzbekistan and Kyrgyzstan by overseeing the 1924 national territorial delimitation, which laid the basis of the contemporary borders. But to properly ascertain that role, it is necessary to understand the political geography of the Ferghana Valley in the century prior to the heady revolutionary years of the early 1920s.

The ethnic geography of the Ferghana Valley in the mid-nineteenth century was very different from that of today. In fact, to use the modern word *ethnicity* of that period is anachronistic. Although historical accounts are patchy and difficult to evaluate, with historians sharply disagreeing on the meaning of terminologies used, it would appear that people identified themselves with others in a range of registers and at a variety of scales. Self-identifications could be made on the basis of language spoken, village/town/region inhabited, sovereign allegiance, religion adhered to, kin group, and broader groupings and alliances of these divisions. Designations such as Uzbek, Kyrgyz, and Tajik were in currency, but, being used in different ways in different contexts, their meanings were more fluid than the rigid distinctions they have come to signal today. Much like the rest of Eurasia, the Ferghana Valley had been conquered and settled numerous times by different groups, in this case from Greeks and Arabs to Mongols and Turks, all of whom had left a greater or lesser imprint on the social and political geography of the valley. As Northrop contends, "Indigenous identities were complex, multifacted and changeable, and they corresponded poorly to these new political borders."[4]

By the mid-nineteenth century, Central Asia was ruled by three dynasties, the Khanates of Khoqand and Khiva and the Emirate of Bukhara, with the Ferghana Valley under the control of Khoqand (figure 3.2). Based on settled communities of farmers, traders, and craftspeople, these polities had developed from the division of Tamerlane's great empire following his death in 1405 and did not legitimize themselves as ethnic dynasties. Rather than linguistic or ethnic unity, these dynasties sought to cultivate a sense of personal loyalty to the ruler. Their territorial extent changed over time through internecine warfare and bore little relationship to present-day boundaries. To the west of these polities were Turkmen nomads; to the south, Afghanistan; to the east, Chinese Turkestan; and to the north, the northern steppe, roughly above an east-west axis drawn through the Aral Sea. The steppe was controlled by different confederations of Kazakh nomads.

By the end of the nineteenth century, however, these polities had been subdued as the Russian empire advanced southward. This was an age of territorially based industrial imperialism as states such as Britain, Germany, France, the United States, and Japan consolidated and expanded territo-

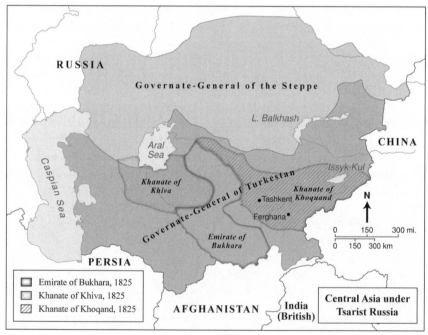

FIGURE 3.2
Central Asia under Tsarist Russia. Cory Johnson of XNR.

rial control in order to secure access to economic resources and markets, a process that would eventually culminate in the clashes of World Wars I and II.[5] Russia expanded eastward into Siberia and southward into the Caucasus and Central Asia. The culmination of this latter push was the conquest of Tashkent in 1865, the defeat of the Bukharans and Khivans in 1868 and 1873, respectively, the annexation and abolition of Khoqand in 1876, and the crushing of Turkmen resistance in 1881.[6] The Russian authorities orchestrated a wholesale political geographical reorganization of the region, dividing it in two. The area formerly controlled by Kazakh nomads became the Governate General of the Steppe, while that of Khoqand, Khiva, Bukhara, and the Turkmen nomads was subordinated to the Governate General of Turkestan, with the Khivan Khanate and the Bukharan Emirate maintaining autonomous vassal status.

The Bolshevik Revolution

The Central Asia of World War I and its aftermath, the Bolshevik Revolution, was an area of turmoil. Rebellions against conscription for war service, ideological and religious revolutionary and counterrevolutionary strife, and anticolonial struggles made the period between 1916 and the early 1920s one of great violence and significant population displacements. Although sporadic armed anti-Soviet resistance continued until the 1930s, Bolshevik control was firmly established by 1924.

Bolshevik rule brought further significant geopolitical transformations. In 1920 the Turkestan Autonomous Soviet Socialist Republic was created. For all the bravado of the name, it was largely a territorial continuation of the tsarist Governate General of Turkestan. Indeed, the Khanate of Khiva and the Emirate of Bukhara survived as "People's Soviet Republics." But this was to change dramatically with the process of national territorial delimitation that culminated with a complete redrawing of the map of Turkestan in 1924.

National Territorial Delimitation (NTD)

The process of national territorial delimitation (NTD) began with discussions in the Politburo of the Central Committee of the Russian Communist Party in 1920 concerning the possible division of the region into national units, in line with Stalin's concept of the nation as "a historically constituted, stable community of people, formed on the basis of a common language, territory, economic life, and psychological make-up manifested in a common culture."[7] Opinion was sharply divided as to the wisdom of this mooted move, with some arguing that this would only help the "nationalist bourgeois" elements of anti-Bolshevik opposition against Lenin, who proposed that Turkestan be divided into Uzbek, Kyrgyz (Kazakh), and Turkmen areas.[8]

Little came of these discussions for some years, possibly due to the ongoing opposition. However, by 1923, Russian force had taken the sting out of the most determined resistance, and the creation of the Union of Soviet Socialist Republics in 1922 provided a unique political geographical framework within which NTD could be reconsidered. This framework was that of a federal system ideologically committed to the construction of a non-nationalist humanity, the Soviet Union, composed, ironically, of nationally defined union republics (the Ukrainian, Georgian, Moldovan, and so on Soviet Socialist Republics). This novel approach was highly paradoxical, enshrining in one system both a commitment to an antinationalist vision of humanity and government by nationally constituted elites. Soviet ideology could justify this in part as a coming together of workers of the world into a project that would eventually weld a common sense of identity but which, in the meantime, worked with existing realities. Nationality was considered to be historically contingent upon capitalism and would wither away as a socialist society was constructed, but in the meantime, accommodation with it was a strategy to gain power.[9] It was arguably a masterpiece of political geography, but the ultimate irony of history was that the Soviet Union fell apart precisely along these national lines.

Whatever its paradoxes, the creation of the Soviet Union provided an obvious structure within which to incorporate Turkestan along national lines. Thus in January 1924 the Central Committee of the Russian Communist Party decided to re-examine the proposal for a division of Turkestan on national lines, a proposal approved by the Politburo that established a special commission for the national territorial delimitation. The Central Committee's Central Asian bureau proposed that Uzbek and Turkmen Soviet socialist republics (SSRs) be created as full constitutive members of the USSR. It also proposed that a Tajik autonomous region be formed within the Uzbek SSR, which in 1929 was to achieve full union republic status as the Tajik SSR. Present-day Kyrgyzstan was incorporated into the Russian Soviet Federative Socialist Republic as the Kara-Kyrgyz Autonomous Region, attaining full union status in 1936 as the Kyrgyz SSR. The already formed Kyrgyz (Kazakh in today's terminology) Autonomous SSR was also incorporated as the Kazakh SSR in 1936. The 1924 proposal on NTD was formally approved at a meeting of the general committee of the Russian Communist Party in October. The Turkestan Autonomous Soviet Socialist Republic was abolished, and the five Central Asian republics, three in their embryonic outline and two in their definitive forms, were born.[10]

National Territorial Delimitation—Drawing Boundaries

If the ideological debates behind NTD had largely been resolved by early 1924, the process of actually drawing boundaries among the new mosaic of Soviet socialist republics and autonomous regions was to prove highly contentious. A number of criteria were used in the division of territory between the new entities. The major ones were that administrative units within the new republics have *geographical* unity, for example, that water resources not be split between new units; have an *economic* rationale, being oriented toward a particular market town; and, as far as possible, be *ethnically* homogeneous.[11]

It was all but impossible to satisfy these requirements because they could often be mutually contradictory, but also, as shown above, ethnicity was often indistinct and fluid. As Hirsch argues, citing the work of the Soviet ethnographer Bartol'd, "Tajiks and Uzbeks were so ethnographically intermixed that in some regions it was difficult even for locals to differentiate between them."[12] How could Turkestan be divided along such lines? Decisions were often made on the basis of rudimentary, incomplete, and simplistic censuses. People were simply presented with a number of options by census takers and obliged to choose one, and one only, for themselves.

Furthermore, ethnicity, or nationality, was malleable in the hands of census takers. Thus late Tsarist and early Soviet censuses contained large numbers of people who identified themselves by categories such as "Sart," "Kurama," or "Kipchak," which were later removed from censuses, thus forcing people to reascribe themselves as Uzbek, Kyrgyz, or some other permitted category. As mentioned above, in 1920 Lenin had proposed that Turkestan be divided into Uzbek, Kyrgyz (Kazakh), and Turkmen republics. His failure to mention sizable groups such as Tajiks, Turks, Sarts, Kurama, and Kipchaks deprived them of any form of Soviet statehood.

In spite of this fluidity of ethnic ascription, NTD meant that nationality had become a significant factor for the newly refashioned emerging elites in terms of access to land, resources, and power.[13] NTD involved fierce political battles between the leaderships of the nascent states that determined how boundaries would be drawn and redrawn, as well as control of disputed areas. These battles occurred before the announcement of the division in October 1924 and continued in a series of appeals against the initial determination over the following three years, overseen by a parity commission.

For the Uzbek and Kyrgyz SSRs, this was particularly the case along sections of the south and east of their boundary. Leaders pointed to supposed ethnic majorities of certain areas, arguing that groups such as Sart, Kipchak, Kashgarlik, or Kurama be properly regarded as either Uzbek or Kyrgyz to sway the argument. The city of Osh, initially allocated to the Kara-Kyrgyz

ASSR, was claimed by the Uzbek SSR on the basis of a supposed Sart/Uzbek majority. A meeting of the parity commission in 1926 rejected this claim for a number of reasons. Geographically, its irrigation system was tightly bound to the neighboring Kyrgyz regions. Economically, it was the only trade and administrative center for the South Ferghana region, which had been allotted to the Kyrgyz.[14] The boundary was thus drawn at the site of the present-day Uzbekistan-Kyrgyzstan boundary, to the chagrin of many Uzbeks in Osh.

Kyrgyz appeals for the region of Aravan, west of Osh, to be ceded on the basis of ethnicity (counting Turks as Kara-Kyrgyz) were accepted by the commission. On May 3, 1927, the central executive committee of the USSR largely confirmed the findings of the parity commission, except for deciding to redraw boundaries to cede Isfara, Uch-Korgon, and the exclave of Sokh to Kyrgyzstan. Behind the scenes, actions by pro-Uzbek factions sought to nullify this verdict. Thus on May 4, Isfara and Sokh were returned to the Uzbek SSR, although it was confirmed that Uch-Korgan and Aravan would pass to the Kyrgyz. The committee declared that territorial claims should be considered settled and sought to ban further attempts to raise the question.

However, the Kyrgyz persistently called for some decisions to be revisited. In particular, they pointed to what they regarded as the illegal Uzbek exclave of Shahimardon. Established when Uzbek authorities took control of two villages immediately following NTD, the Kyrgyz authorities instructed administrative organs in Osh to liquidate the enclave in 1927. These moves were blocked by Moscow, and the exclave remains to this day.[15] According to Koichiev, this whole process left around fifty majority-Uzbek settlements on the Kyrgyz side of the disputed boundary sections in the east and south of the valley and one hundred Kyrgyz settlements on the Uzbek side; not to mention dozens of Sart, Kipchak, Kurama, and Kashgarlik settlements that would eventually be counted as Uzbek or Kyrgyz.[16]

Hence, in a process driven by ideological vision and pragmatic accommodation, actualized through political struggles over ethnographic interpretation and local geographies, the highly complex Uzbek-Kyrgyz boundary, with its numerous anomalies and contested enclaves, came into existence. The boundary itself was certainly an artifact of a state commission, but the extent to which it reflected or created national divisions on the ground remains disputed among historians.

Ferghana Valley Boundaries 1927–1991

The borders established in 1927 were largely to persist until the dissolution of the USSR in 1991. However, as they were never intended to be international boundaries, Soviet economic planning designed electricity, gas, irrigation, and transport networks on an integrated basis. The industrial, urban, agricultural, and transport planning projects of one state spilled freely over into the territory of its neighbor. The Uzbek SSR rented tracts of land from the less densely populated Kyrgyz SSR for use in agricultural and industrial developments. Although sometimes formalized by interstate rental contracts, rents were seldom collected, nor was land always reclaimed when the period of tenure expired. Why should it be? This was one country. This meant that settlements of two or three generations developed on land that was intended to house only temporary workers.

Although the republic's boundaries had little impact on daily movement, administrations were not indifferent to territorial questions. Minor alterations were initiated at various points. For example, a joint Uzbek-Kyrgyz SSR border demarcation commission was established in 1955 to resolve outstanding interrepublican disputes, although this commission never completed its work.[17] According to Brendan Whyte's study of enclaves in the Ferghana Valley based on Soviet atlases, Vorukh was enclaved at this time by the transfer of territory from the Tajik and Uzbek SSRs to the Kyrgyz SSR.[18] A Kyrgyz SSR decree of 1989 created a border delimitation and demarcation committee which established that Tajikistan's Leninabad oblast was using 636 hectares of land in Leylek (in the far west of what is now Batken province), and the people of Leylek in return were utilizing 164 hectares of Tajik SSR land.[19] The legacy of the 1924 delimitation and the subsequent patterns of economic development was a highly complicated mosaic of land use that wantonly transgressed the administrative boundaries of the republics. This situation would bequeath numerous headaches to the independent republics that would appear in 1991.

Post-Soviet Boundaries

The Uzbekistan-Kyrgyzstan Boundary at Independence

The collapse of the USSR was not triggered by the "Muslim nationalism" that anti-Soviet scholars such as Bennigsen, perhaps wishfully, predicted.[20] Nevertheless, independence presented, as we have seen, a complicated and unclear boundary geography. Different maps produced at different periods showed different boundaries. Kyrgyzstan shared a border of 1,375 kilometers with Uzbekistan, the majority of which wound through the Ferghana Valley.

The effects of the Soviet boundaries becoming the lines between independent states were not greatly felt in the years immediately following independence. One notable exception was a brief crisis in 1993 when President

Karimov closed Uzbekistan's border with Kyrgyzstan to prevent Russian rubles from flooding the valley after Kyrgyzstan exited the ruble zone and introduced its own currency.²¹ Some border and customs posts were established, but control checks were minimal or nonexistent and daily transboundary life in the valley continued almost uninterrupted. Social and familial cross-border links were very strong, with large numbers of people regularly crossing the boundary to visit families, parks, sanatoriums, and shrines. In fact, as shown in the next section, a fuller active awareness of the existence of international boundaries did not dawn on many inhabitants of southern Kyrgyzstan until the events of 1999–2000.

The 1999–2000 "Border Crisis"

The benign impact of the Uzbekistan-Kyrgyzstan boundary on borderland dwellers came to an abrupt halt in 1999. Toward the end of 1998, Uzbekistan began to tighten control of its border, severely hampering cross-boundary mobility. Many cross-boundary roads were closed by the demolition of bridges over canals and ditches or the placement of concrete blocks. Cross-border bus routes were terminated, customs inspections stepped up, noncitizens attempting to cross were denied access or seriously impeded, and eventually a (short-lived) visa requirement was introduced. Unmarked minefields were laid in some mountainous areas. Tensions often flared between border control guards and local inhabitants who suddenly found their traditional routes of movement hampered or even terminated. In some cases, these tensions erupted into violent confrontations.

Most dramatically in terms of the visual border landscape, Uzbekistan began erecting a two-meter-high barbed wire perimeter fence along large stretches of the valley boundary. In many cases, this fence went through village communities, although the sight of numerous places where it had been cut through showed that people could be imaginative in finding ways to circumvent it. The rapid and unilateral construction of this fence led to widespread accusations within Kyrgyzstan that Uzbekistan was actually corralling tens of thousands of hectares of Kyrgyzstani land, a legacy of the poorly regulated land leases of the Soviet period. At the same time, arguments over natural resource allocation intensified. Kyrgyzstan depended on Uzbekistan for gas supplies, which were regularly turned off during the winter months by an Uzbekistani government impatient at the failure of the impoverished Kyrgyzstani government to pay the bills. Many in Kyrgyzstan thought this unfair as Uzbekistan did not contribute financially to the upkeep of dams and reservoirs in Kyrgyzstani territory that primarily watered Uzbekistan's agricultural (cotton) heartland in the Ferghana Valley. Border disputes thus became a key factor in mutual relations in 1999 and into 2000.

Explanations of the Kyrgyzstan-Uzbekistan Border Crisis

How can we account for the events of 1999–2000, when the Uzbekistan-Kyrgyzstan boundary emerged from being an abstract line on a map to a brute reality in the everyday lives of people who lived alongside it? The majority of explanations have suggested that the inherited poorly—or maliciously—drawn boundaries would inevitably trigger territorial conflicts after independence. Babakulov's version of this thesis is typical:

> When Uzbekistan and Kyrgyzstan declared independence, an international border suddenly sprang up between the two former Soviet republics. With an international border, came border posts. And with border posts came guards, whose conduct has bred such resentment among Kyrgyz and Uzbek travellers that some analysts are warning that frontier disputes could sow the seeds of inter-ethnic violence.[22]

Similar accounts emphasize divergent macroeconomic policies, the maldistribution of resources, and security concerns. All of these perspectives tend to envisage the border as geographical, economic, and techno-managerial questions requiring techno-managerial solutions.

Without doubt, all of these explanations can make some contribution toward accounting for the circumstances that enabled the dispute to occur. For example, Uzbekistan's actions to tighten border controls were partially motivated by an attempt to restrict the circulation of capital, labor, and goods that became problematic due to the inconvertibility of its currency. Undoubtedly, the chaotic land use patterns that emerged along the boundary created by the 1924 national territorial delimitation provided abundant raw material for disputes and tensions. The threat of antistate terrorism from dissidents taking refuge in neighboring Tajikistan was also real. However, the political significance that this held in both Uzbekistani and Kyrgyzstani domestic politics, as well as the precise course that the dispute took, suggests that these factors alone are inadequate to fully explain the significance of the border. They do not sufficiently explain why a supposedly inevitable conflict took almost a decade after independence to explode, or why it became significant when it did. They do not trace how what was locally termed "the border question" came to subsume a range of issues, including disputes over natural resources, customs regimes, transport, and the personal relationships between presidents, that became part of this interstate crisis. Border disputes do not happen simply because of cartographic confusion; they are made. In short, a fuller explanation of the 1999–2000 border crisis must include an analysis of domestic politics as well as historical political geography.

It is exactly this sense of the political function of boundaries that has rejuvenated border studies over the past two decades. As Newman has argued, boundaries are vital in constructing senses of identity, demarcating self/other and inside/outside.[23] The state border, although physically at the extremities of the polity, can be at the heart of nationalist discourse about the meaning of the nation, of arguments about who should be included in the nation and who should be excluded, and in struggles over the power to make those decisions. This is illustrated in the following two sections, which consider the place of the border in domestic politics in Uzbekistan and Kyrgyzstan, respectively.

Uzbekistan and the Border Crisis[24]

President Karimov of Uzbekistan, the former Uzbek Communist Party leader, has propagated a strong sense of historical destiny around myths of independent statehood, firm leadership, and national identity. His heavy-handed rule tolerates little internal dissent and draws repeated criticism from human rights organizations.[25] In particular, in 1999, the radical Islamist group Hizb-ut Tahrir had stepped up a clandestine leafleting campaign calling for the abolition of Uzbekistan and the creation of a borderless, pan-Islamic caliphate. It is no coincidence that the border crisis occurred at a time of growing opposition to Karimov's rule and an unprecedented crackdown on dissent.

During this period, there were numerous state-controlled television and newspaper reports about increasing efforts to control Uzbekistan's international boundaries. These reports repeatedly framed the state border of Uzbekistan as the boundary between a whole series of binary dualisms: order and disorder, progress and backwardness, stability and chaos, wealth and poverty. The state boundary was not simply a line on a map established by treaty, but a moral border between good and evil. At the same time, it served to script the official vision of Uzbek identity, of who belonged within the new Uzbekistan and who did not.

This complicated ideological vision of post-Soviet Central Asian political space was articulated through a number of discursive strategies. For example, there were numerous reports comparing life on either side of Uzbekistan's boundaries that portrayed plenitude and contentment in Uzbekistan but war, disorder, and poverty over the border in neighboring states. There were also many reports of people apprehended at the border smuggling contraband, particularly narcotics but also "extremist religious literature," into the country. Likewise, citizens caught smuggling goods out of Uzbekistan, such as meat, honey, U.S. dollars, and particularly scrap metal, were also paraded for public approbation. Rather than discussing why people were prepared to risk being caught and imprisoned for these actions, "hooliganism" or criminality/ evil were identified as the motives. To acknowledge that poverty was the main reason behind the smuggling of economically valuable goods would have ruptured the narratives of a rich and happy Uzbekistan that knows deprivation only by the glances it casts from safely behind its border. Similarly, the issue of bribery and corruption of customs officers and border guards, and thus their complicity in smuggling rackets, was entirely ignored. The government was not willing to see its myth of plenitude and satisfaction challenged or to destabilize its key discursive strategy of the geographical imagination of rich land/poor land articulated at the state border. Together they wove a powerful geopolitical vision of what Uzbekistan was, of who was inside that moral commonwealth and who outside.

The strength of Uzbekistan's border was contrasted with the weakness of neighboring states' borders. News media criticized the inability of Tajikistan and Kyrgyzstan to control the flow of drugs across their borders. One article asked whether the same thing could happen in Uzbekistan; "No, in this country control is very strong," argued the main government newspaper, *Halq So'zi,* because it pinches the flow of drugs and has a force of well-trained officials.[26] Firm control of the state border was called for lest it be engulfed by disorder, and President Islam Karimov was the strong leader who was delivering that. The border thus acted as a subtle justification for authoritarian control and as a way to delegitimize those opposing the government.

For the Uzbekistani government, therefore, the border was not merely the location of Uzbekistan's defense of its territory and security. It was also a moral border, a cartography of knowledge mapping a geopolitical vision of vulnerable post-Soviet political space that enabled the Uzbek elite to write its authority over the material and social landscapes of Uzbekistan. The border demarcated a historically continuous binary dualism of a happy and well-governed Uzbekistan from the chaos of neighboring states and legitimized the authoritarian rule of President Karimov as the sole guarantor of the nation's continued welfare. As Paasi argues, "Boundaries are not therefore merely lines on the ground but, above all, manifestations of social practice and discourse."[27]

Kyrgyzstan and the Border Crisis[28]

The Kyrgyzstan of 1999 differed markedly from Uzbekistan. Its then president, Askar Akaev, had earned the reputation of being a relatively liberal reformer. He sought to build a state in which the substantial number of Uzbek- and Russian-speaking ethnic minorities felt fully included, a policy summed up by his favourite slogan, "Kyrgyzstan is our common home," which, illustrated with the image of people from various ethnic groups standing aside the beaming leader, adorned billboards in public spaces. Unlike in Uzbekistan, genuine opposition parties existed, many of which were led by Kyrgyz nationalists who lamented what they saw as the relative weakness of the Kyrgyz nationality. These groups were supported by a vociferous and outspoken nonstate press. Following the dramatic deterioration in relations between Uzbekistan and Kyrgyzstan after Uzbekistan's unilateral closure of the border in February 1999 and the suspension of cross-border traffic, the pages of this press became filled with alarming reports on the impacts.

One of the first examples was provided by a hysterical article published in *Aalam* in February 2000 under the title "Kyrgyzstan—here today, gone tomorrow?" with a dramatic cartoon map depicting helpless Kyrgyzstan being consumed at its borders by ferocious ogres coming from the general directions of Uzbekistan, Kazakhstan, and China (figure 3.3). The author began with a gem of ancient statecraft:

> In the old days a khan would give this counsel to his son: "If, during your reign, you add one inch of land to your country you are a great khan. If you don't even add one inch, but nonetheless lose not an inch, you are an average khan. However if you lose even one inch of the country's land then the people will curse you, you are a bad khan—therefore guard your land like your right hand."

This historical allusion was clearly a challenge to President Akaev to protect the state border of the body politic as one would protect one's own body. The article went on to present evidence that the president had already failed this test. Water was flowing to neighboring states without their paying for it. Tajikistan and Uzbekistan were swallowing up sections of Kyrgyzstan's border area. Chinese herders were penetrating deep into Kyrgyz land for pasture. Uzbekistan was advancing its border posts into Kyrgyz territory. Tajiks were occupying whole areas inside Batken province by settling in land vacated by impoverished Kyrgyz who migrated abroad or to the cities. "Currently it is as if someone drove a donkey-cart through our map, careering all over the place"—not the way a khan should oversee his territory. The article poured scorn on President Akaev's inclusive vision of the state:

> The slogan "Kyrgyzstan is our common home" has sunk deep into the hearts of everyone. You remember it every time you see someone of a different nationality. . . .

FIGURE 3.3
"Kyrgyzstan—here today, gone tomorrow?" ("Bügün Kïrgïzstan Bar: Erteng jok bolup ketishi mümkün?" *Aalam* 7 (259), 24/02/1999–02/03/1999).

This scornful treatment of a key conceptual plank of the president's policy transformed a geographical notion of harmony and tolerance to an ironic indictment of a state policy that failed to protect the country against illegal immigration. The paper continued:

> Another 10–15 years of this "politics of hospitality" and it is possible that we will not be able to find our border at all. But, thanks be to God, we have a number of deputies who take up this matter.

These were opposition parliamentary opponents and hopeful presidential challengers of Askar Akaev, Daniyar Üsönöv, and Ömürbek Tekebaev. For the paper, "the border question is not a joke, it is extremely important, and may be the issue which decides the future of our country."

The relationship between the border and the nation in the minds of the nationalistic opposition was underlined in an interview given to *Asaba* by Daniyar Üsönöv in March 1999. He sharply criticized the government's decision to hold a parliamentary border debate behind closed doors. He expressed fears of the "fifth column" posed by immigration of Uighurs (a Turkic Muslim people) from China across the allegedly open border. For Üsönöv, Uighur women using their wiles to seduce Kyrgyz men threatened the national and territorial integrity of Kyrgyzstan. Conflating a notion of the racially pure Kyrgyz ethnos with the state, Üsönöv concluded that, therefore, the very idea that there was a border was being thrown into doubt. Soon afterwards *Asaba* declared Üsönöv "man of the month." He had started his election campaign and through his outspoken comments on the border made himself the government's prime enemy. He later declared his intention to stand against Askar Akaev in the presidential elections but was prevented from running by what was widely regarded as a politically motivated prosecution for a minor offense committed some years earlier. This meant that he also lost his parliamentary seat in the February 2000 elections.

For the nationalistic Kyrgyz opposition, the border issue functioned to link a range of concerns, including loss of sovereign territory and water resources, immigration, the dilution of the Kyrgyz cultural identity, compromised sexual norms, and flawed foreign and domestic policies, into a coherent and comprehensive assault on President Akaev's claim to be an authentic defender of the body politic of the Kyrgyz nation and territory. Within the context of this bitter power struggle, the opposition's attacks compelled the Kyrgyz government to strengthen its own rhetoric and actions on the border and increase its control of people moving over it. This thus illustrates Ó Tuathail's argument that the geography of the world is "a product of histories of struggle between competing authorities over the power to organize, occupy, and administer space."[29] Just as the emergence of the boundary between 1924 and 1927 was a political process overseen by Stalin, its solidification in the lives of borderland inhabitants in 1999 and 2000 was also, ultimately, about the politics of nationality.

The Impact of the Boundary on Borderland Dwellers

Uzbekistan-Kyrgyzstan Boundary 1991–1998

Throughout this chapter, it has been underlined that boundaries do not simply exist as legal and cartographic entities. They are produced by people, generally elites, and may have enormous consequences on people. This is illustrated not only by NTD between 1924 and 1927, but also by the severing of sections of the Ferghana Valley with the independence of Uzbekistan and Kyrgyzstan in 1991.

The legal emergence of international boundaries at formal independence made little initial impact on the lives of borderland dwellers. However, the cultural and economic landscape of the borderlands gradually began to change as Uzbekistan and Kyrgyzstan increasingly pursued divergent paths toward solidifying independent statehood. For example, agricultural landscapes became perceptibly different as farmers in Uzbekistan remained locked into Soviet-style production of cotton, while the application of more neoliberal economics in Kyrgyzstan led to the breaking up of collectives and a greater diversification into cash crops such as tobacco. Uzbekistan moved to a one-hour difference daylight-saving time scheme. A switch from the Soviet telephone network to independent technologies meant that calls across the border required using international codes. As a result, a call from Osh to Ferghana cost the same as a call to Bishkek in 1997 but cost almost ten times the price of a call to Bishkek in 1999. The abandonment of the Soviet-era Cyrillic alphabet in favor of a European-style Latin alphabet in Uzbekistan in 1995 meant that highway signs and roadside slogans were printed in different scripts, while new national currencies and diverging macroeconomic policies produced a border landscape littered with exchange bureaus and markets. Although independent nation-states emerged with the official declarations of independence, the conscious experience of living in them crept upon the inhabitants of the valley more slowly.

As this gradual differentiation of the boundary landscape emerged, movement across the boundary for work, family, worship, or relaxation was largely unhindered. In fact, arguably the greatest difference was a positive one. To offset some of the economic hardships of post-Soviet collapse, locals could exploit price differentials between the same goods from either side of the border to earn money through shuttle trading. This came to an abrupt end in the border crisis of early 1999, when roads were closed, cross-border bus routes terminated, the boundary fence erected, and stringent new checks on movement introduced.

Uzbekistan-Kyrgyzstan Boundary 1999 and Beyond

The impact on borderland dwellers of the early 1999 solidification of the boundary can be glimpsed from the small agricultural village of Jar, near Marhamat and Aravan. Jar essentially consists of one straight road with a few dozen houses, one school, one mosque, and one cemetery. The inhabitants belong to a single ethnic group (Uzbek), and families are closely interrelated. In these ways, Jar is typical of villages throughout the region. What sets Jar apart, however, is that the Uzbekistan-Kyrgyzstan border cuts through the middle of the village. This abstract line had not been important until late 1998 and early 1999, when the Uzbek state suddenly put up concrete posts and strung a barbed wire fence along it.[30] A checkpoint was positioned some 200 meters into Uzbekistani territory.

The author visited the village soon afterwards while conducting ethnographic fieldwork. The shock, disbelief, and anger of people who gathered at the border and who were speaking to me just after this incident is hard to convey. It seemed difficult for people to accept that their leaders had done this. One inhabitant, Dilshot,[31] exclaimed:

> Why our states and *padeshahs* [emperors, rulers] are not sorting this out amongst themselves, I don't know. How will they resolve this? Just think—that such a thing should happen to towns so closely connected as this!

His words reveal not only a sense of betrayal but also of genuine astonishment. The closure violated the practice of village inhabitants' kinship networks that formed an integral part of meaning and orientation in the world: "This person has an elder brother, that a younger brother, this a father, that a daughter-in-law—it's hard. Everyone lives mixed in with each other," said Farhod, another resident. The point was stressed to the author again and again by different people along the boundary, both Uzbekistanis and Kyrgyzstanis, that everyone here lived inseparably mixed together and the fence showed that the authorities did not understand that. The border crisis can be understood as elites in distant Tashkent imposing a new political geographical logic on the valley over the social geography of kinship as mapped by its inhabitants.

People all across the valley sought ways to circumvent these restrictions. They smuggled goods, livestock, and themselves over the boundary, either away from the watchful eye of guards or under it by bribing them. The inhabitants of Barak, referred to in the introduction, not only smuggled corpses and wedding cars into their village but organized a protest to the Kyrgyzstani state against Uzbekistan's closure of the road connecting them to Kyrgyzstan proper. Following this, the Kyrgyzstani state successfully lobbied Tashkent to open the road to local traffic. Thus, borderland dwellers were not passive. Nonetheless, the concretization of the border in 1999 ruptured senses of orientation and forced people to recognize in their daily life that they lived in separate, independent states. What Northrop said of NTD in 1924 is applicable to 1999: "Borders divide people, but in Central Asia they created people as well."[32]

Whither the Uzbekistan-Kyrgyzstan Boundary?

On March 17, 2008, some 500 people gathered in Kyrgyzstan's Ferghana Valley district of Aksy, near the town of Kerben in the Jalalabat, to hold a "public trial" on the sixth anniversary of a clash between police and demonstrators that left six people dead. The clash occurred as local people protested the imprisonment of their parliamentary deputy, Azimbek Beknazarov, who had become a vociferous critic of then president Askar Akaev's deal to settle a boundary dispute with China by allegedly ceding significant tracts of land to Beijing. The police shooting of demonstrators led to the resignation of Akaev's government, including Prime Minister Kurmanbek Bakiev. Bakiev became an opponent of the regime and used the shootings to galvanize an opposition movement based in the Ferghana Valley part of Kyrgyzstan that would eventually topple Akaev, who fled the country as demonstrators stormed the presidential administration building in Bishkek in 2005. Bakiev himself became president in the aftermath of Akaev's ouster. However, no one has been successfully prosecuted for the shootings. Opposition activists staged the March 2008 "public trial" against the backdrop of a crackdown on dissent by an increasingly beleaguered Bakiev. Bakiev himself was among a number of top officials declared guilty of "organizing and carrying out" the killings by the "court."[33] The question of Kyrgyzstan's post-Soviet boundary has thus played a role in toppling its first president and, if the demonstrators have their way, may also have a part in unseating its second.

Although political actors in both Kyrgyzstan and Uzbekistan continue to use the boundary in domestic struggles for control, a bilateral commission is quietly seeking to resolve ongoing disputes. As Uzbekistan began erecting fences in October 1998, Kyrgyzstan requested that the two countries begin demarcation of the common boundary, a request that, Polat claims, was initially turned down.[34] However, in 2000 a bilateral boundary commission was eventually formed.[35] The commission's work appears to have progressed steadily ever since, and by 2006 only around 300 kilometers of the 1,375 kilometres boundary lacked demarcation.[36] This is remarkably swift progress. Russia's boundary dispute with China, for example, dates back at least to the Treaty of Nerchinsk in 1689 but was not resolved until 2004.[37] Thus, in spite of the boundary's role in generating enormous friction between Uzbekistan and Kyrgyzstan, political dramas within each state, and the disruption of daily life for those who live alongside it, Polat felt able to claim that, following the demise of the USSR, "the conversion of the old administrative divisions into new international boundaries turned out to be remarkably uneventful, particularly so in Central Asia."[38]

The Uzbekistan-Kyrgyzstan boundary may have its origins in Stalin's geography, but its recent remaking has as much to do with the political geographical visions of Uzbekistan's president, Islam Karimov, and political actors in Kyrgyzstan. This history shows that, more than a line on a map, the boundary has been crucial to elite struggles over the definition of the identity of the space of the Ferghana Valley by setting up borders of inside and outside and the power to rule that space. Borderland populations have been caught up in these dramas as active participants as well as victims. Johanson concludes her legal study of self-determination and the Ferghana Valley's anomalous boundaries by suggesting that, in the title of her book, there is an "obligation to show consideration for the interests of others."[39] As the bilateral boundary commission continues its work, that is an obligation that elites in Uzbekistan and Kyrgyzstan would do well to remember.

4

The Wakhan Corridor

Endgame of the Great Game

William C. Rowe

O N AUGUST 13, 1891, WHILE on reconnaissance in the Pamir Mountains, Captain Francis E. Younghusband made the following observation:

> As I looked out of the door of my tent, I saw some twenty Cossacks with six of-
> ficers riding by, and the Russian flag carried in front. I sent out a servant with
> my card and invitation to the officers to come in and have some refreshments.
> Some of them came in, and the chief officer was introduced to me as Colonel
> Yonoff. . . . I gave the Russian officers some tea and Russian wine . . . and I then
> told Colonel Yonoff that reports had reached me that he was proclaiming to the
> Kirghiz that the Pamirs were Russian territory and asked him if this was the case.
> He said it was so, and he showed me a map with the boundary claimed by the
> Russians coloured on it. This boundary included the whole of the Pamirs except
> the Tagh-dum-bash, and extended as far down as the watershed of the Hindu-
> Kush by the Khora Bhort Pass.[1]

This cordial meeting between Captain Younghusband of the Indian Staff Corps and Colonel Yonoff (or Yanov) of the Russian Imperial Army at Buzai-Gambad (or Bozai-Gumbaz) near the mouth of the Wakhjir River in modern-day Afghanistan, where they exchanged tea and wine (and later din- ner and vodka in Colonel Yonoff's tent), became the catalyst for the ending of a protracted war of nerves, territory, and diplomatic sleight of hand played out over Central Asia between Great Britain and Russia. This conflict had commonly become known as the "Great Game," a term coined by Arthur Conolly but immortalized by Rudyard Kipling.[2] What followed this chance meeting would eventually halt the final Russian advance into Central Asia

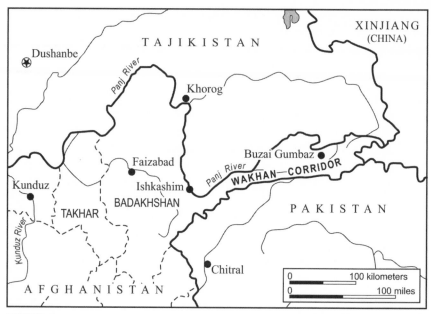

FIGURE 4.1
Northeast Afghanistan and the Wakhan Corridor. Louisiana State University Cartography Laboratory.

through the "Pamir Gap," cause the delineation of the final northern border of the buffer state of Afghanistan, and end a period of enmity between Great Britain and Russia. This border would also include the anomalous entity that would become known as the Wakhan Corridor, which stretches from Afghan Badakhshan to the border with China between modern-day Tajikistan and Pakistan (figure 4.1). Though extremely remote and largely inaccessible, this odd border construction essentially served one important purpose in the geopolitical (and occasionally violent) struggle between European powers by ensuring that the British and Russian Empires did not touch at any point.

The Physical and Demographic Setting

In referring to the area from which the Amu Darya River and its tributaries debouch, Captain John Wood, one of the earliest European explorers to travel into the Wakhan Corridor, succinctly points to the primary consideration of physical geography. The chief governing geographical feature in this field is the great mountain mass so often spoken of, dividing the basin of the Oxus

(Amu Darya) from that of the (Chinese) Yarkand River—the northern Imaus of Ptolemy, the Tsungling of the Chinese—and its confluents.[3]

The Wakhan Corridor, covering 8,936 square kilometers (3,451 square miles) but in some places barely 15 kilometers (10 miles) across, is a part of the overall Pamir Mountain region. With an average elevation of about 5,400 meters (17,716 feet), the preponderant part of the corridor is above 3,000 meters (9,843 feet), with only the Panj and parts of the Wakhan (or Sarhad) River Valleys below that.[4] Due to its altitude and extreme isolation, one author has characterized the corridor as "the most elevated, the wildest, the most inaccessible, and the least populated" place in Afghanistan, argu-ably the country in and of itself with the greatest claims to many of those adjectives.[5]

Due to the varied alluvial and glacial deposits and its generally arid cli-mate, vegetation is scarce in the Pamir region, but notably so in the Wakhan Corridor. Vegetation is restricted to "low-growing plants that are adapted to severe conditions" (or, according to Sir Aurel Stein, a noted archaeolo-gist of China and Afghanistan in the early twentieth century, "stunted trees and brushwood") that can accommodate a growing season of only 100–120 days.[6] This paucity of vegetation causes hardship for the inhabitants in find-ing fuel for cooking fires, with brushwood and animal dung generally the only sources.[7] These conditions are the general trend throughout the Pamir region, where vegetation outside of the river valleys is extremely limited, the only exception being in the narrow adjacent alluvial land and terraces along rivers, where irrigation is possible on a severely restricted (and orographically defined) basis. On this land, such products as barley, potatoes, short-grow-ing-cycle vegetables, and melons are grown (Captain Wood noted only peas and barley with limited wheat in his explorations), along with alfalfa for herd animals. In the Tajik Republic, these small farms were further limited during the Soviet era as the Pamir region was dedicated almost exclusively to breed-ing cattle and other livestock. Small farms and the cultural knowledge of subsistence farming were generally lost until independence.[8]

Altitude does not constitute the only restriction on vegetation growth, as the region in general is arid. Although the mountains do cause the orographic lifting of clouds, creating the necessary dew point conducive to precipitation, this usually occurs in winter and collects as snowfall that melts in warmer weather and then funnels through precipitous river valleys in the late spring and summer. Otherwise, annual precipitation is estimated to be between 8 and 15 centimeters (3 and 6 inches), thus further restricting vegetation growth in nonirrigated areas.[9]

These characterizations have effects far beyond that of vegetation. During his travels in the region in 1838, Captain Wood estimated there were less than one thousand people living permanently in the valley of the Great Pamir upriver of Ishkashim, located at the easterly bend of the Panj River at the start of the Wakhan Corridor, along with some one hundred nomadic Kyrgyz who were summering there.[10] In 1905, Aurel Stein (who claimed to be the first European to visit the Wakhan Corridor since the Pamir Boundary Commission set it up) traveled through the corridor and reported on a key historical precedent of the region that would soon become problematic. In his estimation, there were some 190 households (about 2,000 people) of Wakhi in Russian territory and more than that on the Afghan side.[11] Of the Kyrgyz, he noted about a hundred families whose nomadic range included what was then the Russian-, Chinese-, and Afghan-held Pamirs. The area being used depended on favorable grazing grounds and who had the lowest taxation.[12] This showed that although the Russians and British held these borders to be in place, they obviously did not concern either the Wakhi, who continued to have relations on both sides of the river, or the Kyrgyz nomads, who moved their sheep and yaks easily from Russia to Afghanistan to China.[13] This dramatically illustrates the problematic nature of using a river as a strategic border. Historically, no group would settle on only one side of a river, although different groups might inhabit the length of a river. Effectively, this border, stretching across most of northern Afghanistan, divided every ethnic group that depended on this river and its tributaries. Wakhi, Kyrgyz, Tajiks, and Uzbeks all were divided between Russian (and later Soviet) Central Asia and Afghanistan, thus severing family and economic ties.

Not until 1979 would a clearer description of the region be written. In that year, M. Nafiz Shahrani published the seminal text on the Wakhan Corridor entitled *The Kirghiz and Wakhi of Afghanistan: Adaptation to Closed Frontiers and War*. In this text, Shahrani goes into great detail about the adaptation strategies used by both the indigenous Wakhi people and the native and transplanted Kyrgyz (of Turkic origin), along with related socioeconomic and cultural issues. From his work and that of other works that deal tangentially with the Wakhan Corridor, it is possible to discern a historic geographic narrative of both the people and environment of this isolated region down to recent times. Shahrani reports that nearly 250 families augmented the number of Kyrgyz reported by Stein in the corridor following the success of the Bolsheviks in Central Asia. This occasioned a population of some 2,000 Kyrgyz in 1921;[14] however, due to Soviet incursions, which potentially lessened the number of Kyrgyz, and further migrations (including some from China after its 1949 Communist revolution), an estimated 1,825 Kyrgyz inhabited the corridor. The native Wakhi, who are of Iranian origin and unlike the generally Sunni Kyrgyz, follow the Ismaili (Shiite) sect of Islam, and Shahrani estimates that some six thousand lived in the region during his time of study there.[15] Today, official estimates by the United Nations and the Agha Khan Rural Development Network put the population at approximately 10,590, of which approximately 1,200 are Kyrgyz.[16]

Historical Context of the Border's Creation

According to Lord George Curzon, a noted statesman and author of the period who served as viceroy of India from 1898 to 1905, throughout the European imperial age and down to the late twentieth century, the question of frontiers and borders has caused more vexation and anxiety than any other issue since the advent of the nation-state. It has, therefore, been the "subject of four out of every five political treaties or conventions that are now concluded."[17] In the later nineteenth century, an area fraught with danger and mistrust was the ever-dwindling area that separated the British Empire from the Russian Empire. Although the extent of this danger was perhaps magnified by the British (and to a lesser extent, American) press and known Russophobes, there is no question that it dominated many headlines of the time and caused headaches for the various British governments. Great Britain ran India as a business venture under the British East India Company, and from the earliest years, India had been the most important and economically profitable area within what would become the British Empire after the Sepoy Rebellion in 1857. Great Britain would, therefore, go to any length to protect this valuable asset from covetous eyes.[18] As the source of so much wealth, leaders that included such disparate people as Russian tsars (from Peter the Great to Nicholas II), Napoleon Bonaparte, and Heinrich Himmler's SS commanders wanted to wrest India from the British or at least keep them from profiting from it.[19] Fear (or dismissal) of invasions, therefore, dominated diplomatic discussions of India throughout the late eighteenth and nineteenth centuries. However, no country dominated these discussions more than Russia. This led both the Royal Geographic Society and its Russian counterparts to commission an extensive number of exploratory missions into the region, most often under the aegis of scientific research that incompletely masked their imperial importance.[20] At the same time that these explorations were occurring, the Russian "bogey" advanced ever farther into Central Asia by annexing or making vassals out of the lands held by the Khans of Khoqand and Khiva and the Emir of Bukhara.[21] This caused certain British politicians and citizens to grow increasingly alarmed. These discussions in turn gave rise to two distinct types of politicians in both the English parliament and in the British imperial center of Calcutta: those who advocated the "forward policies"[22] toward Russia and Afghanistan (led by the conservative Sir Henry Rawlinson) and those

who advocated the school of "masterly inactivity"—a sneering title leveled at
Sir John Lawrence and his fellow Whig politicians who wished to negotiate
the extent of Russian incursions into Central Asia.[23] What this meant practically for the people of Afghanistan—and to a lesser extent Iran, which was
also seen as a bulwark against other European powers[24]—is that they had to
negotiate a different policy with each successive British government. New
leadership in London and Calcutta could be more aggressive toward an ill-
defined Afghanistan and its rulers (forward school) in the hopes of monopo-
lizing policy there and bringing the loose conglomeration of tribes that made
up the "country" firmly within its sphere of influence as a buffer state. The
Afghan border, though artificial, would therefore constitute the "advanced
strategic frontier."[25] The alternative entailed backing away from Afghanistan
with the idea that Russia could not successfully invade from that direction,
given the difficulties it would inevitably have with the different tribes and the
terrain. Given the psychology of British imperialism, neither the promoters
of the forward school nor the proponents of "masterly inactivity" thought
that the British would lose a battle against an enemy and/or an uprising that
might be sparked by an invasion. What the East India Company did fear was
the *cost* of prevailing in either scenario.[26]

The question was then neither how a party or a politician felt about war (as
the ultimate motives of Russia remained unclear) nor the waxing and waning
virulence of Russophobia in the British press due to the seemingly ever-expanding nature of the Russian Empire in Eurasia. Rather, it was whether the
British East India Company and later the British colonial government wanted
to incur the expense of a full-scale invasion of Afghanistan in order to keep
the Russians out. The answer to this was a resounding yes on two major occasions in the nineteenth century, appropriately called the First and Second Afghan Wars. Although in each of these wars Great Britain won decisive initial
battles, it was never able to hold Afghanistan, although it certainly tried after
the First Afghan War. In that conflict, the British held Kabul for two years
and installed "their man," Shah Shujah, on the throne; however, they were
soon to lose their hold of Afghanistan in one of the most "spectacular and
humiliating" disasters in British history. Their army was forced to leave Kabul
due to strengthening Afghan opposition in the face of cultural insensitivity by
the British and a correct perception by Afghan tribes that Shah Shujah was a
British stooge.[27] Although scores of officers, officers' wives and children, and
some "2000 sepoys and camp followers" were kept behind as hostages,[28] out
of the 16,000 "British and Indian troops, wives, children, nannies, grooms,
cooks, servants, and assorted hangers-on"[29] who began the march through
the Khoord-Kabul Pass, only one person, Dr. William Brydon, made it to the
British fort at Jalalabad alive.[30]

Although there would be two more wars (in the eyes of the British) with Afghanistan (including one in the twentieth century that was not caused by perceived Russian aggression), the British would never again contemplate holding the country. As a consequence, it became more and more apparent to successive British governments during the nineteenth century that Afghanistan could no longer have nebulous boundaries for fear that Russia would continue to use this as an excuse for continued advances south through Central Asia. This realization meant securing two borders, one between British India and Afghanistan, and the other between Russian Central Asia and Afghanistan. Both were of equal importance to the British because whatever was not held outright by the British or by the Afghan king was potentially open to annexation by the Russians. Given the two borders' importance, there were two (of a potential five[31]) paths into northern India that most concerned the British: the western path through Herat and Kandahar, and the eastern path through the Pamir Mountains, the Wakhan Valley, and directly into northern India.[32] The trouble was that the British knew little about the approaches to the Wakhan Valley, and what they knew of the approaches to Herat had been gathered by individuals, led initially by young men like Arthur Conolly, reconnoitering the area during the early and middle 1800s, sometimes with, sometimes without the consent of the government. More of these "private citizens" and "individualists" would be needed in order to determine the feasibility of an attack through Wakhan.[33] This need was further spurred by the Russian conquest of the oasis of Merv and a subsequent outpouring of Great Game (and Russophobic) literature in 1884–1885 in Great Britain.[34] The map in figure 4.2 illustrates where the British and the Afghan king, Abdur Rahman Khan, believed the limits of Afghan authority extended. This map was published in a book titled *Russian Projects against India: From the Czar Peter to General Skobeleff*, by H. Sutherland Edwards, as a call to action by the British government to halt Russian advances. What is important about this map is that the Russians were already pushing in both the directions the Russophobic authors and the conservatives feared most, toward Herat and the Pamir Plateau, and both were determined that the Russians would push no farther.

However on March 31, 1885, the liberals under Prime Minister William Gladstone were to receive a severe shock when the Russian army attacked the oasis of Panjdeh, about halfway along the route from Merv to Herat, and slaughtered much of the Afghan military guarding it (see figure 4.3). War seemed imminent between Russia and Great Britain[35] as the British Foreign Office prepared announcements of the outbreak of hostilities and dispatched engineers to "place the fortifications of Herat in a state of defence."[36] What proved most surprising, though, was the nonchalance with which the emir

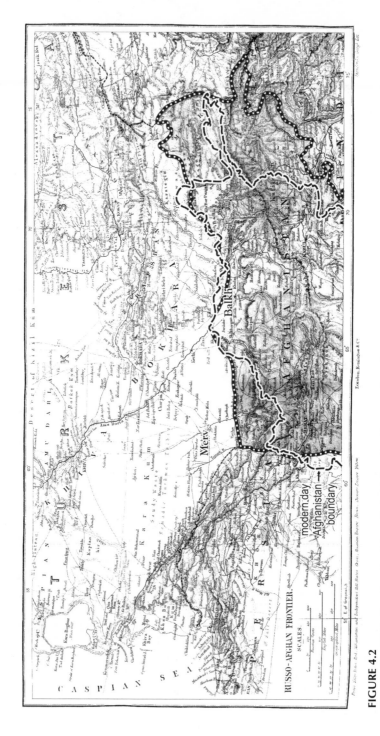

FIGURE 4.2
The Russo-Afghan Frontier. Louisiana State University Cartography Laboratory.

FIGURE 4.3
The Borders of Afghanistan. Louisiana State University Cartography Laboratory.

of Afghanistan, Abdur Rahman (then on a state visit in India), received the news. As a nominal ally of Great Britain, he almost certainly could have provoked the outbreak of war, but what the incident did provoke was the will by both Afghanistan and Great Britain to fix the northern border, which followed the border of the Edwards map along the Amu Darya (the Oxus River in ancient literature),[37] except for the dip southward to include the oasis of Panjdeh, which the Afghans and British conceded to Russia.[38] The only issue left now was the worrisome passes through the Pamir Mountains.

Because ongoing diplomatic problems between Britain and Russia concerning the creation of a border north of Herat, as well as China and Tibet, had barely lessened, official reconnaissance by British citizens of the area was largely discouraged. That did not mean, however, that native Indians in the service of the British could not go into the region; albeit with the understanding that the colonial government would claim no knowledge of either them or their mission. These explorers (known as pundits) provided valuable information to the British government about the possibility of moving an army through the region as well as the movements of Russians in the region.[39]

Among the few British officers and citizens who were intermittently allowed to reconnoiter the area was Francis Younghusband, who as early as
1890 was warning of Russian agents moving through this area and what that
could mean for India.[40] The British government allowed Younghusband
to travel from Beijing to Kashgar in western China and then to proceed
overland to India. En route from Kashgar back to India, Younghusband
heard from local Kyrgyz about a Russian force on its way to annex the
Pamir Plateau for Russia. Alarmed, he proceeded on through the Wakhjir
Pass to the Little Pamir and into the Wakhan area, where he famously met
Colonel Yonoff. However, three days after this meeting, the cordial nature
of the meeting was abruptly terminated when Colonel Yonoff was sent
back to order Younghusband to leave "Russian territory" by the way he
had come and not by way of any passes south of the Pamirs (thus delaying the news of Russian movements in the area). Younghusband complied
and upon returning to India immediately informed the government of the
situation. Thirteen days after the second meeting with Yonoff, the British
ambassador at St. Petersburg strenuously protested to the Russian government of Younghusband's treatment and of the flagrant violation of the
Anglo-Russian Agreement of 1873 in which Russia agreed that Badakhshan
and Wakhan belonged to Afghanistan. This forced the Russians to publicly
state that Buzai-Gambad (site of Younghusband/Yonoff's first meeting) was
outside of Russian influence and that "the Russian officer had violated the
elementary principles of international law."[41]

The British government was not mollified by this pronouncement, and to
add further worry, Aman-ul-Mulk, the leader of the remote city of Chitral,
died in 1892, leaving no clear successor. Chitral's primary importance was
that it contained the series of valleys stretching from Wakhan to British-held
India.[42] Fear of this area as a possible invasion route went back to 1874, amid
the claim that Russia could be in British territory in thirteen days with an
army if it held Chitral; hence Great Britain should maintain a presence there.[43]
Britain had a treaty with Aman-ul-Mulk, but his successor was unknown,
as leaders in the region do not follow primogeniture, and Great Britain
feared that a bloodbath among his sons would make an invasion through
the Wakhan irresistible to the Russians. When the British-backed claimant
Nizam-ul-Mulk was assassinated, the British government's disquiet immediately translated into troops being hastily dispatched into Chitral, where they
became enmeshed in the violence around the succession and had to call in
reinforcements. Among these was Captain Younghusband, who had warned
of the dangers of an unoccupied Chitral.[44] The British ultimately were able to
secure Chitral, but the continued presence of the British there remained in
doubt until the conservatives once more took power in 1895 and Chitral, the

northern extent of which was only twelve miles from Russian-held territory, was incorporated into British India.[45]

Although there had been disagreement earlier as to whether the "key to India" was Herat or Kabul, with boundaries essentially set north of both of these cities, and after the worrisome Chitral episode, the Russophobes in India and London now became united in their call for action on the Chitral front.[46] Because of the lessening of tensions from the previous decades and the knowledge on the British side that setting the boundary was the only way to keep the northern frontier of India itself secure,[47] England and Russia agreed to form the Pamir Boundary Commission in 1895. The Russians sent General Schveikovskii to survey the northern approaches, and the British sent General M. G. Gerard to survey the southern approaches from Chitral. The commission configured a territory, much of which was inaccessible except for the valley by which merchants and travelers (most notably for Westerners, Marco Polo) navigated the southern route of the Silk Road, which would thereafter lie within the domain of the emir of Afghanistan, Abdur Rahman.[48] It further stated that:

> Her Britannic Majesty's Government and the Government of His Majesty the Emperor of Russia engage to abstain from exercising any political influence or control, the former to the north, the latter to the south, of the above line of demarcation. . . . Her Britannic Majesty's Government engage that the territory lying within the British sphere of influence between the Hindu Kush and the line running from the east end of Lake Victoria (Zor Koul) to the Chinese frontier shall form part of the territory of the Ameer of Afghanistan, that it shall not be annexed to Great Britain and that no military posts or forts shall be established on it.[49]

Neither Afghanistan nor China took part in the surveys or the negotiations; therefore, this boundary was created purely to allay British fears of a Russian invasion of India. The treaty, however, only set a line (the Russian-Afghan border), but the British considered the area south of the line up to the Hindu Kush to be "within their sphere of influence" yet recognized as Afghan territory.[50] From the Russian side, they professed that gaining the Pamir Plateau was the end result they desired as they saw that area as firmly within the frontier of the former Khanate of Khoqand (absorbed by Russia in 1875). The Russians claimed that the British did not want to recognize this motive so as to "keep (the Russian) frontier at a distance from India."[51] This appears to be backed up by Barbara Jelavich's analysis of Russo-British relations that Russia, quantitatively unable to match Britain's naval power, always drew up plans to invade India by land in order to exert pressure on Britain to allow Russia to implement what otherwise seemed like small-scale designs in Central Asia or elsewhere in the world.[52] To this end, Russia got everything it professed to wanting, that is, a set boundary encompassing all lands north of the Amu Darya as well as most of the land claimed by the Khanate of Khiva, including the approaches to Herat, and all the land claimed by the Khanate of Khoqand, including the Pamir Plateau.[53]

Now thanks to the "Amir's acceptance of the narrow district of Wakhan," at no point did the British or Russian empires touch.[54] How much of this was "acceptance" as opposed to "coercion" is left for speculation. Because Afghanistan was a state within Great Britain's sphere of influence, the British controlled all of its foreign policy.[55] Afghanistan had protested that the whole of the Pamir Plateau rested within its authority, but the British ignored all Afghan claims to these areas while disregarding the fact that they nominally at least claimed to support the interests of Afghanistan. In point of fact, they were simply relieved to halt Russian expansion toward India. According to the noted Afghan expert, Louis Dupree, Abdur Rahman was not pleased with the tiny section he was to administer and "objected to the gift (of the Wakhan), exclaiming he had enough problems with his own people and did not wish to be held responsible for the Kirghiz bandits in the Wakhan."[56] This attitude continued down through successive administrations, and the Wakhan would continuously suffer from neglect by Kabul.[57] Although Abdur Rahman signed the agreements setting both the Wakhan Corridor and the earlier "Durand Line" that separated British India's western boundary with Afghanistan, he claimed that he thought it set up only "areas of responsibility," not an unwanted, official border. This contention was actually shared by Sir Mortimer Durand, after whom the Durand Line was named, as well as by Lord Curzon.[58] Nevertheless, in setting these boundaries, the final act of the tense game played out by the British and Russian governments came to a close. The only items left to be resolved would mostly be handled in 1907 as almost an anticlimax (though they would have far-reaching repercussions), when Russia agreed to deal with all matters relating to Afghanistan only through the British government and both the Russian and British governments agreed that Tibet, a further place of intrigue between the two governments, would rest secured under Chinese suzerainty.[59]

Though arguably both sides could not have foreseen it at the time due to mutual distrust of the other's motives, both the Durand Line and the Wakhan border would hold until the present day, and only with the disastrous invasion of Afghanistan in 1979 would Russian forces trespass south of these borders.[60] The only open-ended issue from those commissions, therefore, remained the border between Afghanistan and China. At the eastern point of the Wakhan, the boundary moves over several glaciers "of perpetual ice and snow" that neither Afghanistan nor China had ever properly mapped or agreed upon.[61]

Although the British government tried to include the Chinese government in talks, it could not be included within any practical length of time. This long delayed final frontier would have to wait until 1964, when the border was officially demarcated by the government of the king of Afghanistan, Zahir Shah, and Chairman Mao Tse-Tung's government in China.[62]

The Effect of the Border on Proximate Groups of People Both Geographically and Socially

During the British and Russian colonial period, it was clear that this demarcation was an expedient to lessen tensions between those two great powers and not a hard-and-fast barrier to regional ethnic groups migrating through the region. With the advent of the Soviet Union, its policies toward collectivization, and the impediments it placed on travel outside the country, the northern border was effectively sealed. This crisis for the nomadic herders was greatly increased with the Chinese Communist revolution of 1949, which sealed the eastern border. This caused hardship not only for herders but also for traders as the Silk Road was now officially closed in both its northern and southern routes. The Wakhan Corridor essentially became a dead end while the two sides of the Panj River entered radically different economic phases. The northern side fell under a heavily subsidized Communist regime that nonetheless brought the people politically and economically, through new transportation and communication routes, into larger systems, albeit ones that led ultimately to Russia and away from southern and eastern Asia. The southern side of the river, on the other hand, fell into a subsistence-only lifestyle cut off from historic trade routes. This condition became an even larger problem in 1978, when the Communist coup in Kabul (and subsequent Soviet invasion in 1979) caused increasing hardships for all Afghans and caused many of the Kyrgyz to flee once more, but this time into Pakistan. Although a small percentage would eventually return to Afghanistan, for the majority of these Kyrgyz, the stress of staying one step ahead of Communist governments convinced them to accept a resettlement scheme by the Turkish government that translocated them completely out of Central Asia and into Kurdish territory in eastern Turkey, where they remain.[63]

It might have been hoped that with the fall of the Soviet Union and the opening of China to trade and commerce, the isolation of the Wakhan Corridor would end. This, however, did not prove to be the case as almost immediately after the fall, the newly created Republic of Tajikistan devolved into a brutal civil war that included the people (and co-religionists of the Wakhi) of the Tajik Badakhshan region north of the Wakhan Corridor in the conflict.[64]

This caused economic conditions to rapidly deteriorate through a process of "demodernization" to the north, while the Afghan Civil War and the subsequent Taliban interlude caused hardship throughout the rest of Afghanistan.[65] Not until the ending of the civil war in Tajikistan in 1997 and the cessation of violence between the Taliban and the Northern Alliance (which had held nominal sway in the Wakhan Corridor) in the north of the country caused by the events after September 11, 2001, would prospects for improved economic and material conditions arise. These prospects, however, have proven severely limited and finite. The main cause of this is that the only current connection to the rest of Afghanistan is a dirt track that connects to the regional city of Ishkashim. While bridges have opened between Tajikistan and Afghanistan, most notably for the Wakhan Corridor at Ishkashim, this continues to leave the residents at the mercy of politics, particularly as the national Afghan government remains weak.[66] Due to ongoing conflicts involving a rejuvenated Taliban, the borders with Pakistan are currently closed. Although there is no navigable road to China, one has been completed between the Tajikistani city of Badakhshan and China. Yet border crossings with Tajikistan remain difficult for local residents because of transnational drug organizations that use Tajikistan as one of the main transit routes for Afghan opium. Therefore, a reliable road to the rest of Afghanistan remains a top priority.

Unfortunately, at the present time, the Afghan government has little incentive to augment the infrastructure of this region. Far more politically sensitive areas such as Kabul and Kandahar are in need of large expenditures to counter the frequent blackouts that hit these cities, especially in summer, and to rebuild destroyed infrastructure. The government therefore allocates the lion's share of small-scale development projects throughout Afghanistan to nongovernmental organizations.[67] As the largest part of the population in the Wakhan Corridor is Ismaili, the Agha Khan Development Network has invested a considerable amount of money there; however, this has alternated between food subsidies and (more lately) food-for-work programs that have improved transportation within areas of the Wakhan but have yet to produce an all-weather road to the regional capital of Faizabad and thus on to the rest of the country. Because the available goods to trade from the area are limited and mostly restricted to the breeding of fat-tailed sheep (especially among the remaining Kyrgyz), this road would be potentially more favorable to future trade and perhaps the impetus to develop tourism further, either around a national park scheme for wildlife viewing, as proposed by the USAID-funded Wildlife Conservation Society, or by mountaineering as an immediate aid to the region.[68] At the current time, tourists arrive through Tajikistan, whose archaic visa restrictions make movement into the Wakhan Corridor extremely difficult.

With this in mind, it is important to note that the Afghan government has allowed a form of control, typical outside of the capital region, to evolve in the Wakhan Corridor—that of the "commander" system, whereby regional warlords have taken over the economic means of set areas and rule them as personal fiefdoms. As the commander for this region is not even from the Wakhan region, this de facto relationship with the government is seen as overtly exploitative with no discernable benefit. The direness of individual situations is dramatically illustrated in a survey of six hundred households conducted by the Wakhan Development Partnership that found 92 percent of men in households describing themselves as subsistence farmers with an average family holding of approximately one acre.[69] Clearly, there is little besides farming for the residents beyond the rare professional occupation, such as teacher, or village specialists, such as a *mirob* (irrigation supervisor) or blacksmith.[70] These circumstances have created the need for other coping strategies, which for most families has involved some form of migration (both temporary and long term). Migration, until recently, meant finding work as wage laborers in the nearby cities of Pakistan, particularly the Ismaili settlements of Chitral and Gilgit. However, since 2002, the charged nature of Afghan-Pakistani relations has forced migrants to northern Afghan cities such as Faizabad, where there are mining and similar hard labor jobs.[71] From this working framework, one cannot belabor the point enough that the potential for development for inhabitants and the region in general is severely curtailed by this colonial border construct that contributes to geographic isolation and the lack of marketable skills and products among the inhabitants.

Conclusion

Since the 1990s, borders have become a major topic of political geographers. The measure of whose interests are served by the creation of borders and how and why they are maintained has given rise to important new literature that speaks to these ethical questions.[72] Both geographically and historically, the interests and maintenance of the borders enclosing the Wakhan Corridor cannot be extricated from either its colonial past or the geopolitical situation of modern Central Asia. There was never any intention by Great Britain or Russia to consider either the inhabitants or the viability of the region they were setting off. As a classic "buffer state," Afghanistan as a whole was merely a plot of land to keep the great powers from conflict. Since both countries were displaying a notably imperial mindset toward Afghanistan, neither power would seriously consider its economic viability. Both were recent industrial powers, and each had hoped to dominate the market in Afghanistan, much like Great Britain had done in India and Russia was beginning to do in Central Asia. Consequently, when the borders became set with the onset of the Soviet Union and the independence of Pakistan and India, Afghanistan as a whole was left with isolated and ethnically diverse populations, no ports, and few avenues to expand its economy to make up for the loss of transcontinental trade.

The Wakhan Corridor is a microcosm of this situation. While nearby settlements in Tajikistan and China have experienced heavy subsidization from Communist leaderships who have attempted expensive and expansive endeavors to make those areas feel part of a greater whole (however imperfectly realized), the Wakhi and Kyrgyz were left with their traditional survival techniques of subsistence herding and small-scale farming, but without the range of pastureland previously available or the transcontinental trade of the Silk Road (however diminished over time) that augmented this lifestyle. In such circumstances, because of its remoteness both physically and politically from the center of administrative power, the population feels alienated and has never been made to feel part of a larger group (i.e., as "Afghan"), something many disciplines claim as the intended process of border determination.[73] One can therefore cite the Wakhan Corridor as an important example of both the consequences of colonialism on divided and marginalized ethnic groups and, because of isolation, conflict, and the continuous indifference of the government of Afghanistan, the extreme difficulty these groups have in expanding their livelihoods outside of basic subsistence or of ever joining the global community of the twenty-first century.

5

The Caprivi Strip of Namibia

Shifting Sovereignty and the Negotiation of Boundaries

Robert Lloyd

To those who show a penchant for perusing atlases, the political map of modern Africa is a puzzle. The continent is divided into a bewildering and colorful profusion of states. Borders are arranged in lines that appear at first glance to be without order or meaning (figure 5.1). This initial observation has some truth, but delving into the history of Africa does eventually provide clear meaning, order, and context to the delineation of borders. The states in West Africa, for example, are often narrow and deep, which reflects the efforts of different European colonial powers to tap into interior markets. States in eastern and southern Africa are relatively larger and, adjusted for variations in local terrain, look broadly rounded. These borders were drawn up later and were intended to aid the practical subdivision of the continent among leading European states.

Although the African continent presents a number of promising candidates for a study of unusual, anomalous borders, Namibia's so-called Caprivi Strip jumps to the front of the line in any study of seemingly odd borders (figure 5.2). Named after the Namib Desert along Africa's southwestern coast, Namibia was officially born on March 21, 1990, after South Africa relinquished control of what had formerly been called South-West Africa. Broadly geometrically shaped, Namibia's borders are conventional for countries in southern Africa, albeit modified to account for certain natural features such as rivers. The Caprivi Strip, the narrow panhandle jutting out to Namibia's east for about 450 kilometers (280 miles), is one notable exception and the topic of this chapter.

Robert Lloyd

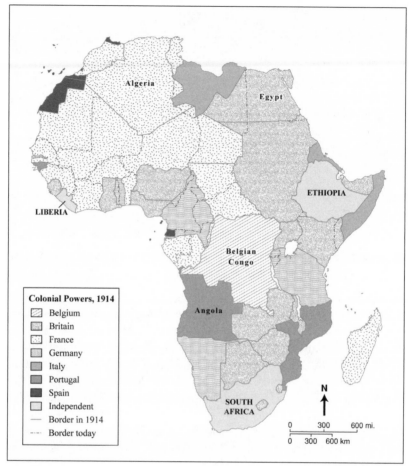

FIGURE 5.1
Africa—Colonial Powers 1914. Cory Johnson of XNR.

The Caprivi Strip is a puzzle, like many other borders of Africa, but the sheer oddness of its borders pique curiosity. How and why was such an odd-shaped territory created? Why does the easternmost terminus of the Caprivi Strip reach nearly to Victoria Falls in Zimbabwe? Why was this territory, so remote from the rest of Namibia, eventually attached to South-West Africa/Namibia and not simply to the geographically closer states of Zambia, Botswana, or Angola? Alternatively, why did the Caprivi Strip not simply become an independent state, separating itself from a Namibia to which it had been linked somewhat tenuously? These questions are answered through an examination of the circumstances that led to the creation of these borders, the actors who created the borders of the Caprivi Strip and Namibia, the importance of these borders to those who managed them, the impact of the borders on the people who live within and outside their confines, and the way the meaning of these borders that structure the Caprivi Strip have evolved over time.

The Caprivi Strip

Some essential background on Namibia and the Caprivi Strip is necessary to begin this inquiry. Namibia has a surface area of 823,144 square kilometers (317,818 square miles) and is roughly similar in size and shape to the American states of California, Nevada, and the western third of Utah combined. The large and arid country is sparsely populated with approximately two million people. Namibia's population is nearly 90 percent of African descent and overwhelmingly Christian. About half of Namibians are Lutheran, reflecting its heritage as a former German colony. English is the official language, but Afrikaans is widely spoken due to the former rule of South Africa. The economy is based to a large degree on the extraction of export commodities, notably diamonds and uranium. The agricultural sector consists of large, white-owned commercial farms, although subsistence farming provides a living for about half the population. One result of this economic structure is both a relatively high per capita gross domestic product (GDP) and a high income inequality for its citizens.[1]

Supporting only 4 percent of Namibia's population and occupying approximately the same area as the country of Macedonia in Europe, the Caprivi Strip is divided into two administrative regions (figure 5.2). The eastern part is the Caprivi Region. With the exception of its northern border with Angola, it is bounded by rivers: the Zambezi River on the northern border with Zambia, the Chobe and Linyanti rivers on the southern border with Botswana, and the Kwando River on the western border with the western Caprivi Strip. The 2001 population was approximately 80,000 people, and the region comprises 19,531 square kilometers (7,541 square miles), or an area slightly smaller than Wales. The administrative center and largest settlement is Katima Mulilo.

The western Caprivi Strip is administratively part of the Okavango Region. Rundu, the administrative center and largest city, with a population of about 50,000 people, is not located in the strip, but farther west along the Okavango River. The entire Okavango Region encompasses an area of 43,419 square kilometers (16,764 square miles) and had a 2001 population of just over 200,000. The western Caprivi Strip itself lies between the Kwando River on the east and the Okavango River on the west. Both its northern border with Angola and its southern border with Botswana run straight, as if drawn with

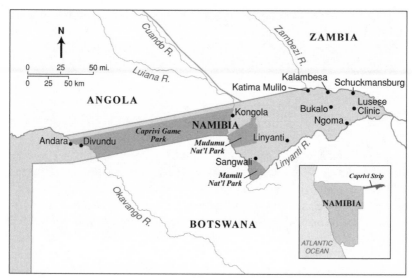

FIGURE 5.2
The Caprivi Strip. Cory Johnson of XNR.

a pen and ruler. The western Caprivi Strip is approximately 5,698 square kilometers (2,200 square miles), or slightly smaller than Delaware.

The inhabitants of the Caprivi Strip represent a diverse array of tribes differentiated by custom, status, history, and language. Ethnic groups in the area may generally be divided into two broad groups based on language family. The Caprivi area east of the Kwando River has been historically dominated by the Lozi (also called the Luyi or Barotse) ethnic group, who speak a Bantu language. The Bantu language groups share a number of common cultural features, including agriculture, cattle herding, and social organization. In the middle of the eighteenth century, the Lozi conquered tribes living in the eastern Caprivi area and imposed a harsh and humiliating feudal system of government over the conquered tribes.[2] The Caprivi was considered part of the southern reaches of Barotseland, a kingdom that included a large part of present-day Zambia.

The borders of this time and region were fluid. Hundreds of miles to the south in what is now called KwaZulu-Natal Province in South Africa, a warrior and king named Shaka initiated a series of wars that consolidated the Zulu nation, created an empire, caused widespread suffering, and was a major factor in large-scale population displacement and migration throughout southern Africa. Later referred to as the *Mfecane*, a Zulu word for "the crushing," this was a period of widespread warfare and suffering that lasted from

1815 to 1840. One Sotho group in South Africa fleeing the Zulus during the *Mfecane* was the Makololo (sometimes called Kololo). This group gradually moved north beginning in the 1820s, migrating hundreds of miles across what is now Botswana, and finally crossing the Okavango and Chobe rivers in the 1830s. There they fought and conquered the Lozi. The Makololo ruled the eastern Caprivi region for thirty years, eventually being decisively defeated by the Lozi in 1864. Their continuing influence is still seen in the Lozi adoption of a Sotho language.

Other Bantu speakers in the eastern Caprivi Strip include the Subiya and the linguistically closely related Fwe and Totela speakers.[3] Khoisan ("click" languages) tribes consist of the numerically smaller Yeyi and Kxoé groups. Khoisan groups, traditionally being pastoralists or hunter-gatherers, are culturally distinct from the farming and cattle herding Bantu language groups. The Khoisan groups were the original inhabitants of southern Africa before the Bantu migration that gradually moved down the eastern and southern parts of the continent. The western part of the Caprivi Strip is much less populated than the eastern part. Khoisan speakers are widespread. The western part of the Caprivi Strip, located between the Okavango and Kwando rivers, is considered the heartland of the Kxoé. The Mbukushu, a Bantu-related group, is also located in this area.

Scramble for Africa

The area now known as the Caprivi Strip and the borders that define this territory did not exist prior to 1890. Most of the Caprivi Strip was part of the southern frontier of the Barotseland state, which spanned what are now western Zambia, southeastern Angola, the Caprivi Strip, and areas immediately adjacent to the strip in Botswana and Zimbabwe.[4] Since the mid-1700s the Barotseland state had defined the patterns of social, economic, and political relations for the various tribes located within its borders. Even after the temporary defeat of the Lozi regime and the establishment of Makololo rule between the 1830s and 1864, certain elements of the state itself proved resilient. The later introduction of European rule into the region, for example, did not eliminate traditional leadership but actively sought its integration into colonial-era policies through a deliberate policy of indirect rule. Through this governing strategy, colonial administrators recognized the legitimacy and role of traditional leaders provided they in turn recognized the paramount authority of the European monarch and cooperated on matters of general administration.

On the foundation and frontier of a preexisting African kingdom, the modern borders of the Caprivi Strip arose from a series of negotiated agreements concluded by influential states outside the African continent. In 1884, some three thousand miles north of the Barotse Kingdom, high-ranking representatives of several powerful Western European states met in a conference to discuss how best to divide the African continent into their respective spheres of influence. While European contact had existed since the Portuguese pioneered the sea route to Asia in 1498, European interest in the African continent had been limited primarily to the extraction of tropical products and slaves. In the latter part of the nineteenth century, after the international slave trade was abolished, European interest in Africa itself grew due to a confluence of technological inventions, organizational innovations, commercial promise, and ideological motivations. One such motivation for the European conquest of Africa was an ideology of imperialism engendered by a social Darwinian view of international relations in which the stark choice was dominate or be dominated. At the same time, a growing missionary movement sought to spread the Gospel to the unreached tribes in Africa. Overall, Africa was no longer viewed as a source of slaves but as what might be called today an "unevangelized emerging market."

A conference to discuss European interests in Africa was sought by Portugal, which, although not a major power at the time, had nevertheless amassed sizable colonial possessions in various strategic parts of coastal Africa during the sixteenth century. Portugal was concerned about increasing French and Belgian interest along the Atlantic coast of central Africa. It also sought to consolidate its African empire by connecting its two colonial possessions of Angola on the Atlantic Ocean coast and Mozambique on the Indian Ocean coast with a land bridge through what is now Zambia, Malawi, and Zimbabwe. This so-called Pink Map included all of Barotseland, except for the future Caprivi Strip as it was located south of the map's Zambia River border. This claim did, nonetheless, mark the first time the northeastern border of the Caprivi was delimited. Germany, a rapidly growing world power that had come quite late to the world stage, organized the conference.

The Berlin Conference of 1884–1885 sought to establish formal ground rules for Europe's subjugation and partition of Africa. It was hoped this diplomatic effort would reduce the chances that competition over Africa might spark a conflict between the European powers. This subjugation was internationally recognized based on a principle of international law termed *uti possedetis* (as you possess). This principle permits a territory acquired through conquest to be legally recognized as belonging to the victor. Since *uti possedetis* required the actual possession of the territory, the Berlin Conference triggered what is known as the Scramble for Africa, as European powers rapidly sought to establish treaties with local leaders and extend their administration into the areas they claimed. Within ten years of the signing of the treaty of the

Berlin Conference, only four independent states remained in Africa: Ethiopia, Liberia, and the two Boer states of the South African Republic and the Orange Free State (figure 5.1).

The Caprivi Strip was essentially an interstitial area for the competing claims of the European states, and its unusual shape reflects this ambiguous status. Germany had established commercial interests in Lüderitz, South-West Africa, in 1883, and on August 16, 1884, declared a protectorate over the southern part of South-West Africa based on this presence. Germany rapidly expanded its claims in South-West Africa, eventually bumping into Portuguese claims in the north of the protectorate. In accordance with Berlin Conference principles, on December 30, 1886, Germany and Portugal agreed on the northern border of German South-West Africa and southern border of Portuguese Angola as being from the mouth of the Kunene River inland to the Zambezi River. This agreement effectively established a northern border to what was to become in a few years the Caprivi Strip.[5]

Through the Berlin Conference, Britain gained large swathes of territory in eastern and southern Africa. British imperialists soon began calling for the creation of a "Cape to Cairo" railroad to link its colonial possessions from Cape Town on the southern tip of Africa north to Egypt. Portuguese claims were one obstacle to this aim. On January 11, 1890, the British government issued an ultimatum to its historic Portuguese ally to cede the Pink Map claims of the territory between Angola and Mozambique, although these claims had been recognized by all the governments at the Berlin Conference except Britain. The ultimatum was also a serious legal violation of the 1386 Treaty of Windsor that pledged mutual support between the two countries. A humiliated Portugal submitted and transferred the territories of Northern Rhodesia (including Barotseland), Southern Rhodesia, and Nyasaland to Britain.

German colonial interest in Africa was a second major obstacle to British aims. Germany, unlike Portugal, was a powerful rival that had the ability to frustrate Britain. The two powers had similar aims in terms of consolidating their African empires. Britain was persistent in its goal of acquiring a contiguous swath of territory from Cape Town to Cairo. German claims in eastern and southern Africa, however, threatened this goal. Since the Berlin Conference, Germany had established control over Tanganyika and the small state of Witu that straddled the current Kenya-Somalia border along the Indian Ocean coast.

Importantly, Germany had established a claim on the Buganda Kingdom (present-day Uganda) and retained some influence on Zanzibar, just off the coast of Tanganyika. Britain was concerned that Germany would seek to link this string of possessions, thereby encircling its Kenyan possession with a contiguous German territory that would block its Cape to Cairo objective. In southern Africa, Britain was apprehensive that Germany might extend its influence from South-West Africa to the east and north, thus blocking the Cape to Cairo goal in southern Africa. Of particular unease was the possible linking of the independent and fiercely anti-British Boer state of the South African Republic (in current northern South Africa) with Germany via South-West Africa.

Thus, imperial appetites and geopolitical rivalry provide the context for explaining the creation of this unusual appendage of land attached to Namibia. The creation of the Caprivi Strip itself arose as but one of a series of land swaps between Britain and Germany. These swaps related to larger questions of both the overall management of colonial possessions (especially territorial consolidation) and cordial international relations. The Caprivi Strip (from the German *Caprivizipfel*) was named after the German chancellor Count Georg Leo von Caprivi. A career military officer, Caprivi had become chancellor on March 18, 1890, after Kaiser Wilhelm II dismissed his predecessor, Prince Otto von Bismarck, from office. The new chancellor wished to improve relations with Britain as a hedge against a growing Russia. Thus, Anglo-German negotiations over territorial holdings in Africa moved relatively quickly.

The resultant Anglo-German Treaty or Heligoland-Zanzibar Treaty (July 1, 1890) clarified borders and spheres of interest of Germany and Britain in western, eastern, and southern Africa. Article III (2) of the treaty marked the official creation of the Caprivi Strip as an extension of German South-West Africa:

> To the east by the line that commences at the aforementioned point and follows the 20th degree of east longitude to its intersection point with the 22nd degree of south latitude. The line then traces this degree of latitude eastward to its intersection with the 21st degree of east latitude, follows this degree of longitude northward to its intersection with the 18th degree of south latitude, runs along this degree of latitude eastward to its intersection with the Chobe River. Here it descends the thalweg of the main channel until it meets the Zambezi, where it ends. It is understood under this arrangement Germany shall be granted free access from its protectorate to the Zambezi by means of a strip of land not less than twenty English miles wide at any point.[6]

This agreement marked the southern border of the Caprivi Strip as four years earlier Germany and Portugal had agreed on its northern border. Germany had insisted on acquiring the narrow extension of land as a corridor to link the colony to the Indian Ocean via the Zambezi River. This would, in theory, allow German waterborne trade between South-West Africa on the Atlantic Ocean with German Tanganyika (present-day mainland Tanzania) on the Indian Ocean. Although the Zambezi eventually reaches the ocean in Mozambique, at the time a Portuguese colony, Germany did not realize that the Zambezi was not navigable to the sea from the Caprivi.

Two other treaties soon clarified outstanding issues related to the Caprivi Strip (also referred to at this time as German Barotseland). On August 20, 1890, the Treaty of London, signed by Britain, Portugal, and Germany, de-limited the territorial limits of Angola and Namibia, including the northern border of the Caprivi Strip. Another treaty between Britain and Portugal signed on June 11, 1891, addressed the issue of the precise location of the Barotse state's boundaries in the Caprivi Strip (figure 5.3). Britain declared that the Barotse Kingdom was in its sphere of influence. Thus, by 1890, a scant five years after the Berlin Conference, Germany had established the

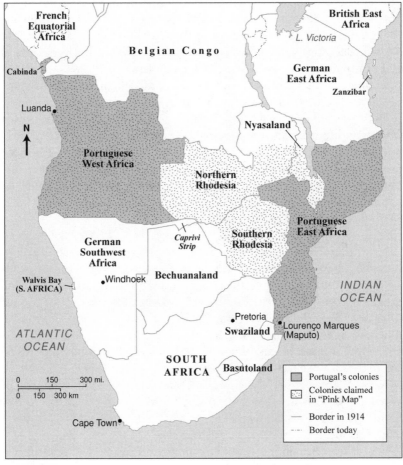

FIGURE 5.3
"The Pink Map." Cory Johnson of XNR.

internationally recognized colony of South-West Africa. Subsequent German policies turned toward establishing actual control over its inhabitants. The German subjugation of Africans living in South-West Africa was effective but brutal, especially in the case of the Herero people in central South-West Africa.[7]

The German Era

The creation of the Caprivi Strip out of a southern region of Barotseland and its attachment to South-West Africa was part of Germany's broader international strategy aimed at rapprochement with Britain, developing its maritime clout, and consolidating its African holdings. In the case of the Caprivi Strip, however, Germany gave short shrift to the actual fine points of what it had acquired. The Caprivi Strip was both culturally distinct and geographically distant from the rest of South-West Africa. Crisscrossed by rivers that flooded in the rainy season, no bridges would connect the length of the Caprivi Strip with South-West Africa until the 1950s. Although the Zambezi River connected the eastern edge of the Caprivi Strip to the Indian Ocean, the presence of rapids and the magnificent Victoria Falls prevented navigation downriver from the Caprivi Strip. The only overland access road to the Caprivi Strip was through the British Bechuanaland Protectorate. All these factors made administration from the South-West Africa colonial capital exceedingly difficult and expensive, delaying the actual occupation and development of the Caprivi Strip for several years.

Britain, being more familiar with the region, was aware of the challenges of administration for the Germans. Both Germany and Britain soon explored the possibility of a new agreement to exchange the Caprivi Strip for another territory. In 1902 a German officer, after visiting the region, recommended a scientific expedition to the Caprivi Strip as a way to enhance its value for exchange by demonstrating continued German interest in the Caprivi Strip and assessing any valuable resources in the territory.[8] In 1905, Britain and Germany unofficially began discussing a possible territorial exchange. Championing the idea of a territorial exchange was Hamilton Goold-Adams, Commissioner of the Bechuanaland Protectorate. He informally proposed that Germany cede to Britain that part of the Caprivi Strip east of the Kwando (Mashi) River in return for a piece of territory in northwest Ngamiland in the Bechuanaland Protectorate. Germany was aware of the strategic value of the Caprivi Strip to Britain but was still uncertain as to the territory's intrinsic worth. Germany therefore decided to send an exploratory expedition to the region that year to assess the value of its resources.

In July 1908, Lord Selborne, the British high commissioner in South Africa, formally proposed exchanging the Caprivi Strip for a piece of land in the Kalahari Desert of southwestern Bechuanaland. Germany rejected this initial offer but did decide to establish an official administrative presence in the Caprivi Strip to assess its importance. This task was entrusted to Captain Kurt Streitwolf, who set out on an arduous journey to reach the strip. In a report in late 1909, Captain Streitwolf stated it unlikely that the Caprivi Strip held mineral resources of any value. He noted, nevertheless, that the strip had great value to Britain given its strategic location between the British territories of Northern Rhodesia and Bechuanaland. He proposed exchanging the British-controlled territory around the port of Walvis Bay in German South-West Africa for the Caprivi. This exchange would have given the Germans access to the only natural port on the coast of South-West Africa and allowed Britain to connect its two territories directly. It was a reasonable proposal, but British objections and the subsequent transfer of South-West Africa to the new Union of South Africa in 1910 ended negotiations on this possible territorial exchange.[9] The ultimate failure of these negotiations between 1905 and 1909 meant that the Caprivi Strip was henceforth attached to German South-West Africa permanently.

Captain Streitwolf established his headquarters in the new settlement of Schuckmannsburg on the south bank of the Zambezi River in the far eastern section of the Caprivi Strip.[10] The reason for this location was largely related to accessibility. It was not yet known whether the Caprivi Strip could be transversed from South-West Africa, and the British had already established an administrative center nearby in Sesheke-Mwandi, on the north bank of the river. This provided a route to Livingstone in Southern Rhodesia and then on to South Africa by rail. The distance from South-West Africa and the unprofitability of the Caprivi Strip meant that funds were scarce. Despite these obstacles, Streitwolf embarked on a number of expeditions from his base in Schuckmannsburg and found it was possible, but very difficult, to reach South-West Africa via the entire length of the Caprivi Strip.

Upon arriving in the eastern Caprivi, Streitwolf discovered that the region had been recently depopulated due to prior news of the expedition's arrival and resultant local fears of German atrocities against Africans. Streitwolf proved very effective in encouraging the refugees to return to their homes in the Caprivi Strip and, surprisingly, proved fair and sensitive to local customs while administering the Caprivi. He was instrumental in forging a Caprivian identity separate from the Lozi of the Barotse Kingdom, keeping white hunters and farmers from settling in the region, and laying the basis for social reforms and indirect rule that continued for decades after the German period of control ended. Later administrators ably followed the example of exploration and organization set by Captain Streitwolf.[11]

On June 28, 1914, the Serbian nationalist Gavrilo Princip murdered Archduke Franz Ferdinand, heir to the Austro-Hungarian throne, in the Bosnian city of Sarajevo. This triggered a sequence of diplomatic and military actions and reactions that led the countries of Europe to war on August 1, 1914. These cataclysms eventually reverberated all the way to a far-off and isolated corner of southern Africa, leading within a few weeks to the end of German control over South-West Africa and the Caprivi Strip. On September 21, 1914, British forces crossed the Zambezi River from Sesheke-Mwandi into the Caprivi Strip and accepted the peaceful surrender of the two German officials stationed in Schuckmannsburg. This marked the first loss of German territory in the war. In October 1914, the British appointed an administrator to oversee the Caprivi from Kasane on the south side of the Chobe River in nearby Bechuanaland. This period of interim British administration continued until 1920. During this time there was some discussion of transferring the land to Barotseland, but the Subiya tribe living in the Caprivi was concerned about the Lozi (or Malozi) returning to the strip for raiding and settling scores.[12]

The Caprivi Strip as a Mandate

Legally, the Caprivi Strip remained German territory until the victorious Allied delegates to the Paris Peace Conference of 1919 (led by Britain, France, the United States, and Italy) signed the Treaty of Versailles on June 28, 1919, stripping Germany of all its colonial possessions. The Treaty of Versailles awarded all of German Tanganyika to Britain. This at long last filled in the gap in eastern Africa that separated British territory in southern and eastern Africa. Separate developments since 1890, however, meant that British control over the entire Cape to Cairo route was not possible. In 1902 the British had defeated the two Boer Republics of the South African Republic and Orange Free State in the Second Boer War. These two states were subsequently incorporated into the Union of South Africa. This new and largely pro-British state received its independence in 1910 and was to play a pivotal role in South-West Africa and the Caprivi Strip in the period between the end of World War I in 1918 and the Cold War in 1989.

During the war, German South-West Africa had been occupied by forces from the Union of South Africa, which was keen to add the territory into its new union. After the war, the status of the German territory was addressed in the Treaty of Versailles. The newly created League of Nations designated South-West Africa as a "Class C" mandate. This category addressed those cases in "which, owing to the sparseness of their population, or their small size, or their remoteness from the centres of civilisation, or their geographical contiguity to the territory of the Mandatory, and other circumstances, can be best administered under the laws of the Mandatory." This decision prevented South Africa from legally incorporating South-West Africa into the union but did permit the South African government to basically administer the territory as if it were an integral part of the country.[13] The South-West Africa Mandate Act 49 of 1919 gave executive and legislative power over South-West Africa to the governor-general of South Africa but did not resolve the ultimate status of South-West Africa. Over the next fifty years, South Africa and the League of Nations (and its successor, the United Nations) debated whether the territory would be incorporated into South Africa as a "fifth province," become independent, or hold some in-between status.[14]

The Caprivi Strip, distant both from the South-West Africa capital of Windhoek and the new mandatory power of South Africa, was from the beginning treated quite differently from the rest of South-West Africa. First, South-West Africa had become an area of substantial European settlement while European immigration to the Caprivi Strip was strictly limited. A second factor was due to the historical circumstances of the war. The Caprivi Strip had been occupied by British military forces while the rest of the territory had been occupied by South African forces. While the mandate had awarded the Caprivi Strip to South Africa, its remoteness made practical administration difficult. Thus, South Africa authorized the British high commissioner of South Africa to administer the entire Caprivi Strip (east of longitude 21 degrees) as part of the Bechuanaland Protectorate from 1922 to 1929.[15]

South African Control of the Caprivi Strip

In 1929 administrative responsibility for the entire Caprivi Strip was transferred from Britain to South Africa.[16] The governor-general gave the administrator of South-West Africa both legislative and administrative power to govern the Caprivi Strip. At the same time laws applicable in South-West Africa were extended to the Caprivi Strip.[17] These actions in 1929 marked the first time that the Caprivi Strip, since its creation nearly four decades earlier, was treated administratively as integrated with South-West Africa. This was not to last long. In 1939 administrative responsibility for the Caprivi Strip was split in two. The western Caprivi continued to be administered from Windhoek. The eastern Caprivi was the sole responsibility of the South African minister of native affairs (later minister of Bantu administration and development) based in the South African capital of Pretoria.[18] Subsequent

South African legislation in 1951 and 1968 continued to distinguish between laws applied to South-West Africa and the eastern Caprivi Strip. Interestingly, the administrators sent to the eastern strip were English speaking, in marked contrast to the use of Afrikaans in government administration in South-West Africa.[19] This, combined with the use of English in the neighboring territories, led to the widespread use of English as a lingua franca, creating stronger linguistic divisions between the eastern Caprivi Strip and the rest of South-West Africa.

Meanwhile, continued South African efforts to obtain international recognition of South-West Africa as integral to South Africa were increasingly unsuccessful. In the face of growing opposition to colonialism and white minority rule in Africa, the United Nations approved Resolution 2145 (XXI) in 1966, ending the South African mandate over South-West Africa and in 1968 officially changed the name to Namibia. The United Nations Security Council subsequently requested an advisory opinion from the International Court of Justice, which declared in 1971 that South Africa's occupation of South-West Africa was illegal and that the former mandatory power should vacate the territory immediately. The South African government rejected withdrawing from South-West Africa/Namibia immediately, but in 1977 it did begin to make plans for the eventual independence of Namibia.[20] This act also included the transfer of administrative responsibilities over the eastern Caprivi Strip from the South African government to the South-West African administration in Windhoek. From this point forward, the Caprivi Strip was linked administratively with Namibia, although these ties were tenuous given the distance from Windhoek.

Despite the closer administrative ties, the Caprivi Strip became increasingly isolated from the rest of the territory due to growing insecurity along the border of South-West Africa and Angola in the 1970s. A major contributing factor was instability in Angola following the sudden collapse of Portuguese colonial rule there in 1975, which left a power vacuum as various liberation groups battled for control. Angola became a proxy battleground of the Cold War as a Marxist faction took control of the capital, supported by Cuban troops and Soviet equipment. Another faction led by Jonas Savimbi drew on traditional tribal support in its battles with the new government. South Africa, concerned about radical, black-led Marxist countries on its borders, intervened on behalf of Savimbi in 1975. South African forces used the strip as a rear base to support military intervention in Angola.[21] A second factor was that the South-West Africa People's Organization (SWAPO), seeking the independence of Namibia under black rule, began using Angola as its main base for armed incursions into South-West Africa. These two conflicts militarized the strategic Caprivi Strip border.

Namibian Independence and Caprivian Separatism

South Africa withdrew its forces from Angola in 1988 as part of a comprehensive agreement that included the independence of Namibia. As a result of
these negotiations, South Africa agreed to implement the provisions of UN
Resolution 435 from September 29, 1976, that laid out the basis for a transition to independence. On April 1, 1989, the South-West Africa administrator-
general was subject to the "supervision and control" of the UN special representative and the United Nations Transitional Assistance Group (UNTAG).
Elections followed in November 1989, with SWAPO Party presidential candi-
date Sam Nujoma winning 76 percent of the popular vote. Namibia, including the Caprivi Strip, became an independent state on March 21, 1990.

Although Caprivi was internationally recognized as part of independent
Namibia, the region had nonetheless developed and retained an independent identity due to its historical isolation, separate administrative status,
and cultural distinctiveness. During the war for independence, for example,
growing anticolonial sentiment in Africa led to the establishment of the
Caprivi African National Union (CANU) in Zambia in 1962. This organization advocated independence for the Caprivi Strip and began to mobilize the
region's population in early 1964. The organization had been suppressed by
the South African government within the year, but CANU militants joined
forces with SWAPO to infiltrate the Caprivi and commit sabotage and terrorism. Although denied by SWAPO, CANU claimed that SWAPO agreed,
in return for its support in the struggle against South African rule, to permit
either autonomy or independence for the strip following the establishment of
an independent Namibia.[22]

Recognizing the distinctiveness of the region, South Africa gave the eastern
Caprivi Strip a degree of self-rule in the Constitution of 1971. Accordingly,
Caprivi was granted its own legislative council in 1972. To this was added an
anthem and emblem, which depicted two elephant bulls representing the two
chiefs of the area. The motto, written in the Lozi language, is translated as
"We stand together." Yet the local population was not consulted in these developments, and many South-West Africans continued to see the Caprivi as a
"foreign country."[23] South African reforms after 1977 allowed representatives
from Caprivi to participate in the new government for the first time. These
developments, however, took place in an environment where the security
situation was deteriorating, and emergency regulations were introduced in
response.

Secessionist sentiments in the Caprivi Strip continued after independence.
Former CANU leader Mishake Muyongo had championed the political slogan
"Revival of the Lozi Culture in Caprivi." He joined the Democratic Turn-

halle Alliance (DTA), eventually becoming its leader in 1991. The DTA had emerged as the largest opposition party to SWAPO after the elections in 1989. In 1998 it became public that Muyongo had negotiated with South African officials regarding the secession of the Caprivi Strip. He was quickly dismissed by the DTA for these actions. Muyongo subsequently changed strategy and began planning attacks to obtain an independent Caprivi.[24] Within the eastern Caprivi Strip, local support for SWAPO and the DTA was split along tribal lines. In this politically and ethnically contested area, grievances against the government by the pro-DTA Fwe tribe (with whom Muyongo held a high tribal status) grew, laying the groundwork for an armed struggle. In 1994, the Caprivi Liberation Army was formed to seek the unification of the Lozi people. The organization sought external support and began military training.[25] By late 1998, however, the Namibian government had arrested its leaders, and many of its followers fled the country. The movement still had some strength, attacking Katima Mulilo Airport on August 2, 1999. The attack was repulsed but nevertheless indicated the commitment of the rebels to the cause. After a second attack ended in failure a month later, Muyongo went into asylum in Denmark, effectively ending the separatist movement.

The western part of the Caprivi Strip, in contrast, has remained relatively calm since independence. Land title disputes between the Bantu Mbukushu, San Kxoé, and the Namibian government did, however, emerge. In late 2007 the government proclaimed the entire western Caprivi Strip as part of the new Bwabwata National Park, incorporating the former Caprivi Game Reserve. This park includes the traditional lands of the Kxoé, raising the issue of dispossession.[26]

Missed Opportunities

The failure of the separatist movement indicates that the Caprivi Strip will remain an integral part of the Namibian state. In hindsight, the continued existence of the Caprivi Strip is a testament to the power of borders to shape both the dynamics of a region and the internal identity of the people who live within the confines of these borders. Nevertheless, it is surprising that the Caprivi Strip continued its existence in the midst of the major reconfigurations of identity and politics in southern Africa. The actual creation of the Caprivi Strip was not unreasonable, given the geopolitics of the Scramble for Africa period and Germany's incomplete understanding of the region. Thus, Germany's desire to have a river shortcut linking its colonies in southern and eastern Africa made sense.

After Germany ascertained the unsuitability of the Zambezi River for transport and lack of valuable resources, the Caprivi Strip became an isolated and unprofitable piece of German territory. Germany was not opposed to land swaps for the Caprivi, but in negotiations with the British the two parties could not agree on the appropriate value of the Caprivi Strip, thus making it difficult to find a suitable piece of territory to swap. The most auspicious time to deal with the Caprivi Strip issue would have been in the negotiations at the Paris Peace Conference or soon after, in the early sessions of the League of Nations. Title to South-West Africa was now available. The Caprivi Strip could have been detached from South-West Africa and assigned to either Northern Rhodesia (Zambia) or northern Bechuanaland (Botswana). Had the Caprivi Strip been awarded to the British in Northern Rhodesia, the southern border of the Barotse Kingdom would essentially have reverted to its precolonial status. Had it been awarded to the Bechuanaland Protectorate, then the separate identity of the Caprivians first established by the Germans would have continued under a future Tswana-dominated state. Essentially, such an award would have been a decision to keep either the strip's northern border or southern border as the final international border. In either case, the isolated Caprivi Strip would have remained a distant region of either Zambia or Botswana.

Over time, the isolation of the Caprivi Strip deepened its sense of a separate identity as successive governments ruled the territory under a different basis from the rest of South-West Africa. The militarization of the border between the 1960s and the 1980s gave the Caprivi Strip great strategic value for all sides in the conflict. This cemented the strategic value of the strip to South-West Africa/Namibia. The growth and subsequent defeat of the Caprivi separatist movement illustrates both the strength of a Caprivi identity and also the value of the Caprivi Strip to the new Namibian government. Thus, in the relatively short 110 years of its existence, the Caprivi Strip had proven surprisingly resilient, surviving the colonial era, great power negotiations in Europe, South African occupation, wars of decolonization, and a separatist movement from newly independent Namibia. One possible explanation for this robustness is that since the isolated Caprivi Strip had very little strategic value for the first seventy years of its existence it did not really matter to the interested powers that controlled the territory. Beginning in the 1960s, the Caprivi Strip had enormous strategic importance, but by that time its key value related directly to the larger territory of South-West Africa/Namibia. After Namibia's independence, this link was internally challenged, but its proponents had no realistic chance of success given strong African norms against subnational secession in the postcolonial era and the defeat of any friendly sources of support in neighboring Zambia and Angola. The Caprivi Strip, however oddly shaped and distant from Namibia, was now an integral part of the new state. In this new era, colonial-era borders were no longer European but international borders between independent African states.

This chapter has shown the process by which Caprivi was created and attached to Namibia through colonial-era treaties signed by Europeans, how subsequent attempts to "fix" the problem failed, and how the identity of groups living within the Caprivi Strip was affected by the political boundaries imposed by "outsiders." Of great importance in the continued existence of the strip was its varying strategic value in different times and political conditions. Finally, although the political status of the Caprivi Strip is legally established, the force of traditional identity was seen in a separatist movement, not fully supported by all inhabitants of the Caprivi Strip, that drew on both Caprivian and Lozi identity from the Barotse Kingdom.

6

The Renaissance of a Border That Never Died

The Green Line between Israel and the West Bank

David Newman

ON THE ROAD NORTH FROM Beersheba to Jerusalem, the traveler arrives at the Shoqet junction and is greeted by a road sign that offers two alternatives for the onward section of travel to Jerusalem. Either one can continue via the Hebron bypass route and get to Jerusalem after 75 kilometers (47 miles), or one can choose to travel via Qiryat Gat, a distance of 120 kilometers (75 miles) (figure 6.1). Over 90 percent of the travelers opt for the latter route, despite the fact that it is almost twice as long and that they will eventually have to enter Jerusalem via the main Tel Aviv highway and encounter severe traffic holdups. The shorter route is more pastoral, the roads are virtually empty, and a traveler would enter the city from the south, along a road that rarely has traffic problems.

So why, indeed, would the traveler opt for the longer, busier route? The answer is simple. The shorter route means traveling through the West Bank and the Occupied Territories, while the longer route, bypassing the West Bank altogether, remains within the sovereign territory of Israel. The vast majority of Israeli travelers, fearful for their physical safety, despite the army patrols and the semiseparate road system that has been constructed for the benefit of the settler population, choose to remain on "their" side of the border—a border that even after sixty years of statehood is no more than an armistice line, not recognized in any international treaty and that, until recently, did not even have a fence or a physical barrier to denote its presence.

The "Green Line," as it is known, has come to denote the line of separation between Israel and the West Bank and most probably will be identical, or at least very similar, to the line that will eventually demarcate the border between Israel and an independent Palestinian state as part of a two-state

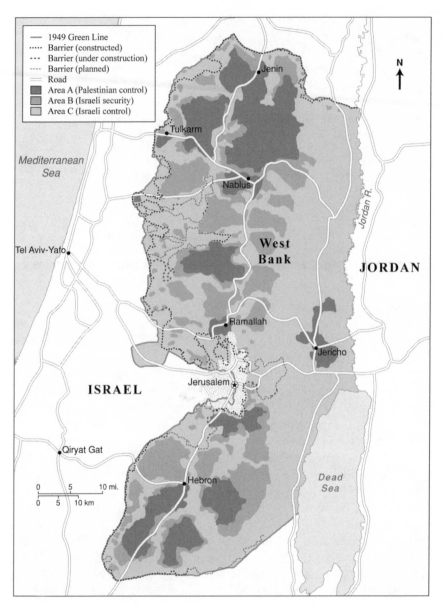

FIGURE 6.1
The Security Barrier/Transportation Routes/Control Areas. Cory Johnson of XNR.

solution to one of the world's bloodiest and longest ongoing conflicts (figure 6.2). It is, in all senses, an "odd" border. It was imposed on the landscape in 1949 as a result of the establishment of the state of Israel and the subsequent Israeli War of Independence (the Palestinian Naqba), was overrun and "opened" in the Six Day War of 1967, and was removed from all official maps by the Israeli government and declared dead while, at the same time, it continued to be a line of administrative and political separation for both Israelis and Arab-Palestinians. Most recently, it has become the subject of renewed controversy as Israel's separation/security barrier has been constructed in some parts along the line, but in other parts has deviated from the line inside the West Bank, thus potentially annexing Occupied Territory to the state of Israel.

This chapter seeks to retrace the political and geographic history of the Green Line during its separate phases of development.[1] The chapter discusses

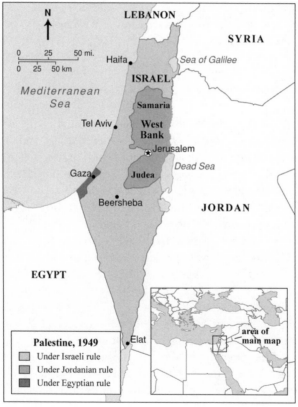

FIGURE 6.2
The Green Line—Israel 1949. Cory Johnson of XNR.

the strange demarcation of the line and the way that this impacted local populations, resulting in economic and social dislocation for thousands of people. The chapter analyzes the political significance of the line, both before and after the Six-Day War of June 1967 and looks at its administrative and legal status from both internal (Israeli and Palestinian) and external (the international community) perspectives. The importance of the line in determining the routing of the recently constructed security/separation fence/barrier/wall and the significance of the deviations between these two lines for the daily life practices of thousands of people who are caught as spatial hostages between the two is discussed. And, finally, the chapter assesses the importance of the Green Line in the negotiations leading up to the possible implementation of a two-state solution to the Israel-Palestine conflict and addresses the question of whether this is the default line for the future political boundary or whether it will be possible to determine an alternative line through bilateral negotiations between the two sides. Such a line would have to take account of the geographical and political changes that have taken place in the region since the Green Line was first demarcated some sixty years ago.

Maps of Partition: A Brief Historical Background

The demarcation and delimitation of the Green Line took place on the island of Rhodes shortly after the cessation of armed conflict and direct warfare between the newly established state of Israel and its Arab neighbors in 1949. Israel conducted separate but parallel negotiations with each of the four surrounding countries, Egypt, Jordan, Syria, and Lebanon. The area that prior to the establishment of Israel in May 1948 had been part of the Palestine mandate under British control was negotiated between Israel and Jordan, resulting in the creation of a new political territory to the east of the River Jordan to be administered by the state of Jordan and to be separated from Israel by a border. This border became known as the Green Line because of the color of the ink that depicted the borders on the first (and all subsequent) maps.

The idea of partitioning the Palestine mandate territory was not a new one. The original mandate had been granted by the League of Nations to Britain following the final disintegration of the Ottoman Empire after the end of World War I. The mandate included the current Israeli and West Bank territories as well as the much larger area of desert regions to the east of the River Jordan. In 1921, the British government decided to create the new state of Transjordan, encompassing all of the mandate territory to the east of the river and redefining the outer border of the area known as Palestine along the course of the river itself.[2]

The remaining territory, including all of those areas today covered by Israel, the West Bank, and the Gaza Strip, occupied an area of no more than 25,000 square kilometers (9,653 square miles). As tensions grew between the Jewish and Arab populations of the Palestine territory during the 1920s and 1930s, the British government began to examine, from the mid-1930s onward, proposals aimed at dividing this territory into two political entities—one Jewish, and one Arab. In the late 1930s, successive royal commissions, the Peel and the Woodward Commissions, presented a series of proposals aimed at territorial partition, which took into account the location of the respective Jewish and Arab populations and tried to assess the expected demographic growth and territorial expansion of both national groups.[3] Following a hiatus during the period of World War II, tensions between the two national groups became even more extreme, especially because of the desire of the post-Holocaust Jewish people to be allowed to establish their own state in their ancestral and biblical homeland.

In the late 1940s, the British government decided to relinquish its mandate and return it to the United Nations, who in turn sent out its own committee to draw up a map of territorial partition. The UNSCOP (United Nations Special Committee on Palestine) proposal presented a map in which both the Jewish and Arab states would consist of two territorial sections, while the area of Jerusalem would remain under international administration.[4] It was this partition proposal that was voted on by the United Nations General Assembly in November 1947 and that legitimized the subsequent creation of the state of Israel in May 1948. The high governor and the last British troops departed immediately thereafter.

The Arab refusal to accept the partition proposal resulted in armed conflict between the new state of Israel and its neighbors. During the war, Israeli armed forces succeeded in gaining control over large tracts of territory beyond those proposed by UNSCOP, including the relatively unsettled areas of the Negev desert to the south, reaching as far as Aqaba at the northernmost point of the Red Sea.[5] At the same time, because of the relatively dense Palestinian population in the interior upland areas, coupled with the absence of Jewish settlements in these areas, the army did not attempt to take control of those areas that would eventually become the West Bank. It was during the war that the roots of the Palestinian refugee problem were created, with the outflow of approximately seven hundred thousand refugees, soon to be demographically countered with the inflow of a similar number of Jewish refugees and migrants from countries in the Middle East and North Africa, most notably Iraq, Morocco, and Yemen.[6] This resulted in a radical change of the Jewish-Arab demographic balance within the state of Israel (approximately 80 to 20 percent, respectively). This balance has been maintained until today and, as explained in the final section of this chapter, is a major consideration for Israeli policy makers in drawing up the future, and final, line of political separation between Israeli and Palestinian independent states.

During the nineteen-year period between the imposition of the Green Line and its opening in 1967, the settlement landscapes on both sides of this sealed border underwent differential processes of spatial development. On the Israeli side, Arab-Palestinian villages were caught up in the general development that took place during the formative years of the state, while villages on the West Bank side found themselves totally cut off from their former spatial and economic hinterlands in Israel. Moreover, the state of Jordan saw the new border region as a zone of confrontation and did not invest any major development resources into these communities over and beyond the influx of military installations and army camps. This resulted in the outward flow of many West Bank Palestinians, especially those in close proximity to the border, to find alternative economic and educational opportunities outside the region, especially in the Gulf states. By the time the border was opened in 1967, the demographic, educational, social, and economic profiles of the Arab-Palestinian villages on both sides of the border were vastly different from each other, where only nineteen years previously they had been part of a single ethnospatial area.[7]

The Demarcation and Imposition of the Green Line

The demarcation and delimitation of the new border separating Israel from the West Bank was carried out at the Rhodes armistice talks in 1949. The key factor determining the course of the border in a region that had never previously been divided was the location of the respective armed forces at the end of the war. This, in turn, had been influenced by the spatial distribution of Jewish settlements prior to the establishment of the state of Israel. The Haganah army had set as its first priority ensuring control over all the settlements and only afterwards determining which additional areas to conquer as future development areas for the new state. One of the mythological stories of the time asserts that one of the army commanders, Yigal Allon, requested permission to move his troops eastward as far as the Jordan River, to include the area that became the West Bank. The prime minister at the time, David Ben Gurion, forbade him doing so on the grounds that this was a densely populated upland region that would only create a demographic problem for the new state. Instead, he ordered the army to move southward and capture the whole of the Negev desert region, which by comparison to the West Bank was less densely populated with indigenous inhabitants and also provided spatial potential for the establishment of new agricultural settlements and communities.

True or otherwise, Israel's War of Independence had resulted in an area west of the River Jordan under the control of the Jordanian Legion, with a small section in the north controlled by Iraqi forces. Allowing for a few minor territorial changes and swaps, plus the inclusion of a major transportation artery between the Israeli towns of Hadera and Afula (Wadi Arah), the Green Line largely reflected the outcome of the war. Given the extremely small spatial scale of the region in question and the thickness of the pen that was used to draw the line, a number of problems arose during its implementation, necessitating localized changes in its course.[8] This resulted in the splitting of some Arab villages in two, one part remaining inside Israel and the other part in the newly created West Bank territory. In many cases, the village found itself on the West Bank side of the line in the lower slopes of the upland region, while its fields and agricultural hinterland remained on the Israeli side in the low-lying and relatively flat coastal plain. In the early years of the state, the result was a great number of cross-border infiltrations, with Palestinian landowners attempting to farm their fields and pick their produce. Eventually, the Israeli army prevented them from crossing the border altogether, and the lands were gradually transferred to new Israeli settlements that had been established in the late 1940s and early 1950s.[9] Equally, Palestinians who had fled their villages during the war with the intention of returning when the fighting was over were unable to do so. They ended up in Palestinian refugee camps throughout the West Bank and neighboring countries while most of their villages were gradually erased as the landscape of the new state underwent substantial ethnic change.[10]

Israel saw its new border areas as regions within which it was necessary to establish a civilian presence over and beyond its military installations. This was perceived as an ideological position on the part of the state to lay claim to all of the land area that it now controlled through an active process of land colonization, similar to that which had taken place in prestate Palestine and which had brought areas of the state-to-be under Jewish control.[11] Thus, the 1950s and 1960s witnessed an active process of settlement construction along both the Lebanon border in the north and the Green Line border in the center of the country.

Closed, Open, and Closed Again: Stages in the Evolution of the Green Line

The Six-Day War of June 1967 resulted in the Israeli conquest and occupation of the West Bank, the Gaza Strip, and the Golan Heights. The Green Line was, in effect, opened, enabling the movement of people from one side of the line to the other. In the short term, this was beneficial for Palestinians on both sides of the line who wished to visit their families, while in the longer term it resulted in Palestinians from the West Bank commuting into Israel to find employment, mostly as cheap and menial labor at construction sites and in the restaurants, and as cleaners. By the late 1980s, prior to the outbreak of the first Intifada, it was estimated that upward of 120,000 Palestinians were working in the Israeli labor market, the majority of whom crossed and recrossed the Green Line boundary every morning and evening.[12] It was a common sight to drive by the major crossroads and intersections leading into Israel from the West Bank in the early hours of the morning and find a ready pool of available labor seeking daily employment.

The opening of the Green Line did not simply enable movement in one direction. For Israel's Jewish population, especially those who were inspired by religious-nationalist values, the Israeli conquest of the West Bank was no less than the "liberation" of the key places and sites of the ancient biblical and Israelite kingdoms. It was, in their view, essential that Israel not relinquish the conquered territories as part of any future peace agreement. As a means of preventing this from happening, a new wave of settlement took place from the mid-1970s onward. Under the auspices of the right-wing Gush Emunim movement, the goal was to create new communities throughout the West Bank to ensure the retention of this territory through classic means of settlement colonization and territorial control.[13] This was initially opposed by the Labor governments of the time, which saw the West Bank as a territorial pawn to be used as a bargaining chip with Jordan in return for a peace agreement. But this position underwent a change following the rise to power of the right-wing Likud government of Prime Minister Menachem Begin in 1977, which gave the green light for expansive settlement construction throughout the region.

Not only was the Green Line crossed daily in both directions, but gradually the physical elements of the pre-1967 border were removed. There was a conscious attempt by policy makers to argue that the artificial Green Line boundary had been erased and that it no longer existed. By order of the government, the Surveyors Department, responsible for the country's mapping authority, removed the Green Line from all official maps, while school textbooks also displayed maps without any internal borders. They would not appear again until almost forty years later in 2007 by order of the education minister Yuli Tamir.[14]

Public and government statements to the effect that the Green Line had been erased and no longer constituted a border were contrary to the functional and administrative realities of the line. Israeli governments, even those of a right-wing creed who desired to retain long-term control over the Occupied Territories, did not attempt to pass any act of formal annexation. This was partly because they were aware of the huge international outcry that such a move would bring in its wake, but also because the West Bank contains a large and rapidly growing Palestinian population. Annexation of the territory would mean that the entire resident population of the West Bank would be entitled to full Israeli citizenship, substantially diluting Israel's Jewish demographic majority. Thus, Palestinians residing in the West Bank remained stateless while their Arab brethren and cousins residing inside Israel retained their citizenship in the state. All activities in the West Bank, even of a civilian nature, including the founding of settlement communities, were carried out through the authority of the military administration of the region and not directly through the relevant government ministry in Jerusalem or Tel Aviv. The result was the same as the continued existence of the Green Line border. Even though it was no longer visible for the most part, it had a powerful impact on the way that development took place, infrastructure was created, and public services were provided.[15]

The fact that the Green Line was simultaneously "erased" and "existent" caused a great deal of uncertainty on the part of the Israeli civilian population. Israelis, who refused to cross into the West Bank because they were fearful for their safety and/or because they refused to travel in the Occupied Territories for moralistic antioccupation reasons, were not always sure just where the point of crossing was. The military authorities issued different sets of rules to soldiers concerning the conditions under which they could use live ammunition, depending on which side of the Green Line they were to be found. But when they had to implement these orders, even in training sessions, they were often unclear as to what side of the line they were on and, as a result, did not know whether they were permitted to use their ammunition or not.[16]

The Green Line also came into play with the construction of the first sections of the new north-south Trans-Israel Highway during the late 1990s and early 2000s. This major transportation artery was constructed to enable travelers to avoid the overcrowded metropolitan center of the country and, generally, to ease congestion on Israel's overloaded road system. In the center of the country, the route was planned to be as far as possible from the nearby towns, but equally to remain entirely within Israel. In other words, it would not cross the "nonexistent" boundary. Following its completion, stretches of the highway run parallel to the Green Line, in some places no more than a few hundred meters from the border. Given the fact that the separation fence/wall has also been constructed in this region (see next section), travelers on the highway now see the visible manifestations of the evolving political boundary as they travel to and from work on a daily basis.

There was, however, one map that continued to show the precise location of the border. Since the Israeli government had not attempted any de jure annexation of the West Bank, it followed that local government and municipal authorities could not extend their jurisdictional area from one side of the line to the other. Nor could they create umbrella authorities of neighboring municipalities to achieve economy of size thresholds for the provision of public services if doing so entailed crossing the nonexistent boundary. They could expand only on their own side of the Green Line. Anyone familiar with a map of Israeli local government authorities could simply follow the line of the outer boundaries of the neighboring rural and urban municipalities from north to south to trace the precise course of the Green Line boundary.

The same was true for the construction and expansion of Israeli settlements. They could be built on either side of the Green Line, but they could never cross the line or have the line running through the center of their community. Thus two communities located in close proximity to each other, but on either side of the line, had totally different statuses. One was a legitimate community within Israel while the other was a settlement constructed by Israel in the Occupied Territories contrary to international opinion, which condemned the continued construction and expansion of West Bank settlements. It is perhaps not surprising that the vast majority of West Bank settlers live in communities that are located in close proximity to the Green Line. In this locational preference, they enjoy the financial and tax benefits that the government has given to settlers as a political incentive while at the same time only marginally increasing their commuting distance from the main employment centers of the Israeli metropolitan area in the Gush Dan and Tel Aviv regions. In this way, the Green Line served as a major point of discontinuity on the distance decay effect of land prices, starting in the downtown area and extending into the suburban and exurban areas of the metropolitan region.[17] For anyone who was not opposed on ideological or moralistic grounds to settling in the Occupied Territories, the optimal locational choice with the maximal benefits was to locate just beyond the Green Line. This has been described elsewhere as constituting a process of suburban colonization, wherein political objectives of territorial control were achieved through the colonization of the suburban areas within the metropolitan hinterland.[18]

The Green Line and the Separation Barrier: The Securitization Discourse

During the first twenty years of occupation, Israelis and Palestinians traveled in relative safety within each other's territory, even to the extent that many Israelis undertook commercial activities in Palestinian towns and markets.

Issues of security re-emerged in the late 1980s, following the outbreak of the first Intifada, the popular civilian Palestinian uprising against Israeli occupation. It was from this point onward that many Israelis ceased to travel into the West Bank, especially on Saturdays, when many of the stores in Israel were closed because of the Sabbath restrictions on commerce and business. This effectively dealt a death blow to many Palestinian commercial enterprises that offered cheap goods and services to Israeli consumers.

Prior to the outbreak of the Intifada, it was common for Israelis to cross into both Gaza and the West Bank. But following a number of incidents in which some Israeli civilians were killed, the flow ceased to a trickle. It was at this point that the signpost described in the opening of this chapter first made its appearance on the road from Beersheba to Jerusalem via Hebron and the West Bank. During the 1990s, roadblocks were increasingly set up at entry and exit points from the West Bank. In addition, the West Bank was often placed under curfew by the Israeli authorities during festival periods or following major terrorist incidents. Whenever this happened, the location of the roadblocks and the temporary barriers were invariably at points along the Green Line, reinforcing rather than weakening the image of the line as a border.

The securitization discourse returned in a big way following the outbreak of the second Intifada, which followed the breakdown of the Camp David and the Taba Peace Talks in 2000. But the return of violence to the streets was this time accompanied by the growth of religious fundamentalism in the shape of the Hamas and Hizbollah movements. This led to the use of suicide bombers who blew themselves up along with their innocent victims in crowded buses, street markets, and shopping malls. The use of curfews, coupled with the total cessation of the movement of Palestinian labor into Israel, a process that had commenced during the 1990s as cheap Palestinian labor was gradually replaced by the influx of cheap labor from other countries that did not constitute the same security risk, had only a limited impact on the suicide bombings. It was impossible to hermetically seal the whole of the West Bank.

There was huge pressure on the Israeli government to erect a security fence or barrier that would encircle the entire area of the West Bank and act as a physical obstacle to the movement of people across the border, except for a limited number of heavily controlled crossing points. Initially, the government was not in favor of this policy as it would indicate the construction of a border that would have political implications well beyond the immediate security considerations. This was particularly the viewpoint of Prime Minister Ariel Sharon, who was known for his intransigent position on the issue of territorial withdrawal, his traditional opposition to the establishment of a Palestinian state, and his past track record of ruthlessly dealing with guerrilla and terrorist activities in the Gaza Strip.

Eventually the grassroots pressure from across the political spectrum, a rare case of consensus in the fragmented politics of Israel, resulted in the government's acquiescing to the demands of the public. In 2002, Israel commenced the construction of its security barrier (the official term), which very soon became known by its other name, the separation fence or wall.[19] The fence/wall was constructed in sections starting in the northern and central regions of the West Bank, which were considered to be most vulnerable. It was intended to eventually encompass the whole of the West Bank, except for the very steep cliff areas in the southern Judean Desert area overlooking the Dead Sea, through which it was almost impossible to cross anyway (figure 6.1).[20]

Sharon and other government officials insisted that the security barrier was precisely that and that there were no broader political implications. But this flew in the face of reality, given the way in which the fence/wall and the limited number of transit points were constructed, as well as the considerations given to rerouting the fence/wall away from the Green Line and into the West Bank. Here it served the political objectives of the state, namely, ensuring that as many of the Israeli settlements as possible would remain on the Israeli side of this new border.

At the time the road sign at the Shoqet junction was erected in the late 1980s, a traveler could still cross the Green Line into the West Bank without being aware of that fact. But today, with the arrival of the separation fence/barrier to even the southern, relatively untroubled parts of the West Bank, this is no longer possible. Five kilometers to the north of the road sign, just beyond the suburban community of Meitar, one reaches what can only be described as a major international crossing point. Heavily controlled gates and barriers prevent travelers from driving onward unless they have the right documents, car license plates, or accent. Palestinians cannot move beyond the barrier into Israel unless they have one of the precious few work permits. Even then, they have to leave their cars on the Palestinian side of the border and wait for their Israeli employer to pick them up on the other side. On each side of the transit point, the new triple barbed-wire, electrified fence stretches beyond the horizon, while parallel to the fence, the road has been improved and widened, mostly for the use of Israeli travelers. It is, for all purposes, a political boundary that has been erected, even though Israel and the Palestinian Authority have yet to reach a political agreement.

There are five such transit points along the route of the fence/wall. With one exception (the Gush Etzion region south of Jerusalem), the border crossing points have all been erected at places where the fence coincides geographically with the Green Line. But this does not hide the fact that the fence has, in many areas, deviated from the Green Line, eating into parts of the West Bank and in reality annexing pieces of territory to Israel. This has happened in those areas where there is a significant Israeli settlement in close proximity to the Green Line. In any future political arrangement, Israeli withdrawal from the West Bank will have to be accompanied by the evacuation of Israeli settlements from the Palestinian side of the line (see the final section of this chapter). Regardless of the legal status of these settlements in the first place, this is a very difficult scenario for any Israeli government. The forced evacuation of settlements in the Gaza Strip was, with all its difficulties, a relatively easy process compared with what is to be expected in the settlement heartlands of the West Bank. Knowing this, Israel has attempted to reduce the number of settlements that will have to be evacuated by including them on the Israeli side of the fence.

It is precisely in these areas where the International Court of Justice and even the Israeli Supreme Court have ruled that the unilateral construction of this barrier is illegal and that it has to be rerouted. This is less because of the issue of settlements than it is because of the functional hardships that it has caused for the Palestinian residents of the "twilight" zones, who have become spatial hostages in the strips of land between the Green Line to the west and the separation fence/wall to the east. They are prevented from crossing into Israel, and they are unable to move with ease into the West Bank. They are subject to border checks and, in some documented cases, humiliation for simply trying to get to their workplaces, schools, medical care, or local shopping centers. The courts have ruled that this constitutes a basic denial of their human rights and has ordered the Israeli government to reroute the fence in some of these areas.[21]

Some of the most absurd results of the construction of the barrier have taken place in the middle of built-up urban areas like Jerusalem. It is in these areas where the physical distance between Israeli and Palestinian houses is so relatively small that the fence has been replaced by the wall. In reality, these walls account for only approximately 7 percent of the entire length of the border; however, media images of the separation barrier concentrate on the ugliness of the concrete wall. The construction of the wall has not only created a landscape of ugliness and new graffiti within Jerusalem, but it has resulted in the imposition of a physical, impassable barrier for Palestinians, who now have to spend up to an hour simply to get to their workplace or school on the other side of the wall. In the past, it would have taken no more than a few minutes. Politically, the wall has redivided Jerusalem into two parts, a Jewish/Israeli West Jerusalem, including some Palestinian neighborhoods in close proximity to the Old City, and a Palestinian/Arab East Jerusalem (figure 6.3). The media images of the grotesque concrete wall and the associated graffiti led the government to invest in a more aesthetically pleasing wall, built in Jerusalem stone, to the south along the road to the Gush Etzion region. This section of the wall separates Israeli travelers from the city of Bethlehem as they

FIGURE 6.3
Separation Wall. Photo by David Newman.

drive to and from work each day. The notion of "aesthetics" in such a violent and conflictual environment transforms this section of the wall into one of the strangest of contemporary political borders.

The Palestinian town of Qalqiliya, located in the center of the region, is another border absurdity. The outer residential areas of the town border the Green Line and are no more than a few hundred meters from the outer residential areas of the Israeli town of Kfar Sava, with the Trans-Israel Highway running between the two. The fence/wall completely encircles the town on three sides, enabling only a single point of entry and exit from the town into the West Bank to the east. All other points of entry have been blocked off by the new barrier, leaving an overcrowded bottleneck of cars and pedestrians entering and leaving the town at all hours of the day.

The Palestinian township of Baq'ah el Gharbieh on both sides of the Green Line now has a ten-foot concrete wall running down the middle of the road where there was a cross-border spontaneous market. This township was split in two by the imposition of the Green Line in 1949, underwent some functional and family (although not administrative) reunification after 1967, and has now been split in two again by the new wall.

If the security barrier has had one positive effect, it is that the concept of a boundary between two separate states is now a tangible and concrete, rather than abstract, idea. Israelis and Palestinians encounter the fence and wall on a daily basis. The idea of a political border is no longer just a line on a map but a geographical fact on the ground. Eventually, the line may have to undergo a process of redemarcation, but it has become a reality and, as such, may serve to bring a political agreement between the two sides a few steps closer.

The Failure of Cross-Boundary Cooperation

Following the signing of the Oslo Accords in 1993 and 1995, there were some initial attempts to increase the level of economic development in the Palestinian territories. Much of this was based on international investment and, to a lesser extent, attempts by Israeli entrepreneurs to become involved in the Palestinian economy.[22] There were a number of proposals aimed at creating and strengthening the level of cross-border cooperation between the two sides across the Green Line. These covered a wide range of functions including joint environmental protection (the mosquitoes that cross the boundary do not require visas and are an equal hazard to people on both sides of the boundary), the creation of cross-border commercial and/or industrial zones, markets in close proximity to the border, and even the idea of a borderline maternity hospital ("Birthing Together") somewhere along the line dividing the Gaza Strip from Israel. Most of these projects never went beyond the planning stages, either because of the rapid deterioration in political relations or because the two sides were unable to create the appropriate planning and fiscal agencies that would enable efficient management in an atmosphere of political mistrust and technology asymmetry.

One example of these cross-border ideas was the proposal of the Lev Hasharon Regional Council to create a "peace park" along the border interface. The purpose of the venture was to establish an industrial zone encompassing one thousand dunams (one hundred hectares) that would provide employment for the area's residents on both sides of the border. The location of the venture corresponded to one of the crossing points (Sha'ar Efraim), thus providing the perfect opportunity for cooperation and cross-border activity. The venture failed to progress and, following the worsening political environment and the later construction of the separation barrier, the designation of the project was changed to a terminal-support employment area rather than a joint industrial zone. The fate of this project was typical of all of the proposals during this period.

Another dimension relating to the crossing of the border concerns the link between the Gaza Strip and the West Bank. Although this chapter has concentrated on the line separating the West Bank from Israel, it is important to remember that the Palestinian territories consist of two disconnected areas: the West Bank and the Gaza Strip.[23] The distance between the two is no more than forty kilometers (twenty-five miles) at the shortest point, but any link necessitates the crossing of the border in and out of Israel and a land passage through Israeli sovereign territory. Two "safe passage" routes were designated in the immediate post-Oslo period in the mid-1990s: one crossing into the West Bank in the south near Meitar, with a second route farther north, by-passing the Israeli town of Qiryat Gat and the Tarqumiya crossing point near Hebron-Al Khalil (figure 6.1). Israel insisted that no transit route would cross through, or be in close proximity to, Jerusalem because of its desire to emphasize the retention of long-term Israeli control over the city.[24]

For a period of five years, tens of thousands of Palestinians traveled in both ways along these routes without any major problems. Residents from the extremely densely populated and poverty-stricken Gaza Strip traveled to the West Bank on a daily and weekly basis for economic, family, or educational purposes. Many West Bank residents traveled to the Gaza area to enjoy the beaches. In the future, the Gaza Strip may be a place where independent port installations for the Palestinian state will be developed to serve the residents and factories of both areas.

But following the closing down of both territories in the wake of the outbreak of the second Intifada in 2000, these routes ceased to function. The Erez and Karni crossing points from the Gaza Strip into Israel also closed down, although these had been important transit points for both people and goods. Because of the security issues, trucks carrying goods into the Gaza Strip had to unload at Karni and be reloaded onto Palestinian trucks. Special back-to-back transfer platforms were initially constructed for this process, but these were replaced at a later stage with "sterile" areas that could be opened or closed on each side. Israeli trucks would drive into these areas, unload their goods, and drive out. Once their side was closed, the gates to the Palestinian side would be opened, and trucks would drive in and be loaded with the goods. When the process operated in the opposite direction, from Gaza into Israel, the entry of the Israeli trucks into the sterile area would be preceded by the use of sniffer dogs trained to detect explosives.

Demarcating a Border for Conflict Resolution: The Two-State Solution

Since the early 1990s, there has been growing consensus, both within Israel and among the international community, that the solution to the Israel-Palestine conflict has to be based on a two-state solution. This necessitates the withdrawal of Israel from the Occupied Territories and the establishment of an independent Palestinian state. The internal discourse within Israel has shifted in favor of accepting the principles of this solution because of the demographic discourse which has suggested that continued occupation will eventually result in Israel's losing its Jewish majority and, hence, the raison d'etre of the existence of the state in the first place. By equating demography with the securitization discourse, Israelis now see the imperative of territorial withdrawal as a means through which the long-term "security" of the state is ensured.

The move toward implementing the two-state solution was strengthened following the unilateral Israeli disengagement from the Gaza Strip in August 2005. But the establishment of two neighboring states requires the clear delineation of the physical border that will separate the two respective territories. Various proposals for the demarcation of a border have been proposed during the past decade, but they have invariably remained as no more than lines on a map.[25]

One of the more professional attempts to determine the principles that governments and negotiators would have to take into account if and when high-level bilateral negotiations were to restart was taken up by a group of professional geographers, planners, and cartographers in 2005 as part of a border project sponsored by the EU.[26] The objective of the working group was to identify the key problems involved in boundary demarcation and to suggest alternative methods of dealing with these problems. The group did not aim to come up with a single optimal line of separation. Rather, the main purpose of the exercise was to suggest alternative courses for the boundary in those areas where the course of the Green Line is no longer deemed appropriate. A number of key working assumptions provided the framework for the demarcation project.

First, while the Green Line constitutes the default border, the specific course of the Green Line is not sacrosanct, nor is its international legal status clear.[27] It is a boundary artificially imposed upon the landscape only sixty years ago. The course of boundaries can be redrawn according to contemporary demographic, geographic, and political realities. Moreover, it is assumed that any alternative line drawn up as a result of bilateral negotiations and agreement between the two sides will have international recognition, regardless of the extent to which such a line may or may not deviate from the existing Green Line.

Boundary demarcation must, as far as possible, take account of existing infrastructural realities, not least the location of major transportation arteries, water sources, agricultural land, and so on, in such a way as to cause as little human and economic dislocation as possible. This includes consideration of Route 6 (the Trans-Israel Highway), which runs parallel to much of the Green

Line, as well as the five major boundary transit points that are currently under construction.

Demarcation of boundaries should be carried out in a way that will ensure a compact and contiguous territory for both Israel and the Palestinian state, avoiding as far as possible the establishment of exclaves, enclaves, or bypass transit routes, except the route(s) that will link the West Bank with the Gaza Strip. This means that Israeli settlements on the Palestinian side of the boundary will have to be evacuated. One of the major problems of the transitional maps drawn up at the Oslo Accords was the highly fragmented nature of the Palestinians' internal territory, with Palestinian Autonomy Areas A, B, and C separated from one another by bypass roads, safe transit passages, roadblocks, and Israeli settlements (figure 6.1). In retrospect, it was clear that this constituted a cartographic recipe for political instability.

Because of the way the security fence/separation barrier has been unilaterally superimposed upon the landscape, including deviations away from the Green Line into the West Bank, it does not constitute a political boundary and, as such, is not taken as a de facto border. Notwithstanding, the security fence constitutes a geographical reality in the landscape and, unlike all other border proposals of the past decade, it has been implemented on the ground. However, that does not rule out the demarcation of an alternative boundary that will deviate from the Green Line in certain areas, providing that this is part of a bilateral, rather than unilateral, process and that there is territorial exchange or compensation for those areas desired by Israel. Annexation of territory to Israel would have to be met with a fair exchange of territory such that the Palestinian state will encompass the same areal extent as exists within the existing boundaries of the West Bank and Gaza Strip (figure 6.2).

Based on these ground rules, the group worked its way around three spatial scenarios:

1. The course of the Green Line with minor territorial changes, reflecting the course of the line demarcated in 1949. This option took into account the fact that the original demarcation of the Green Line closely followed the armistice line without considering numerous geographical features, such as the value of different types of land, the location of wells and water sources, the route of transportation arteries, and so on. Even though some changes were made in the course of the line as part of the "officers' agreement" in 1949–1950, further changes would be necessary to make it more "user friendly" for the local inhabitants.
2. The course of the Green Line with major territorial changes that allowed the inclusion of some Israeli settlement blocs inside Israel in exchange for the transfer of comparable territory on the Israeli side of

the border to the Palestinian state. The expected difficulties facing an Israeli government undertaking mass evacuations of settlements, likely far larger than those in the Gaza Strip, makes territorial withdrawal a highly unattractive proposition for many Israeli policy makers. While this does not make the settlements any less illegal or immoral than in the past, any form of border revisions that takes this factor into account would make its implementation much easier, assuming that a fair territorial exchange is offered to the Palestinian side. Whatever territorial changes are negotiated, it is clear that a significant number of Israeli settlements will remain on the Palestinian side of the border and have to be evacuated.

3. The demarcation of a completely new line that would reflect the existing geographic and demographic realities of the region. This would be based largely, although not exclusively, on the patterns of population dispersal, both Israeli-Jewish and Palestinian-Arab, in Israel-Palestine. Such a proposal could result in the silent transfer of Israel's Arab-Palestinian residents to the Palestinian state, despite the fact that they have stated categorically that they desire to remain within Israel. This most contentious of solutions is backed by some of the right-wing parties in Israel who, while they only begrudgingly accept the notion of two states, want the number of Palestinian citizens inside Israel to be as low as possible.

Conclusion: From Armistice Line to Conflict Resolution

This chapter has demonstrated the way in which socially constructed boundaries become strongly imprinted on the landscape and on the mental cartographic imaginations within a relatively short period of time. Prior to the 1930s, there had never been any talk of partition within Palestine west of the River Jordan. The de facto partition in 1949 as a result of the establishment of the state of Israel and the subsequent conflict and armistice agreements took place no more than sixty years ago. Of that sixty years, the Green Line was a sealed border for only nineteen years. Since then it has been an administrative line of separation within the area controlled and occupied by Israel. As security issues have come to the fore again during the past twenty years, the Green Line has served as the focus for the re-establishment of a de facto border, starting with roadblocks, the construction of fences and walls, and finally the vision of the Green Line as the de facto line that all future border and territorial negotiations should use as their source of reference. The armistice line that was haphazardly demarcated in Rhodes in 1949 may well prove to be the eventual course of the border between separate and independent Israeli and Palestinian states, regardless of whether this accords to the demographic, settlement, land use, and other realities of the geographic landscape. It is a lesson in the way that political and human landscapes are formed and the extent to which physical land borders remain a central part of the political discourse even in the so-called emerging borderless world.

Epilogue

In May 2008, Israeli and Palestinian peace NGOs organized a three-day "Walk the Green Line" walkathon. This was intended to raise awareness of the existence of the line as a default political boundary as well as raise funds for pro-peace NGOs. Thousands of people from both sides of the line joined in the event. IPCRI (the Israel Palestine Center for Research and Information), the organizers, noted as follows:

> November 29 marks 60 years since the United Nations decided to partition the Land of Israel/Palestine into two states—one Jewish (Israel) and one Arab (Palestine) [UN General Assembly Resolution 181 (Nov 1947)]. Israel was created in 1948 but the Palestinian state has yet to be created. The Green Line border set in the armistice agreements of 1949 marks the line that designates the basis of the future border between Israel and Palestine. Since the beginning of the occupation of the West Bank and East Jerusalem following the June 1967 war, the green line border has been gradually disappearing. Walk the GREEN LINE is a political statement aimed at marking the line where the future border should be so that Israeli-Palestinian peace can emerge and develop.[28]

7

Locating Kurdistan

Contextualizing the Region's Ambiguous Boundaries

Karen Culcasi

A̲LL BORDERS ARE TO SOME degree perceived in our geographical imaginations, but unlike many other national or international borders,
Kurdistan's boundaries are particularly difficult to locate, both on the ground
and on a map. Ambiguously defined as spanning parts of Iraq, Iran, Turkey,
and Syria (and sometimes Armenia, too), Kurdistan does not have walls,
fences, or border crossings to demark its territory.[1] This vague region is not
an internationally recognized state. Instead, it is a transnational region where
approximately twenty million to twenty-five million Kurds make up a large
percentage of the area's population.[2]

Even though Kurdistan's boundaries are undetermined, the region has a
very real geopolitical and national existence, which has been manifested in
both war and contention between numerous states, factional Kurdish groups,
and the everyday lives of Kurds and their neighbors. Generally, the debate and
conflict over Kurdistan is not whether the region exists, but rather the extent
of the region, its unity, and its potential independence.[3]

This chapter seeks to locate Kurdistan's ambiguous and varied boundaries
and explain the importance of these elusive boundaries in modern geopolitical conflict and the Kurds' continued marginalization. Beginning with the
Allies' formative decisions after World War I and the fall of the Ottoman
(Turkish) Empire, this chapter examines the geopolitical processes that were
involved in denying the Kurds their autonomy while concurrently creating
many of the states of the modern Middle East. The goal of this chapter is to
historically and politically contextualize why the Kurds do *not* have their own
state and also to show how border delineations (and the lack thereof) have

been pivotal to the status of the Kurds and Kurdistan across internationally recognized borders.

Pre–World War I Kurdistan

Kurdistan has never been a clearly defined region, but generally, its geographical center is considered to be in the Zagros and Taurus mountainous region of Anatolia. Spanning approximately 518,000 square kilometers (200,000 square miles), this extensive region was inhabited by nomadic Kurds as early as 6,000 BC.[4] Though the Kurds were never a unified or homogeneous group, the Kurdish language distinguished them from their Turkish, Persian, and Arabic speaking neighbors.[5] Kurdish historian Mehrdad Izady estimates that between the fifth and sixth century BC, the term *Kurd* acquired an ethnic connotation that was different from Arab, Turk, and Persian as well as Lur, Georgian, Armenian, Azeri, and Turkmen.[6] Many empires, such as the Hurrians, Aryans, Medes, Romans, and Persians spread through and ruled over Kurdistan, but each empire's influence on the Kurds was minor. However, the seventh-century Islamic invasions had a substantial impact.[7] Most Kurds converted from their tribal belief systems to Islam, and today most Kurds are Sunni Muslims. With the exception of religion, few other cultural or political traits were absorbed from the Muslim invasions, and the Kurds, though never homogeneous themselves, remained a distinctive group.

In the early sixteenth century, Kurdistan was absorbed into the expanding Ottoman Empire. The Ottomans maintained a policy of tolerance toward the various minority groups in their empire, and though the Kurds may have been an ethnic minority, since they were Muslims, they were at least theoretically considered part of the majority.[8] Living in approximately fifty different Ottoman *sanjaks*, which were small feudal provinces with their own princes and tribal loyalties, the Kurds prospered under relative autonomy. David McDowall, a specialist on Middle Eastern affairs, refers to the mid-sixteenth century as the Kurds' "golden age."[9] But in the latter part of the century, the Kurds were caught between the feuding Ottoman and Safavid (of Persia) empires. Much of their land was devastated, and many Kurds were forced to relocate. This time of hardship arguably inspired early attempts at Kurdish independence. For example, in 1596 Kurdish Prince Sharaf al-Din of Bitlis wrote *Sharafnama*, the first work that called for the political unification of the Kurdish homeland and the elimination of invaders from their land.[10] Then, in 1639, the Ottomans and Safavids signed the Peace Treaty of Zohab, which drew a boundary between the two empires, essentially dividing the Kurdish region. As a result, the Kurds were further fragmented, and burgeoning attempts at unification stagnated.

In the early to mid-nineteenth century, the Ottoman Empire was losing control of its hinterland. In an attempt to regain power and centralize their rule, Ottoman officials instituted the Tanzimat reforms (in 1839), which abolished the autonomous regions of their empire. Some Kurds revolted after these reforms, and a semblance of Kurdish nationalism began to emerge.[11] In the 1880s, Shaykh Ubaydullah (often written Ubayd Allah) led a revolt in the name of the Kurdish nation, and soon afterwards, the nationalistic Kurdish League was formed in an attempt to gain independence from the Ottomans, Persians, and Armenians.[12] However, this experiment in modern nationalism weakened their traditional tribal and princely ruling houses, which historically had provided leadership and maintained order within Ottoman Kurdistan.[13] Feuds soon erupted between different Kurdish groups vying for power, and neither clear leaders nor unified groups emerged to speak on behalf of the Kurds. The lack of strong Kurdish leadership would prove detrimental to the Kurdish cause during the decisive post–World War I period, when the Ottoman Empire was carved into the new states of the Middle East.

The Near Creation of Kurdistan

World War I reached Kurdistan in October 1914, when the Ottoman Empire joined the Central Powers and declared war on Russia. Four years of fighting plagued the region, ending in 1918 with the Armistice of Mudros. After the war, European politicians (American politicians, too, but to a lesser degree) engaged in years of negotiations over how to divide the fallen Ottoman Empire. During this pivotal time when much of the world was remapped into independent states, many minority groups within the former Ottoman territories sought their own sovereign territories. Guided by Woodrow Wilson's Fourteen Points (January 1918), the postwar territorial negotiations were theoretically based on individual groups' right to self-determination (or independence). In particular reference to the former Ottoman Empire, Wilson's twelfth point asserted that "The Turkish portions of the present Ottoman Empire should be assured a secure sovereignty, but the other nationalities which are now under Turkish rule should be assured an undoubted security of life and an absolutely unmolested opportunity of autonomous development." This "unmolested opportunity of autonomous development" was supposedly extended to the Kurdish minority as well as the Arab majority. However, European and American diplomats viewed the Kurds and many other marginalized groups as a weak, violent, and clannish people unable to rule themselves. Thus the Kurds and their ambitions for autonomy were quickly disregarded during the postwar territorial negotiations.[14] Ultimately, the British, French, American, and Turkish decision makers divided the empire to reflect their own self-interests of strategic regional control.[15]

The former Ottoman Empire was a much lesser concern during peace negotiations than the Austro-Hungarian and German empires, but nevertheless, the division of the Ottoman Empire was the subject of intense debates, which dragged on for seven years. As early as 1916, three years before the Paris Peace Conference, British diplomat Mark Sykes and French diplomat Georges Picot signed a secret agreement that divided Ottoman lands between British and French powers, with some limited autonomy granted to the Arabs, but none to the Kurds. At the signing of the Sykes-Picot Agreement, most of Kurdistan was parceled under French control. Though it was greatly altered during the seven years of negotiations that ensued, the premature Sykes-Picot Agreement served as an overarching template for the division of the Ottoman Empire. During the many years of debate during and after the war, the possibility of creating a sovereign Kurdish state was considered. Indeed, some European decision makers proposed and mapped various boundaries for an independent Kurdistan.

During the 1919 Paris Peace Conference, some Kurdish leaders mobilized in order to assert their territorial claims.[16] Though the Kurds were not united politically or culturally and even among different Kurdish leaders there was no consensus of the ethnic and political boundaries of Kurdistan, they had some brief success in lobbying for an independent Kurdistan.[17] Led by General Sherif Pasha, the Kurdish delegation in Paris proposed an independent Kurdistan and legitimized the proposal by citing Wilson's principle of self-determination. In his *Memorandum on the Claims of the Kurdish People*, presented to the Paris Peace Conference on March 22, 1919, Sherif Pasha argued that "in virtue of the Wilsonian principle everything pleads in favor of the Kurds for the creation of a Kurd state, entirely free and independent."[18] In this memorandum, he also outlined and justified his delineation of Kurdistan.

> The frontiers of Turkish Kurdistan, from an ethnographical point of view, begin: in the North at Ziven, on the Caucasian frontier, and continue westwards to Erzeroum Erzindjian, Keman, Arabkir, Behismi and Divick; in the South they follow the line Haran, the Sindjihar Hills, Tel Asfar, Erbil, Kerkuk Suleimanie, Akk-el-man, Sinna; in the East Ravandiz, Bash-Kale, Vizir-Kale, that is to say the frontier of Persia as far as Mount Ararat. From the remotest periods of history these tracts have been occupied by the Kurds under various names, and for the last thirteen hundred years under that of Kurds [see figure 7.1].[19]

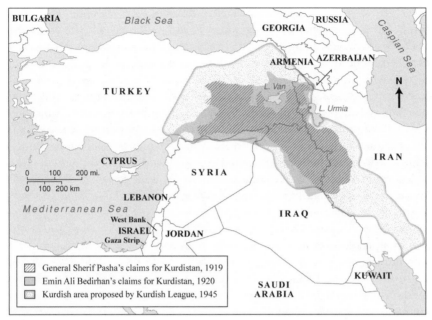

FIGURE 7.1
Kurdistan Claims 1919, 1920, and Proposal of 1945. Cory Johnson of XNR.

The extent of Sherif Pasha's territorial claim was not accepted among all Kurds. A particular area of contention was the Van region (in modern-day southeast Turkey), which Sherif Pasha had excluded from his boundaries even though it purportedly had a large Kurdish population.[20] Emin Ali Bedirham (also known as Mehmet Emin), another Kurdish leader, created an alternative proposal for an independent Kurdistan that included the region around Lake Van and extended Kurdistan's boundaries to include an outlet on the Mediterranean Sea near the port city of Alexandretta in the Hatay Province of modern-day Turkey (figure 7.1).[21] Sherif Pasha and Emin's different proposals clearly reflect the lack of consensus on the location of Kurdistan. However, what is similar between their claims was the desire to create some form of a free Kurdish state, which was becoming an urgent concern as the emerging Kemalists (the political party of Kemal Atatürk) of Turkey began to argue for complete assimilation of the Kurdish region into secular Turkey.

There were considerable differences of opinion among European diplomats over what to do with Kurdistan, and for a time, Western decision makers agreed on the creation of an independent Kurdish state.[22] The 1920 Treaty of Sèvres, which sought to officially establish peace between the Allies and the fallen Ottoman Empire, delineated an autonomous Kurdistan in modern-day southeast Turkey. The treaty stipulated local autonomy "for the predominately Kurdish areas lying east of the Euphrates, south of the southern boundary of Armenia as it may be hereafter determined, and north of the frontier of Turkey with Syria and Mesopotamia" (section III, article 62–64) (figure 7.2). Kurdistan would initially be under the "influence" of the French and British, but the treaty allowed the Kurds to elect complete independence within one year. However, this proposed Kurdish state was significantly smaller than those proposed by Sherif Pasha and Emin and excluded areas that contained large Kurdish populations.[23] Although granting the Kurds some territory, the independent Kurdish state as outlined in Sèvres omitted much of the fertile areas that Sherif Pasha and Emin proposed, and it is debatable whether or not it was even a viable state.

The Treaty of Sèvres was signed, but it was never ratified because it did not satisfy the demands of all the leaders involved. Immediately following the war, control and power in Turkey was unclear and divisive. Mustafa Kemal Atatürk, the leader of the Turkish National Movement and the founder of modern-day Turkey, was in direct opposition to the sultan and his rule in Istanbul. Though the sultan did grudgingly sign the Treaty of Sèvres, Atatürk quickly rejected the treaty, which he considered an encroachment on the heartland of Turkey. As Atatürk gained more military and political strength in the early 1920s, due largely to his successful attacks on Greek and French

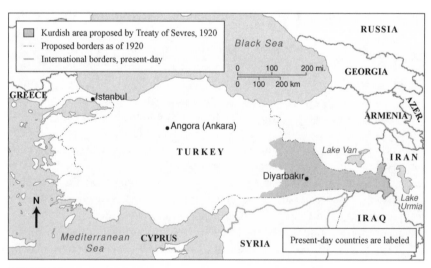

FIGURE 7.2
Treaty of Sèvres—Kurdistan. Cory Johnson of XNR.

forces in Turkey, he began negotiations with European and American leaders over the parceling of land in Anatolia.[24] Unlike the territorial divisions in the Treaty of Sèvres, Atatürk's vision of an independent Turkey included all non-Arab areas of the Ottoman Empire. In order to maintain the territorial integrity of Turkey, Atatürk fought staunchly against its division into Kurdish, French, Greek, and Italian hands.[25]

In 1923, after months of negotiations, the Treaty of Lausanne was signed and ratified, officially establishing peace between the Allies (excluding the United States) and Turkey. In this conclusive treaty, the former Ottoman Empire was partitioned primarily into the independent states of Turkey; the British mandates of Iraq, Transjordan, and Palestine; and the French mandate of Syria (which included Lebanon). The autonomous state of Kurdistan, as proposed in 1920, was dissolved into the new Turkish state (figure 7.2). This decisive parceling of the Ottoman Empire is often considered one the greatest tragedies of the Kurdish people. Though there were some general provisions about the protection of linguistic minorities, there was no stipulation in the Treaty of Lausanne to provide the Kurds or any minority group autonomy or rights (see section III). Ultimately, the vast Kurdish region was divided, and the Kurds were left under the control of Atatürk in Turkey, Reza Shah in Iran, British-appointed Prince Feisal in Iraq, and French politicians in Syria. However, the Kurds did not simply accept these territorial divisions. Inspired by the concepts of nationalism and self-determination, there were various revolts in Turkey, Iran, and Iraq.[26] As early as 1925, Sheikh Said Piran of Turkey and other Kurdish elites led the Sheikh Said Rebellion, which is considered the first large-scale Kurdish national rebellion.[27]

By 1923, the boundaries and states of the former Ottoman Empire began to solidify, but their formation was far from over. For example, the northern Mosul border, between Iraq and Turkey, would remain undetermined until June 1926. Numerous other territorial alterations would also be made between newly created states, but what remained constant was the fragmentation of Kurdistan.

Postwar Autonomy Attempts: Turkey, Iran, and Iraq

Since the establishment of the Turkish state in 1923, Ankara has fiercely denied autonomy to any of Turkey's ethnic minority groups and pursued a policy of "Turkification" of the entire state. In the government's quest for a homogeneous Turkish nation, the Kurds of Turkey have been subjected to various assimilation policies and cultural oppression. Such oppression arguably reached its climax on March 3, 1924, when a law was ratified that banned the use of the Kurdish language in public schools, government offices, broadcast media, and any publications. The Kurds did not acquiesce, and as mentioned above, a full-scale rebellion erupted in 1925.[28] The rebellion was not successful, and after decades of continued oppression, Abdullah Ocalan formed the Partiya Karkari Kurdistan, or the Kurdistan Workers' Party (PKK). Since the 1970s, the PKK has sporadically engaged in systematic violence (labeled as a terrorist organization by the United States) against Turkey, its military, and even some Kurdish groups in northern Iraq.

In 1991, after decades of forced assimilation and systematic cultural oppressions, the draconian Turkish laws were eased, and the Kurds of Turkey were officially allowed to use the Kurdish language in schools and publications. Though it remains unlikely that Turkey will relinquish any part of Kurdistan, Turkey's attempts to join the European Union (EU) have been hindered by the state's condemnable human rights record. Thus it is possible that Turkey's desires to enter the EU will have some positive ramifications between Ankara and Turkish Kurds. Nevertheless, relations between Ankara and Turkish Kurdistan remain hostile. Recent attacks by the Turkish military across Iraq's border in search of active PKK members have revived this decades-old conflict.

In Iran, the situation of the Kurds has been less hostile than in Turkey. Nevertheless, both the Shah's monarchy and the Ayatollah's Islamic republic have opposed Kurdish autonomy and at times have engaged in brutal oppression of the Kurds. Though short-lived, the Kurds of Iran have experienced some independence. With the assistance of the Soviet Union, the autonomous Kurdish region of Mahabad was established in northern Iran on January 2, 1945 (figure 7.3). Though the Shah's forces overtook Mahabad eleven months later, this brief experience with independence facilitated the formation of the Kurdistan Democratic Party of Iran (KDPI), which is still actively pursuing autonomy today.

The Kurds of Iraq, like those of Turkey and Iran, have also had hostile relations with the different ruling powers of their state. During the post–World War I British mandate of Iraq, Mullah Mustafa Barazani (also transliterated as Barzani) mobilized some Iraqi Kurds to revolt against the British administration. After Iraq gained independence in 1932, the Kurds unsuccessfully sought autonomy again. Then, in 1946, fourteen years after Iraq's independence, Barazani formed the Kurdish Democratic Party (KDP), a political group that provided influential and powerful leadership. In the 1970s, after the Ba'th Party had gained control, Iraq attempted to "Arabize" its northern areas by forcefully relocating Kurds elsewhere while moving Arabs into traditionally Kurdish areas. These assimilation policies caused numerous conflicts between Arabs and Kurds, but on March 11, 1970, Baghdadi and Kurdish

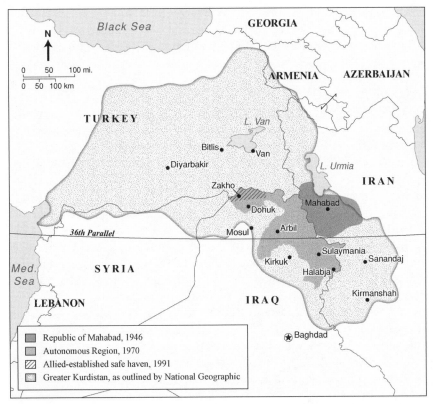

FIGURE 7.3
Kurdish Regions 1946–Present. Cory Johnson of XNR.

leaders reached an agreement that outlined the provisions for a Kurdish autonomous region. Under this agreement, the Kurds gained some control over an area in northern Iraq, which included the historically Kurdish towns of Arbil (also spelled Erbil) and Sulaymaniya.[29] However, four years after its inception, Barazani discarded the agreement and again unsuccessfully attempted to gain complete independence. As a reaction to the KDP's failure, Jalal Talabani formed the Patriotic Union of Kurdistan (PUK), which, like the KDP, remains politically active today.

The 1991 Gulf War generated public attention not only to Saddam's violent onslaught of the Kurds and their mass fleeing but also to the 1988 chemical gas attacks on the Kurdish town of Halabja, which resulted in approximately seventeen thousand Kurdish deaths.[30] Pressured by public concern, the Allies established a safe haven for the Kurds in northern Iraq (figure 7.3). On April 5, 1991, UN Resolution 688 implemented Operation Provide Comfort, in which this safe haven was officially created north of the thirty-sixth parallel in the vicinity of the town of Zakho. The safe haven was substantially smaller than what was outlined as the 1970 autonomous region, but with continued support from the Allies, an agreement was reached between the Kurds and Saddam's government to create an autonomous Kurdish region within the Iraqi state. This newly established autonomous region was similar to that of the 1970 agreement and included the Kurdish cities of Arbil and Sulaymania and much of the oil-rich province of Mosul. In 1992, the Kurds held their first elections for a democratically elected parliament, but the votes were split between Massoud Barazani, the son of Mustafa and leader of the KDP, and Jalal Talabani, leader of the PUK. An agreement was soon reached that split the autonomous region so that the KDP governed Arbil and northern Iraqi Kurdistan and the PUK controlled the southern region around Sulaymania.[31]

The Kurdish Regional Government of Iraq, as it was coined after the 1992 elections, has been considered a successful attempt at establishing Kurdish sovereignty within an internationally recognized state's boundaries. Predictably, since the U.S.-led invasion of Iraq in 2003, the situation in Iraqi Kurdistan has been precarious. Although the Kurdish region has been self-governing for more than a decade and has remained the most stable area during the post-Saddam reconfiguration of Iraq, the formation of an independent Kurdish state has received mixed reviews. A January 2008 *New York Times* article foreshadows that there will indeed be an independent Kurdistan, yet the creation of an independent Kurdish state is unlikely.[32] In order to maintain the status quo with Turkey, Syria, and Iran, the United States intends to maintain the territorial integrity of Iraq's western constructed boundaries.[33] Even Kurdish leaders in Iraq adhere to this policy. Although consensus on the streets of Iraqi Kurdistan is a desire for independence, neither at the end of the 1991 Gulf War nor after the fall of Saddam did Barazani or Talabani seek independence for Iraqi Kurdistan.[34] Instead, the two Kurdish leaders have been working within the Iraqi federal government (Talabani is the president of Iraq) in order to maintain the territorial integrity of Iraq.

The experiences of the Kurds across the internationally recognized states have been diverse, but regardless of some differences, they have all been subjected to some degree of state-sponsored oppression. The governments of Syria, Turkey, and Iran (and, until recently, Iraq) have continually refused to grant autonomy to the Kurds and have staunchly opposed the creation of a unified Kurdistan. Though the reasons for their continued marginalization are numerous and complex, they are firmly rooted in the geopolitical and border discourses of the region, particularly in the attempts of each state to maintain its territorial integrity. For example, each state is fearful that if one state grants the Kurds independence, then each neighboring state would also have to relinquish its Kurdish regions.[35] Second, within each state, if the Kurds were to gain independence, then other minority groups may also pursue similar goals. Relinquishing Kurdish areas would not only question the territorial legitimacy of each state but also threaten its access to essential resources, which would harm its national economy. For example, the Kurds in southeastern Turkey reside within an important watershed, while those in Iraq are in oil-rich land. Thus borders, or more specifically the maintenance of the post–World War I state borders, have a central role in each state's geopolitical policies toward its Kurdish population.

The Meaning(lessness) of Borders in Twentieth- and Twenty-First-Century Kurdistan

Though Kurdistan never gained sovereignty and does not have internationally recognized borders, the region does exist, just not in the classic geographical categories of sovereign states.[36] The division of the Kurds among several states has exacerbated existing differences among Kurds themselves, but nevertheless, the idea of Kurdistan and the sporadic fight for the region's independence has not been hampered by its lack of borders. On the contrary, the lack of borders has perpetuated the Kurdish independence movement.

As mentioned above, Kurdistan was not a unified region, but before World War I neither was Iraq, Syria, Lebanon, Palestine/Israel, Jordan, or the Arabian Peninsula states. These states, which dominate the current geopolitical map of the Middle East, are modern Western creations. Thus it is not surprising that maps of this region generally delineate these internationally recognized states, but only occasionally is the vague region of Kurdistan mapped.

After the geopolitical and historical events that divided Kurdistan among the states that have become much of today's Middle East, maps have been used as powerful, albeit subtle, tools to normalize the way we think of Kurdistan as a stateless region. Before World War I, Kurdistan was mapped by outsiders, often as a label sweeping across an extensive but not clearly defined region.[37] Though it is possible to find maps of Kurdistan with clearly delimited boundaries in books, specifically those about the Kurds, most mass-produced cartography uses a cartographic technique similar to what was used in the early twentieth century in order to denote Kurdistan. For example, the *National Geographic Atlas of the Middle East*'s (2003) political map of the region uses the label "Kurdistan" to indicate a vague, borderless region in the southeasternmost part of Turkey and along the border of Iraq and Iran (figure 7.3).[38] The label is a similar font and size as the similarly ambiguous label of "Mesopotamia" to its south. The larger-scaled national maps of Turkey, Iran,

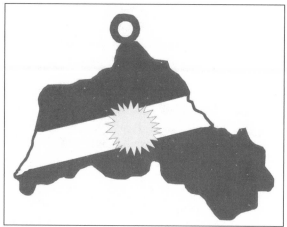

FIGURE 7.4.
Keychain in the Shape of Kurdistan. Illustration by author.

and Iraq each contain a floating label indicating the vagueness of this region's location. Further, the text on the map of Iraq explicitly states that the "Kurdish homeland" spans part of Iraq, Iran, Turkey, and Syria, but oddly, there is no recognition of Kurdistan on the map of Syria. This one example from the National Geographic Society does indeed exemplify the cartographic treatment of Kurdistan in maps produced within the United States.[39]

Unlike common reference maps and atlases produced in the United States, there are several cartographic examples in which Kurdistan has clearly defined boundaries. Maps are powerful tools used to assert territorial claims as well as national identities, and some Kurdish groups have created maps in order to assert Kurdistan's own borders and thus create an image of an autonomous state. As Maria O'Shea wrote, maps have been the "most visible weapon in the Kurdish nationalist arsenal."[40] Though there is no one accepted definition of Kurdistan even among Kurds, their maps show a similar center.[41] The maps created by Sherif Pasha and Emin during the post–World War I peace negotiations readily exemplify these variations. Another similar example stems from a 1945 proposal submitted by the Kurdish League to the first meeting of the United Nations in San Francisco. Stretching from central Turkey and the port of Alexandretta to the Persian Gulf, this expansive state includes geopolitically contentious and resource-rich territory (figure 7.2). Though it differs from Sherif Pasha and Emin's maps, it exemplifies a continued desire for Kurdish autonomy. Yet cartography of a clearly defined Kurdistan has not been limited to postwar peace negotiations. Indeed, some Kurds have recently mapped the boundaries of Kurdistan in a variety of avenues and have disseminated them to wide audiences.[42]

The outline and shape of Kurdistan has become an emblem of a Kurdish nation. Both necklaces and wall maps of Kurdistan can be purchased online or on the street for use as decoration and edification of the region's boundaries (figure 7.4). These cartographic examples, coupled with the above discussion of Kurdish groups fighting for autonomy, demonstrate that the borders of Kurdistan are indeed still important to some Kurds.

Implication and Conclusions

The Kurds are often referred to as the largest nation in the world without a state.[43] While the reasons for this status are numerous, the nonexistent borders of an independent Kurdistan have had a pivotal role. The existing state system imposed upon Kurdish areas was formed less than one hundred years ago by European decision makers and the emerging Turkish government under Kemal Atatürk. As recent as these states' boundaries are, they have been staunchly protected by each state in order to maintain not only its territorial integrity but also oil and water resources. As mentioned above, granting the Kurds independence in any one country would have both national and international implications. Internally, there is a real threat that other minority groups may also attempt secession. Externally, if the Kurds are granted independence in one state, then irredentism, or the uniting of Kurds across state boundaries, is also a concern. As Michael Gunter argues, "No state on earth would support a doctrine that sanctions its own potential breakup."[44]

Even though an internationally recognized state of Kurdistan with clear-cut boundaries is not a common cartographic feature, both the place and idea of a Kurdistan are very real. Its borders may not be visible, but they are part of everyday and geopolitical discourses. Even more conspicuously, these boundaries affect the everyday lives of Kurds in their (in)ability to express their cultural identity or to sustain reasonable livelihoods. Indeed, Kurds across the region have experienced quite different lives largely based on the state in which they became minorities after the division of the Ottoman Empire. For example, Kurds in Iraqi Kurdistan have experienced both autonomy and substantial support from international organizations. These two factors have greatly facilitated political, economic, and cultural development, including the creation of the Kurdish Regional Government and new institutions of higher education. Conversely, the Kurds of southeastern Turkey have experienced much greater political and cultural oppression. Though they have been granted some cultural rights, they are still marginalized by the Turkish government. Further, Turkish Kurds have received little international aid, largely due to the PKK's reputation as a terrorist organization, but also because of the strategic relationship that the United States has with Ankara. Largely due to

their marginalized status and lack of international assistance, Turkish Kurdistan remains relatively poor and unstable.[45] Though the Kurds have been directly impacted by the post–World War I borders, their neighbors' militaries
and military forces ranging from Turkey to Iran to the United States have also
been implicated in this global geopolitical issue.

The different levels of rights and recognition afforded to the Kurds have
pacified and even stunted secessionist movements in some states. As discussed
with Iraq, calculated political attempts to achieve complete independence
have dwindled. The continued failure and even the complacent attitude that
some Kurds have toward independence can be partly attributed to a lack of
internal Kurdish unity, but the boundaries and states we have become so ac-
customed to seeing on the map have also helped create and exacerbate this
divisiveness.[46]

8

Russia's Kaliningrad Exclave

Discontinuity as a Threat to Sovereignty

Alexander C. Diener and Joshua Hagen

O N SEPTEMBER 15, 2005, a flight of seven Russian military aircraft left their base near St. Petersburg on a routine flight to Kaliningrad. While they streaked across the Baltic Sea, one of the pilots veered deep into Lithuanian airspace, prompting the immediate scrambling of NATO fighter jets. Complicating a potentially volatile situation, the Russian plane crashed before the NATO interceptors arrived. The pilot ejected safely and was returned to Russia, but not before Russian and Lithuanian officials exchanged harsh words. While this intrusion was likely accidental, Lithuania, Latvia, Estonia, and Finland have reported dozens of incidences of Russian military aircraft violating their airspace in recent years. Evidence of Russia's determination to maintain unimpeded linkages with its Kaliningrad exclave, these airspace violations have contributed to tense relations between Russia and its Baltic neighbors.

Wedged between Lithuania, Poland, and the Baltic, Kaliningrad is an unassuming, often-overlooked piece of twenty-first century Europe and an unlikely source of international discord (figure 8.1). Indeed, at around 15,100 square kilometers (5,830 square miles), Kaliningrad is only half the size of Belgium. While at first glance Kaliningrad might appear to be an independent state, it is actually the westernmost territory of the Russian Federation. Kaliningrad is what political geographers refer to as an exclave. An exclave is a part of a state that is detached or separated from the main body of that state by foreign territory; that is, it is not contiguous with the rest of the country. Kaliningrad oblast (province) is more than 400 kilometers (nearly 250 miles) away from "mainland" Russia but supports a majority Russian-speaking population totaling approximately 950,000.

FIGURE 8.1
Present-Day Baltic Region. Cory Johnson of XNR.

While many saw the end of the Cold War, strengthening international organizations, and growing economic interdependence between states as heralding a new, borderless world, it is obvious that borders, their functions, and their meanings remain integral to understanding the contemporary international scene. Although small in stature, Kaliningrad and other exclaves provide powerful examples of the continued power of borders since they tend to "influence the bilateral relations between their mainlands and surrounding states in a disproportionate degree to the smallness of both their territory and population."[1] Indeed, Kaliningrad has been a source of recurring disputes between Russia and its western neighbors, as illustrated by the story that opened this chapter.

To understand Kaliningrad's contemporary situation, it is first necessary to understand how this exclave came into being. This chapter begins by reviewing the area's long, troubled history as a German exclave from the Middle Ages to World War II. It then investigates the area's incorporation into the contiguous territory of the Soviet Union after 1945 and concludes by examining the implications of the area's re-emergence as an exclave following the dissolution of the Soviet Union in 1991.

The German Exclave of East Prussia

The territory now known as Kaliningrad has a tumultuous history. The pagan Prussians, the earliest known inhabitants, were a loosely organized people. During the thirteenth century, the predominantly German Teutonic Knights conquered the Prussians and established a monastic state centered on the city of Königsberg. Teutonic control gradually expanded to cover much of the Baltic coast to modern-day Estonia until a Polish-Lithuanian force defeated the Knights in 1410. Teutonic power ebbed until their leader dissolved the order in 1525 and established himself as a secular ruler over the remaining territories, roughly twice the size of modern Kaliningrad. The ruling class of this new Duchy of Prussia retained its ethnic German character, although the territory was initially under the suzerainty of the Polish king.[2] Since the Teutonic state and later Duchy of Prussia were separated from the main body of German-speaking lands by a relatively thin strip of Polish-speaking territory, the area was already a German political and cultural exclave.

After two centuries of relative stability, the eighteenth century witnessed significant political changes as the Polish kingdom slowly declined and the powerful Hohenzollern family inherited the Duchy of Prussia. Based in Berlin, the Hohenzollerns controlled large territories across northern Germany and were rising to preeminence among the German states. Hohenzollern rulers worked to integrate the duchy, now known as East Prussia, and their other territories into a contiguous Prussian kingdom at the expense of Polish territories. During the three partitions of Poland in 1772, 1793, and 1795, Poland ceased to exist as Austria, Russia, and Prussia divided the territory among themselves.[3] East Prussia was now a contiguous portion of the kingdom. Although no longer a political exclave, East Prussia remained something of a cultural exclave since many ethnic Poles remained in West Prussia (figure 8.2).

Pitting the Central Powers of Germany, Austria-Hungary, and their allies against the Allied Powers of the United Kingdom, France, Russia, and their allies, World War I (1914–1918) initiated widespread political upheaval across Europe. Given the huge investment of lives and resources, it seemed natural that the winners would seek compensation through a dramatic realignment of Europe's political boundaries. The collapse of the Central Powers left the Allied Powers responsible for shaping Europe's postwar map. Although none

FIGURE 8.2
Pre–World War I, East Prussia. Cory Johnson of XNR.

of the combatants intended to resurrect Poland when hostilities began, all of the major powers eventually promised Poles some degree of autonomy in exchange for their support in the conflict.[4]

The United States was a late entry in the conflict, declaring war on Germany in April 1917. Despite the comparatively modest American contribution, President Woodrow Wilson played a major role in the reconstitution of Poland. In 1918, Wilson laid out his Fourteen Points for securing a lasting peace. In his thirteenth point, Wilson declared: "An independent Polish state should be erected which should include the territories inhabited by indisputably Polish populations, which should be assured a free and secure access to the sea, and whose political and economic independence and territorial integrity should be guaranteed by international covenant."[5] While seemingly straightforward, Wilson's statement covered two distinct goals that clashed once peace talks commenced. First, Wilson's declaration envisioned border realignments based on nationality. Therefore the Poles, divided among the Russian, German, and Austro-Hungarian empires, should have their own

state, that is, national self-determination. Second, Poland should be economically viable, by which Wilson envisioned open trade facilitated by access to the
sea. While the idea of applying the principal of national self-determination
was somewhat novel, belief in the freedom of navigation on the seas and the
right of access to the sea was widely shared among Western states.[6]

Despite numerous calls for Polish autonomy, the prospects for Polish statehood appeared remote. Victory by the Central Powers would likely result in
continued German and Austrian domination. Russian territorial claims would
have complicated Polish statehood following an Allied victory. Circumstances
changed dramatically toward the end of the war. First, the Russian monarchy
collapsed amid civil war, and the new Bolshevik government ceded its Polish
territories to the Central Powers in early 1918. Yet this arrangement proved
temporary as Germany's government collapsed later that year. Polish nationalists quickly filled this power vacuum and seized many Polish-speaking areas
before the Allied Powers gathered in 1919 to draft a peace treaty.

Since a nascent Polish state already existed, it was no longer a question of
whether to reconstitute Poland but rather a matter of delineating its boundaries. While negotiations leading to the Treaty of Versailles included many
difficult issues, perhaps the most contentious dealt with the German-Polish
border. The main architects of the treaty, French prime minister Georges
Clemenceau, British prime minister David Lloyd George, and United States
president Woodrow Wilson, had conflicting objectives. As noted above, Wilson thought nationality and economic viability paramount. Lloyd George
aimed to weaken Germany's military while allowing its economy to recover.
Clemenceau demanded harsh terms designed to leave Germany prostrate,
which meant restoring Poland to its 1772 boundaries. This would include
areas with majority Polish populations but also areas of mixed and German-
majority populations in West and East Prussia. A rump East Prussia would
become a vassal republic under Polish protection. Lloyd George and Wilson
countered that placing large German populations under Polish control would
lead to another war.

A compromise was reached that allowed the French, British, Americans,
and Poles to achieve some of their objectives, but it left no one completely
satisfied.[7] Predominantly Polish-speaking areas were awarded to Poland. Predominantly German-speaking portions of East Prussia remained in Germany.
While seemingly consistent with Wilson's ideal of national self-determination, the province of West Prussia posed an obstacle. Germans argued that
they represented about 65 percent of its total population and should therefore
retain the territory. Poles countered that they constituted majorities in twelve
of its twenty-nine counties and needed West Prussia, its main port Danzig,
and portions of East Prussia to guarantee access to the Baltic Sea.[8]

There was no way to divide the territory between the two groups coherently, so in the end the belief that Poland's economic viability required a territorial link to the Baltic trumped ethnic considerations. Poland was awarded a narrow strip of land running north through West Prussia to the Baltic coast. This so-called Polish Corridor contained approximately 412,000 ethnic Germans, about 42 percent of the total population. Some areas actually had German majorities.[9] The city of Danzig was an even greater problem. For Poland to have access to the sea, it needed a working port. Yet Danzig and the surrounding area were over 90 percent German. The Allies again reached a compromise that disappointed both the Poles, who favored outright annexation, and the Germans, who clearly preferred union with Germany. Instead, Danzig became an independent free city, although Poland received special transshipment rights (figure 8.3).

The final border settlement placed a sizable German minority within Poland, perhaps numbering as high as 1.1 million. The Free City of Danzig con-

FIGURE 8.3
Interwar East Prussia. Cory Johnson of XNR.

tained another 330,000 Germans.[10] Although Germany retained East Prussia, the territory was bounded by Poland and Lithuania. After nearly 150 years, East Prussia was once again an exclave. Both sides felt wronged and argued for territorial revisions in their favor, yet this arrangement was "probably the least bad solution to an impossible problem."[11]

For most Germans, the Versailles settlement and especially the resulting detachment of Danzig and East Prussia from the rest of Germany constituted an "act of national humiliation."[12] Often relying on sensationalist, highly selective, or outright misleading information, German authors provided a variety of economic, historical, linguistic, and geopolitical arguments for restoring East Prussia's contiguity with the rest of Germany. While some authors claimed that restricted access to East Prussia hindered economic growth, others worried that the exclave's "encirclement" would lead to a complete loss of German sovereignty. Regardless of the exact argument, many Germans felt passionately that East Prussia should be restored to what they saw as its rightful and natural contiguity with Germany.[13] Indeed, most German readers would have agreed that the Polish Corridor was an "absurdity" and "preposterous."[14] This odd border arrangement was proof enough for most Germans that the corridor and the resulting separation of East Prussia were unnatural and unjust. Perhaps surprisingly, public debate concerning East Prussia subsided after the Nazis seized power. Indeed, German-Polish relations stabilized after the countries signed a nonaggression pact in 1934. But rather than actually renouncing territorial claims, Hitler likely viewed the pact as a means to delay a final confrontation with Poland while he focused on other objectives. Ominous German publications calling for a "reckoning with Poland" over the corridor began reappearing in 1939.[15]

Described as "unashamedly nationalist," Poland's foreign policy experts were equally passionate in defense of the corridor and their access to the sea.[16] Like their German counterparts, Polish leaders presented highly selective information to support their claims. Polish authors argued that their access to the sea was tenuous since it was flanked by German territories. While Germans feared that East Prussia's separation would undermine their sovereignty over the exclave, Poles were convinced that Germany would employ East Prussia, "a bastion of German militarism thrust far into the East," to undermine Poland's independence.[17] Perhaps surprisingly, Polish writers agreed that the current border arrangement was unnatural. But based on their interpretations of history, economics, geopolitics, and nationality, it was not the corridor but rather East Prussia that was an "artificial creation" or a "German colony" planted on Polish territory.[18] The natural order of things, from the Polish viewpoint, was for East Prussia and Danzig to be incorporated into Poland.

The Polish Corridor also became a recurring topic of debate in American and British foreign policy circles. Opinion was largely sympathetic to Polish claims and concerned that the corridor dispute could lead to war.[19] Although the Versailles settlement left numerous border disputes across Europe, many predicted that the apparent artificiality of the Polish Corridor and the East Prussia exclave would spark conflict. The corridor was variously described as "the most menacing storm centre on the Continent," "the greatest danger spot of Europe," and a "thorn in Europe's flesh."[20] After visiting the Corridor in 1934, one British journalist even predicted that this "tinder box of Europe" would cause full-scale war to erupt within two years. In his 1933 science fiction history book *The Shape of Things to Come*, H. G. Wells foretold of an imminent world war triggered by the corridor.[21]

Unfortunately, such statements proved prophetic as Hitler turned his attention to the corridor. Backed by France and the United Kingdom, Poland refused Hitler's demands for territorial concessions in the corridor. On September 1, 1939, the first shots of World War II rang out as German troops poured into the corridor.[22] Although the corridor was the immediate cause for war, it is almost certain that Hitler intended to provoke war with Poland eventually. Germany quickly defeated Poland and annexed considerable territory. East Prussia was again contiguous with the rest of Germany. Yet German military success was temporary. As Anglo-American forces closed in on Germany from the west and Soviet forces approached from the east, their leaders began mapping out a new Europe. While much remained uncertain, Polish exiles argued that lasting peace could be achieved only by awarding the East Prussian exclave to Poland and expelling its German inhabitants.[23] But it would be Soviet premier Joseph Stalin who determined the final territorial settlement. The area's long history as a German exclave was at an end.

Creating Kaliningrad

Given the brutality of the German invasion of the Soviet Union, it is not surprising that the Soviet army's first encounter with historic German territory in late 1944 was venomous and punitive. As their troops advanced on East Prussia, Soviet propagandists shifted their focus from "liberation" of occupied territory to "vengeance."[24] The Soviet assault on East Prussia proved costly as German troops exacted four to eight times their own losses, with estimates ranging from 250,000 to 900,000 Soviet casualties.[25] The carnage only hardened Soviet resolve to transform East Prussia from Germany's easternmost territory and the "heartland of Prussian militarism" into Russia's westernmost territory and a bastion of military strength.

The fate of East Prussia was intertwined with broader negotiations among the leaders of the Big Three (United States, United Kingdom, Soviet Union) concerning the postwar realignment of German-Polish-Soviet territories. The 1941 Atlantic Charter attempted to forestall any controversies at the outset of the war by renouncing territorial acquisitions in the event of an Allied victory. The charter was signed by American president Franklin Delano Roosevelt and British prime minister Winston Churchill, but not Stalin. The Soviet Union was, therefore, under no obligation to forego opportunities to extend its territory.

Suspicious of Stalin's intentions, Churchill attempted to block Soviet territorial expansion into Eastern Europe. At the Tehran Conference in 1943, Churchill stated that "the home of the Polish State and nation should be between the so-called Curzon line (eastern border with USSR) and the Line of Oder (western border with Germany), including for Poland East Prussia and Oppeln." Stalin responded that "Russians have no ice free ports on the Baltic," and therefore the Soviet Union required Königsberg and Memel (another port city) to facilitate access to the sea.[26] Although several Baltic ports were already under Soviet control in the recently annexed territories of Estonia, Latvia, and Lithuania, Roosevelt was willing to concede to Stalin's wishes. Despite Churchill's efforts, the fate of East Prussia was all but sealed by the end of February 1945. Only the matter of official sovereignty remained.

In the wake of Roosevelt's death and Churchill's ouster from office in the summer of 1945, Stalin opened the Potsdam Conference aggressively by calling for portions of German territory to be ceded to Poland. As the conference progressed, the Soviet delegation boldly advanced a formal case for acquiring Königsberg and the surrounding areas. Under this plan, the southern two-thirds of East Prussia would be ceded to Poland's pro-Soviet government, while the Soviet Union received the northern third. Combined with the annexations of the Baltic states, Soviet territory now extended much farther to the west. The United States and United Kingdom agreed to endorse this plan at the forthcoming peace conference to officially end World War II.[27] Since the conference never occurred, some have argued that the Soviet Union received only administrative control over Königsberg and its hinterland. De jure control, or full-scale legal sovereignty, may be argued to remain unsettled.

While legal ambiguities remained, the Soviet Union's de facto control of the northern portions of East Prussia, renamed "Kaliningrad" for the deceased Soviet president Mikhail Kalinin, was evident in efforts to transform the area to meet Soviet strategic needs. The first step in this transformation was to cleanse the territory ethnically. Ironically, the other Allied powers endorsed this goal, but for different purposes. Favoring awarding East Prussia to Poland, Roosevelt called in March 1943 for peaceful "arrangements to move the Prussians out of East Prussia. . . ."[28] Beginning in the harsh winter of 1944 and continuing until April of 1945, the rampaging Soviet advance prompted an unmanaged exodus of German citizens. Aware of the carnage inflicted by German troops on Russia and with rumors of Soviet atrocities abounding, East Prussians fled to port cities in hope of evacuation. For many, escape to the Baltic turned tragic as Soviet submarines sank the slow-moving cruise liners used to transport evacuees.[29] Perhaps responding to the ethnic cleansing of East Prussia, the Big Three leaders agreed in the summer of 1945 to support a "humane" transfer of German populations from Czechoslovakia, Hungry, and Poland. It was, however, too late for the Germans of East Prussia, as an estimated prewar population of 2,470,000 was reduced to a mere 600,000 in 1945 (mostly non-Germans remained). Some ethnic Germans returned following Germany's surrender, but by 1947 it is estimated that starvation, disease, execution, and deportation left as few as 30,000 Germans in Königsberg.[30]

As the area emptied of its German inhabitants, Soviet leaders sought to import a population loyal to the Communist cause. Transfers of large numbers of Russians, Byelorussians, and Ukrainians from war-torn regions of the Soviet Union began as early as 1946. Several hundred thousand migrants soon arrived as the population reached 611,000 by 1959. The resettlement of predominantly ethnic Russians altered the sociocultural landscape of what had been German territory for more than six hundred years.[31] In part because of its forward position in Europe, the identity of Kaliningraders was perhaps the most successful fruition of Soviet nationality policy, that is, the creation of the "Soviet man." Though close relationships were generally maintained with friends and family back home, the largely imported population saw themselves as Soviet-Russian, Soviet-Ukrainian, or more simply Soviet citizens. Lacking an indigenous population, Kaliningrad's almost exclusively Russian-speaking population held themselves, and the territory, to be an extension of Russia. Such a perception was supported in the 1940s by Moscow's promotion of a fictive history of Slavic occupation of the region in the early medieval period.[32] Clearly, Moscow thought it important to cultivate a loyal population in this new territory. In retrospect, then, this program of expulsion and forced resettlement was part of a grander strategy to transform Germany's easternmost province into the Soviet "window on the West."

While the area underwent this dramatic demographic transformation, it was also necessary to integrate the territory into the Soviet political system. In theory, the Soviet Union was a union of independent Communist republics based largely on nationality. The largest was the Russian Soviet Republic, but other major ethnic groups, like the Lithuanians, Latvians, or Estonians, had their own republics. In practice, though, strong central control meant that these republics had little autonomy. Since Kaliningrad's indigenous German population had been expelled, no native national group existed. While it was possible to incorporate Kaliningrad into the neighboring Lithuanian Soviet Republic, this was without historical precedent since "the presently truncated northern third of East Prussia had never been included in any Lithuanian state entity."[33] Lithuania's recent history of independence may have also made inclusion of the territory within the Lithuanian Republic undesirable. The addition of a warm-water Baltic port within "Russian" territory may have also been too tempting for Soviet leaders. Lacking an ethnic indigenous people for whom to name a republic, Stalin unilaterally assigned administration of the new Russian-speaking territory to the Russian Republic on October 17, 1945. While the decision appeared trivial at the time, it would have major ramifications after the Soviet Union collapsed.

To mark its sovereignty over this newly acquired territory and emphasize the need for constant vigilance against Western encroachment, Soviet planners launched a program of extensive landscape change. This entailed widespread destruction of traditional Germanic architecture and public symbols that had survived the war. Soviet authorities obliterated hundreds of historical churches, medieval castles, and even entire villages after the war in a purposeful attempt to erase the German cultural landscape. Yet Soviet efforts to recast the landscape of Kaliningrad were not simply destructive. Rather, planners aimed to integrate the Kaliningrad region into the broader structures of the Soviet Union. In terms of economics, agriculture was collectivized, and light manufacturing tailored to military production was fostered. New road and rail connections to the east integrated Kaliningrad's reorganized economy into the broader Soviet framework.[34] Yet this economic system proved inefficient, and Kaliningrad remained a constant drain on Soviet resources.

This lack of economic productivity stemmed partly from Kaliningrad's geopolitical role at the forefront of the Cold War. Apprehensive about the military strength of the United States and its NATO allies in Western Europe, Soviet strategists were eager to establish a strong military presence in Kaliningrad to "serve as a buffer against an attack from western aggressors. On the offense, it would allow Russia to simultaneously attack its enemies in central and western Europe."[35] Reflecting Kaliningrad's designation as the command headquarters for their NATO opposition forces and a key staging area for the Baltic fleet, between 100,000 and 300,000 Soviet troops crammed into the oblast during the immediate postwar period. The total population also grew rapidly (1959, 611,000; 1970, 732,000; 1989, 913,000) in support of the military. As the Soviets' westernmost military bastion, Kaliningrad played a vital role in Soviet Cold War strategy in Europe.

Given the primacy placed on geopolitical considerations, it is not surprising that Kaliningrad was a negative contributor to the Soviet Union's
economic ledger. As relations with the United States improved toward
the end of the Cold War, Kaliningrad authorities and planners working
under Soviet premier Mikhail Gorbachev advocated turning the region
into a free economic zone (FEZ). Rather than its customary military role,
Kaliningrad's proximity to Western Europe would be used to revitalize the
Communist system by luring foreign investment, trade, and business innovation into the Soviet Union through its window on the West. The idea
was approved eventually as a means of attracting foreign and domestic
investors with tax breaks and incentives. Yet the program did little to arrest
the Soviet Union's terminal economic decline. Despite these belated economic reforms, Kaliningrad's primary purpose was to serve as a westward
military fortress and platform for projecting Soviet geopolitical strength
(figure 8.1).

Kaliningrad as a Russian Exclave

Burdened by economic stagnation and growing secessionist movements, the
Soviet Union dissolved in 1991 as its fifteen constituent republics became
independent countries. Since the Russian Republic had administered Kaliningrad, the area fell under the sovereign control of the new Russian Federation. If Kaliningrad had been integrated into the Soviet Union as part of the
Lithuanian Republic or as a separate republic, it is likely that the area would
now be part of Lithuania or its own independent state. Although certainly not
envisioning the demise of the Soviet Union, the decision by Soviet leaders to
administer Kaliningrad as part of the Russian Republic directly contributed
to the emergence of a new political exclave on the Baltic.

Given its previous integration within the broader Soviet economy, it is not
surprising that the collapse of the Soviet Union exacerbated Kaliningrad's
economic plight. From 1990 to 1995, government statistics indicate that
"industrial production fell by 61 percent and agricultural production by 50
percent, compared to 51 percent and 29 percent respectively in Russia as a
whole."[36] Recognizing Kaliningrad's unique geographical position, the new
Russian government awarded it additional privileges, including compensation for transit costs across the new international borders that surrounded the
territory and allowing the region to retain a greater share of its tax revenues
(45 percent in 1992 to 70 percent in 1995).[37] The Kaliningrad FEZ was also
maintained initially but succeeded in drawing only modest foreign investments (only $27 million in 1995).

Reflecting the dire economic scene, some Kaliningraders, led by their new governor Yuri Matochkin, pressed for increased autonomy to take advantage of their proximity to the growing economies of Central Europe. Matochkin argued that because of Kaliningrad's location, it confronted disadvantages unlike any other region of Russia. Opponents in Moscow cited Kaliningrad's negative net contribution to Russia's budget and the area's burgeoning smuggling economy, which was untaxable by either Moscow's or Kaliningrad's governments. Despite the economic difficulties and its physical separation from the rest of the country, Kaliningrad's ethnic ties to Russia and continued dependence on Russian military spending limited widespread calls for secession.

Although separatist sentiment among Kaliningraders remained minimal, Russia also worried about potential irredentist claims. With border disputes throughout the post-Soviet sphere, a variety of scenarios presented themselves for all or parts of Kaliningrad to be claimed by neighboring countries. In the early 1990s, Lithuanian nationalists eyed portions of Kaliningrad. After various Lithuanian leaders suggested that the territory might be reclaimed, a number of Russian pundits responded that Russia could offer its own irredentist claims over Lithuanian territory.[38] This, coupled with the prospect of absorbing Kaliningrad's overwhelmingly Russian population, led Lithuania to renounce all claims to Kaliningrad. Poland also signed treaties renouncing territorial claims in both Germany and Russia. Should it reverse its position, Poland could potentially face the prospect of counterirredentist claims from both countries. Having benefited from the division of East Prussia, Poland has little reason to take action that could jeopardize its sovereignty over the southern portions of that territory.

Perhaps the greatest immediate concern following the Soviet collapse was possible German irredentism targeting Kaliningrad. A unified Germany with its capital relocated to Berlin loomed ominously for the residents of former East Prussia. Though systematically obliterated from the landscape, the territory's German character remained in the minds of many. Even during the late Soviet era, rumors spread of the possibility of converting Kaliningrad into a homeland for Soviet Germans. These plans never came to fruition, and most Soviet Germans left for new lives in Germany. In Germany, however, an aging cohort of East Prussians called for the right of return, compensation for lost property, and, at times, outright reclamation of the territory. Although these movements have diminished with time, organizations such as the Association of East Prussians draw considerable support from the more conservative elements of German society. Nevertheless, the German government, careful to avoid the appearance of revanchist interest in its former eastern territories, officially recognized Russian sovereignty over Kaliningrad in 1990.[39]

Although secessionist and irredentist sentiments concerning Kaliningrad were limited, Russia still confronts the difficulties associated with governing an exclave, while other Baltic states struggle with the implications resulting from this slice of Russian territory in their midst. At times reminiscent of the previous estrangement in German-Polish relations over the East Prussian exclave, Kaliningrad has been a recurring irritant in Russian relations with European Union and NATO members. As a Russian exclave bordered by Poland and Lithuania, now members of both the EU and NATO, one can rightly claim that Kaliningrad "plays a role in international affairs far beyond its size and economic potential."[40]

Transit between Kaliningrad and the rest of the country has been a persistent concern for the Russian government. During the 1990s, Russia went so far as to pressure both Lithuania and Poland to establish special corridors through which Russian citizens could travel between the exclave and mainland Russia. Worried that the accession of Poland and Lithuania to the EU's visa procedures would further limit access to the region, Russian officials used Kaliningrad in an attempt to forestall the EU's eastward expansion. After lengthy and at times contentious negotiations during which both sides voiced Cold War–style rhetoric, Russia and the EU agreed to create a type of transit visa that allowed Russians to cross EU territory to reach Kaliningrad.[41] While generally allowing Russian citizens and goods to travel back and forth, some on both sides continue to argue that the current arrangement places undue burdens on their respective sovereign rights.

Russia also used alleged threats to its sovereignty over Kaliningrad as a pawn "in the game between NATO and Russia over what security architecture should be built in the aftermath of the Cold War."[42] In 1997, Russian leaders proposed a Baltic security agreement that they hoped would forestall NATO expansion in the region. After this failed, Russian officials hinted that tactical nuclear weapons could be deployed in Kaliningrad to demonstrate Russian concern over the exclave's encirclement and to leverage against any possible attempt to deny Russian access. Russian officials also raised this possibility in response to plans for a U.S.-backed missile defense system in Eastern Europe. While it is unclear whether the missile shield will be constructed, Poland and the other three Baltic countries did join NATO. Ironically, Russian attempts to utilize Kaliningrad as a geopolitical pawn against EU and NATO expansion likely strengthened Polish and Lithuanian resolve to join these institutions, while their membership will likely bolster Russia's determination to maintain a large military presence in Kaliningrad.

The apparent EU and NATO encirclement of Kaliningrad and direct borders with Russian territory run counter to long-term Russian geopolitical strategy of maintaining subservient buffer states. Fearing that overland access, especially for military purposes, could be impeded or halted completely, the Russian government has established air and sea routes from St. Petersburg to Kaliningrad. While theoretically allowing Russian aircraft to reach Kaliningrad without crossing foreign territory, the narrow air corridor across the Baltic has led to dozens of instances of Russian violations of Finnish, Lithuanian, Latvian, and Estonian airspace, as noted at the beginning of this chapter. While most were incidental, these flights have contributed to mutual anxiety and mistrust. Indeed, suspicion that Lithuania might limit rail access led the Russian government to establish regular ferry service from St. Petersburg to Kaliningrad. Former Russian president Vladimir Putin called the seaborne link "a matter of national security," while government-controlled media declared that the ferry would "deprive the Baltic states of an instrument of influence over Russia."[43] Conversely, EU and NATO members, especially Poland and Lithuania, worry that the heavily militarized Kaliningrad region will become a type of "Trojan horse" to flex Russian geopolitical muscle in the Baltic.[44]

Beyond its strategic implications, some in the EU have feared that Kaliningrad's location could undermine the rule of law within the EU. These fears are perhaps most acute regarding Kaliningrad's role as a conduit for illegal immigration, narcotics, and organized crime to penetrate EU territory. Although Kaliningrad boasts a burgeoning transportation infrastructure that could position the region as a major transit corridor linking Asian-Pacific and EU markets, as well as serving as an import/export hub for Russian markets, Kaliningrad's budding entrepreneurial class now makes smuggling and shuttle trading a prime occupation. Estimates suggest as much as 20–30 percent of Kaliningrad's population is involved in such activities.[45] Although some doubt the veracity of these figures, it is clear that criminal groups are using Kaliningrad as a base to smuggle everything from illegal drugs to illegal immigrants into the EU. These unregulated border flows lead EU officials to fear that the perceived lawlessness of Russian society will infiltrate their territory, while Russian and Kaliningrad authorities worry about the growth of powerful mafia networks. Ironically, the inability or unwillingness of the Russian government to stem these illegal flows and the reluctance of EU members to grant special economic concessions both serve to constrict Kaliningrad's economic potential and leave residents increasingly dependent on illicit activities.

Kaliningrad in the Twenty-First Century

Given its location, the Kaliningrad exclave has the potential to serve as an important place of cooperative interaction and understanding between Russia and its Western neighbors. Unfortunately, the region has more often been a source of competition and mistrust since 1991. These issues have grown more acute as the expansion of the EU and NATO to include Lithuania, Latvia, Estonia, and Poland has left Kaliningrad an island of Russian sovereignty within these steadily integrating frameworks. Although important differences exist, the stories of the East Prussian and Kaliningrad exclaves highlight some common themes. First, states possessing exclaves, initially Germany and then Russia in this case, tend to view this discontiguity as a potential threat. Faced with images of encirclement, Germany and Russia took extraordinary measures to maintain their sovereignty and secure unrestricted access. Neighboring states have tended to regard demands for transit privileges to and from exclaves as challenges to their own sovereignty. A dynamic of mutual suspicion, if not outright paranoia, can develop all too quickly, as evident in both the interwar and post-Soviet periods.

While the case of East Prussia demonstrates the potential of exclaves to spawn conflict, outright hostilities between Russia and the EU or NATO remain remote. Yet questions remain as to how Russia will utilize its exclave. Will Russia continue Kaliningrad's Cold War role as an "unsinkable aircraft carrier" opposing NATO forces? Or will Kaliningrad emerge as an "assembly workshop," a bridge, and an access point between Eastern and Western markets?[46] Will the EU and NATO come to regard Kaliningrad as a potential threat to be isolated? Or will Kaliningrad's economic potential lead both sides to facilitate cross-border trade and investment? Since 1991, relations between Russia and its Western neighbors have too often unfolded against a backdrop of mutual suspicion and competition, but the present geopolitical complexities surrounding Kaliningrad make it difficult to predict with confidence which option is most likely. Regardless, Kaliningrad continues to illustrate the centrality that borders still occupy at the beginning of the twenty-first century.

9

Defining Liechtenstein

Sovereign Borders, Offshore Banking, and National Identity

Robert Ostergren

IN EARLY MARCH OF 2007, the world's media pounced rather gleefully on a breaking story coming out of Switzerland. It seemed, as reported by the Swiss daily newspaper *Blick*, that the Swiss army had accidentally invaded Liechtenstein. The story was farcical. A company of 171 Swiss soldiers on routine night maneuvers somehow got completely turned around and marched across the unmarked border, penetrating some 2 kilometers (1.2 miles) into the neighboring principality before realizing their mistake and beating a hasty retreat. What made their blunder all the more amusing, as well as embarrassing to the Swiss, was in the details. As it turned out, no one in Liechtenstein actually noticed the intrusion, which occurred in the dead of night and in foul weather, when most sensible locals were asleep. Authorities in Liechtenstein remained blissfully unaware of what had happened until the next day, when the Swiss called to notify them that their border had been violated and to extend an official apology. Moreover, the trespassing army unit, belonging as it did to one of Europe's most famously neutral countries, was a most unlikely aggressor. The recruits were armed with assault rifles but carried no ammunition. A Liechtenstein spokesperson, in an attempt to downplay the incident, was later quoted as saying, "It's not like they stormed over here with attack helicopters or something."[1] In the end, Liechtenstein turned out to be magnanimous in its official reaction, accepting what had happened without taking offense. In fact, no resistance could have been attempted since Liechtenstein has not had an army since 1868. The border between the two countries is normally open, with citizens from both countries passing back and forth daily as if no border existed. Indeed, the principality shares many official ties with its

Swiss neighbor, including a common currency, postal service, and consulate services in other countries. The media nonetheless had a field day, launching droll headlines such as "Whoops! Swiss Accidentally Invade Liechtenstein," "A Wartime Scenario, Starring the Swiss," and "Swiss Miss."[2]

All joking aside, the media hoopla did for a brief time focus popular attention on one of Europe's often overlooked border anomalies—the existence among the larger and more familiar political entities of the so-called microstates. Europe has five of these diminutive sovereign states: Andorra, Monaco, San Marino, the Vatican City, and, of course, Liechtenstein. All of them share some common characteristics, the first of which is their Lilliputian size. Andorra, the largest of the five, has an area of only 468 square kilometers (181 square miles), while at the other extreme, Monaco and the Vatican City are fully contained within spaces of 1.95 square kilometers (.76 square miles) and .44 square kilometers (.17 square miles), respectively. All have long histories as well as specialized and, at times, convoluted political relationships with their nearest neighbors. San Marino traces its existence back to the late Roman Empire and claims to be Europe's oldest existing state. The others are modern-day survivors of a feudal Europe of ancestral fiefdoms and small princely territories. Andorra arose out of a thirteenth-century treaty that created a sovereign territory jointly ruled by a Catalonian bishop and the House of Foix in the south of France. Monaco also emerged in the thirteenth century as a Genoan colony under the control of the House of Grimaldi. The Vatican City is the last remaining parcel of what were once the Papal States; while Liechtenstein emerged from the myriad princely dynastic holdings of the old Holy Roman Empire and can lay claim to being the sole surviving monarchy of the Holy Roman Empire.[3] Finally, all are regarded today as places of relative exclusivity: the Vatican due to its special role as the global headquarters of the Catholic Church, the others by virtue of their highly selective citizenship laws and their reputations as tax havens.

The emergence of each of these microstates and their special status within Europe today are fascinating stories. An important part of each case are the processes by which the territorial borders that delimit these places were created and acquired special functions and meanings to people in different places, at different times, and at different scales. In accordance with the overall theme of this volume, Europe's microstates are a striking example of the fact that borders still matter, even in what we increasingly imagine as a "borderless" world.[4] They are also clear expressions of the fact that borders are more than just static lines drawn on the map. Even seemingly small and unimportant political territories have the capacity to empower, differentiate, and provide meaning and identity, and these qualities can be manipulated by those who live in their shadow as well as by distant forces. The aim of this chapter is to explore the role of borders with regard to just one of these micro-states: in this case, the Principality of Liechtenstein, the story of whose recent and comic border violation by the Swiss army began this chapter. It will do so by focusing on three thematic topics that seem to capture that which is most interesting and unique about the principality and its borders: sovereignty, offshore banking, and identity.

Sovereign Borders

One of the most basic functions of an international border is the role it plays in helping to demarcate and confer the exclusive right of sovereign jurisdiction on the people and territory that it confines. In other words, borders both establish and mark the limits of sovereign power and commonly carry that accepted meaning both within and beyond the territory. In the case of Liechtenstein, however, the sovereign meaning of its borders has not always been so clearly accepted and understood. The story of the principality's creation, which resulted essentially from an expedient move to gain political status on the part of an old-line Austrian noble family, and its subsequent history of close associations with neighboring states have, from time to time, called into question the precise and enduring nature of its sovereign status (figure 9.1).

Long before its formal emergence as a political territory in 1719, the area that is today Liechtenstein was part of a backcountry collection of hereditary fiefs belonging to local feudal magnates, the boundaries of which were often in flux and sometimes even in doubt as holdings were subdivided and combined over time.[5] By the middle of the fourteenth century, however, the area had been consolidated into two entities: the County (*Grafschaft*) of Vaduz and the Lordship (*Herrschaft*) of Schellenberg, both of which were fiefs held directly under the imperial throne of the Holy Roman Empire without obligation to any intermediary lord. By the early fifteenth century, both had fallen into the hands of a single baronial family, the Hohenems. Over the course of the particularly rapacious sixteenth and seventeenth centuries, the family became increasingly impoverished due to the meager revenues that could be extracted from its lands and was forced to consider selling some of its possessions. The financial plight of this family thus set the stage for two purchases that would create the Principality of Liechtenstein.

The purchasers who eventually rescued the Hohenems from their financial woes were the Liechtensteins of Austria, whose family name derives from its twelfth-century ancestral castle built on a chalky white promontory ("*lichter stein*") just south of Vienna. This important and ambitious family played a

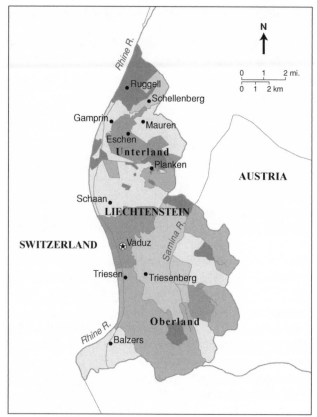

FIGURE 9.1
Liechtenstein. Cory Johnson of XNR.

seminal supporting role in the affairs of the Hapsburg dynasty, which ruled
over Austria and much of east-central Europe. Members of the Liechtenstein
family were notable for holding high political and military offices under the
Hapsburgs. The family was also notable for its considerable landed wealth,
having amassed by the seventeenth century a rather impressive collection of
lands and castles scattered across Lower Austria, Moravia, Bohemia, and Silesia. All of these territorial possessions were, however, enfeoffed in various ways
to other higher-level feudal nobility. What the family lacked (and so earnestly
desired) was a hereditary territory that was both *Reichsunmittelbar*—that is, a
territorial possession under no obligation to any feudal authority except the
Holy Roman Emperor—and situated outside the lands controlled by the Austrian Hapsburgs. This was of utmost importance to the Liechtensteins because
the acquisition of such a territory was the only way to achieve the family goal

of securing a seat in the Imperial Diet, thereby gaining entry to the empire's most exclusive club with all its attendant powers and privileges.

In 1699, after a two-generation-long family quest, the then head of the family, Prince Johan Adam Andreas von Liechtenstein, succeeded in arranging the purchase of the Lordship of Schellenberg from the Hohenems, along with an option to purchase the neighboring County of Vaduz should it become available. In 1712, with the Hohenem family finances still in poor condition, the option was exercised, and the County of Vaduz also fell into the hands of the Liechtensteins. Both estates met the prized requirements of being *Reichsunmittelbar* and located beyond the immediate jurisdiction of the Austrian Hapsburgs. And in 1719, Emperor Charles VI agreed to recognize the merger of these two new family holdings into a single territory and to raise its status to that of Principality (*Fürstendom*) of the Holy Roman Empire with the name of Liechtenstein, thereby securing the family's long sought-after princely seat in the Imperial Diet. The principality thus came into formal existence as an opportunistic act of political expediency on the part of a ruling family with no prior connections or interests in the area. Proof of this lies in the fact that until 1818, no one from the Liechtenstein family even bothered to visit the principality. The first visit by a sovereign prince, as opposed to simply a member of the family, did not take place until 1842. Indeed, for much of its early existence the principality was governed on behalf of its absentee rulers by appointed officials who were not native to the area and often exercised their authority from beyond its borders.

Although now recognized as one of the constituent states of the Holy Roman Empire, the question of sovereignty was still very much up in the air, because technically the principality was still held in fief to the emperor. The issue became clarified somewhat after the Napoleonic invasion of the Holy Roman Empire in 1806, which led to the empire's dissolution along with any feudal obligations owed to its emperor. Even then, the situation was not entirely clear because the small territory remained a pawn of the larger powers. In short order, the principality was duly inducted as the sixteenth member state of the Napoleon-sponsored Confederation of the Rhine, and although Liechtenstein never signed the founding charter, its sovereignty was now constrained by its French protectors. Only after the collapse of the Confederation of the Rhine in 1813 did the issue of sovereignty finally officially resolve itself, as Liechtenstein took its place as a full and independent member of the new German Confederation that was created following the 1815 Peace of Vienna. These developments, along with the subsequent revolutionary wave of liberal reform that swept over Europe beginning in 1848, had the effect of lending Liechtenstein for the first time a certain political and territorial legitimacy in the minds of its citizens and its neighbors.

Nonetheless, given the close ties between the ruling family and the Hapsburgs in Vienna, the country found itself in many ways bound to, and even integrated with, Austria-Hungary. During the latter half of the nineteenth century, a series of bilateral treaties and agreements were concluded that, while careful to uphold in name the sovereignty of the principality, integrated many governmental functions and services. An 1852 customs agreement, for example, put Austrian customs officials in charge of collecting duties on goods crossing the borders of the principality. Liechtensteiners found themselves spending Austrian currency, posting mail with Austrian stamps, using Austrian weights and measures, and carrying out their legal affairs under Austrian law. Workers from Liechtenstein and the neighboring Austrian province of Voralberg moved freely back and forth across the border. In 1872 a rail line that crossed the small country from east to west was opened. The line, which was part of the major trunk line from Vienna to Zurich, was built and operated within the borders of the principality by the Imperial Austrian State Railway. An 1880 treaty enabled Austrian diplomatic and consular offices abroad to represent Liechtenstein's interests.

All of these integrating measures combined to give the impression that the border with Austria-Hungary was somewhat less than real. There was not much on the surface that differentiated life in Liechtenstein from that of Austrian Voralberg on the other side of the border. This misperception was brought home at the outbreak of World War I by the fact that the British government, after declaring war on Austria-Hungary, found itself in a muddle as to whether Liechtenstein should be regarded as a belligerent or a neutral country. After much discussion and repeated inquiries, the British finally concluded that Liechtenstein was, in fact, formally independent of Austria-Hungary and therefore a nonbelligerent country. But even then, the British eventually came to regard the principality as so economically integrated with Austria-Hungary as to be unable to fully assert its neutrality and therefore liable to economic embargo by the Allied Powers. The latter decision caused much hardship in Liechtenstein. Even requests by the Swiss to deliver emergency foodstuffs across the border were turned back by the Allies.[6]

Liechtenstein's inclination to develop integrative border relations with one of its neighbors, which was in part a natural function of its small size, would resume after the 1918 armistice, although this time in a different direction. With the collapse of Austria-Hungary and its ruling Hapsburg dynasty, the principality turned toward Switzerland. Before long, a customs treaty was entered into with the Swiss that shifted the old customs border eastward from the Liechtenstein-Swiss frontier to the Liechtenstein-Austrian frontier. The new border stations were staffed with Swiss rather than Austrian border guards, and the Swiss franc was adopted as the country's legal currency. A new postal treaty was negotiated, which turned over the management of postal and postal banking services to the Swiss, although Liechtenstein retained the right to issue its own stamps. The Swiss also agreed to provide the services of their diplomatic and consular offices to represent the interests of Liechtenstein abroad.

As in the case of the former treaties with Austria-Hungary, care was taken in all of these arrangements to uphold the principle of Liechtenstein's sovereignty. There was no provision, for example, by which the Swiss would militarily defend the principality in the event of an attack. Nonetheless, the ensuing degree of cross-border integration between the two states was considerable enough to raise perceptions of Liechtenstein as being little more than some kind of semi-independent Swiss canton. With the rise of Nazism in Germany, and especially following Germany's absorption of Austria in 1938, tiny Liechtenstein suddenly found itself sharing a border with a threateningly expansive German state. It was at this time that the long geographic separation between ruler and subjects came to an end, as the newest prince, shortly after ascending to the throne, chose to take up residence in the family castle at Vaduz rather than on one of his Austrian estates.[7] The Swiss connection became an asset in preserving the country's independence. On a number of occasions, the threat of impending annexation by Nazi Germany seemed real and imminent. An alarmed Switzerland, which for its own reasons wanted no breach of the principle of neutrality, took every step it could to encourage Liechtenstein to resist its internal Nazi sympathizers' efforts to join the greater German Reich. For its part, the German government chose in the end to respect Liechtenstein's sovereignty and neutrality, partly because of the principality's close association with Switzerland and partly because of the perceived usefulness to the Germans of the two neutrals as safe havens for hiding money, carrying out espionage, and pursuing back-channel diplomacy.

The increasingly tense situation made the Swiss nervous enough to begin fortifying the frontier with Liechtenstein and, as part of their preparations, to propose that the principality surrender to them a strategic mountain, the Ellhorn, which the Swiss wished to incorporate into their defensive system. In an indication that the violability of the border with the Swiss could be taken only so far, the Liechtensteiners refused. The two countries went on to live out the war in a kind of symbiotic relationship; neutral but physically cut off from the rest of the world in the center of Nazi-occupied Europe. The only serious breach of the border came at the very end of the war, when an army of Russian soldiers who had been fighting on the side of the Germans forced its way across the Liechtenstein border to escape the pursuing Red Army. Once inside the principality, the Russians allowed themselves to be interned; but, unlike other countries, Liechtenstein refrained from forcing their repatriation to the Soviet Union, which undoubtedly saved most of their lives.[8] After the war, amid a general atmosphere of Cold War tensions, the Swiss would again take up the issue of the Ellhorn. This time they would do so with much greater insistence, leaving Liechtenstein little choice but to barter away the mountain in exchange for a piece of Swiss real estate of roughly equivalent monetary value.[9]

The unusual and intimate border situation with Switzerland—mutually beneficial to both sides, but not without its occasional tensions—has continued to the present day. In particular, the principality's close associations with Switzerland have allowed it to share in and prosper from its neighbor's traditional strengths; such as its political neutrality, economic and social stability, and sound banking and currency policies. The two countries essentially share a common economic space and political outlook. As Western Europe prospered under the so-called economic miracle of the postwar decades, Liechtenstein joined with Switzerland in entering the European Free Trade Association (EFTA) as a means of lowering trade barriers. And in 1972, when Switzerland brokered a bilateral treaty with the European Economic Community that brought home some of the benefits of the wider European market without formal membership, the principality was included in the deal. At the same time, Liechtenstein has at times moved diplomatically beyond its Swiss connections. In 1995 Liechtenstein chose to join two other EFTA countries as members of the European Economic Area (EEA), the non-European Union members of which agree to enact legislation similar to those promulgated in Brussels in return for free-trade benefits with the EU. In doing so, Liechtenstein broke with its Swiss neighbors, who rejected EEA membership in a national referendum.

Liechtenstein today enjoys an unquestioned acceptance of its sovereign place among European nations. The country's border relations, though, are more complicated than that. Since an open border has been in existence since the 1920s, Liechtenstein has become deeply integrated within Swiss economic space and may be said to be well on its way in becoming deeply integrated within European economic space as well. At the same time, remnants of the old Austrian alignment still persist. Workers, for example, still move freely across the border between Austria and Liechtenstein. Liechtenstein, thus, has managed over the past few centuries to firmly establish itself as a sovereign territory, yet one whose borders have more or less continually assumed unusual qualities of openness and entanglement with those of its neighbors.

Offshore Banking

For such a small and relatively out of the way place, Liechtenstein has a considerable reputation as a nexus for secretive international financial dealings.

Its borders are accordingly commonly understood as instrumental in both facilitating and shielding the international movement and accumulation of wealth. In a sense, this quality may have been established early on by the fact that the ruling family drew its considerable wealth not from within the principality, but from its myriad holdings and interests scattered across a wide swath of Europe. The Liechtensteins were a family that made its way easily among an elite upper crust of European society for whom territorial borders presented few obstacles. Possession of the Principality of Liechtenstein was a critical source of the family's exalted station, and therefore a political investment, but for a very long time the family scarcely felt much need to set foot, much less reside, in the principality. Since then, the family's many interests and dealings have continued to cross boundaries, including various legal efforts to recover properties and holdings in other parts of Europe that were confiscated after World War II. This has included a recent and unsuccessful lawsuit before the World Court in The Hague, in which Liechtenstein sought millions in damages from Germany for improperly handing over to Czechoslovakia as war reparations various land, property, and artwork belonging principally to Liechtenstein's royal family. As one of the world's richest heads of state, the current prince of Liechtenstein has wide-ranging business assets both within and beyond the borders of the principality.

But equally important has been the development of a highly secretive banking industry and favorable tax code that holds great attraction for foreigners in search of a place to shelter financial assets. One hundred years ago, Liechtenstein's economy depended primarily on its smallholding farmers, herders, local craftspeople, and tradespeople. However, in an effort to stimulate economic growth during the difficult times that followed World War I, the principality took two steps to improve the business climate. The first was the founding of a bank in 1920, the main purpose of which was to bring capital into the country by offering a safe place in a neutral country where foreign assets could be deposited. The second step was to introduce new legislation that provided the means by which foreigners could own holding companies registered in Liechtenstein that may not actually do business there and pay a very low tax rate of 1 percent. These companies became known as "letter box" companies, referring to the fact that only a nominal presence in Liechtenstein is necessary. Legislation was also passed that allowed foreign individuals to place their personal assets in "foundations" (trusts) usually registered in the name of a citizen of the country (most commonly a lawyer), that provide extraordinary privacy for the nonresident holder's money. This combination of banking and tax laws, so attractively favorable to outsiders, has persisted with various adaptations and reforms down to the present day. Today, international banking and finance account for 30 percent of Liechtenstein's economy, but as much as 90 percent of the financial services are provided to nonresidents. This influx of capital, in turn, has helped to finance a modern industrial economy, provide the necessary revenues to run the country's modest governmental apparatus, and generate an extraordinarily high level of prosperity and wealth in Liechtenstein, whose citizenry enjoys one of the highest per-capita incomes in the world.[10]

In the eyes of others, however, the principality's generous banking and taxation laws amount to something entirely different. Simply put, the country is generally regarded as a tax haven. This was already true as early as the 1930s, by which time the number of holding companies and foundations had reached roughly one thousand and had become a source of exasperation for authorities in Hitler's Germany who believed that the principality had become a place of refuge for private capital, particularly that of German Jews. Today the number of holding companies and foundations stands at something over 73,000, more than twice as numerous as Liechtenstein's 34,000 citizens. Its attentiveness to secrecy in banking has earned Liechtenstein, along with some of the other microstates of Europe like Monaco and Andorra, considerable negative attention from international financial watchdogs. In 2000, for example, the country found itself on two blacklists; one compiled by the Financial Action Task Force of the Organization for Economic Cooperation and Development, and the other by the G7 group of leading industrialized nations. The principality was cited for its laws that made it difficult for foreign tax authorities to identify assets that should be taxable at home and for policies that made the country an attractive place for money laundering. Liechtenstein responded by altering its banking rules somewhat. Banks are now required to record the identity of their customers and may allow the veil of privacy to be dropped in the case of criminal investigations. The move quickly resulted in a substantial increase in the number of suspected money laundering schemes reported in the principality. Although removed from the money laundering blacklist, Liechtenstein has remained under fire with regard to the charge that its overly opaque banking rules protect assets from scrutiny by foreign tax authorities.

That issue came to a head in February 2008, when German foreign intelligence agents bribed a disgruntled former employee of the trusts division of the principality's LGT Bank to turn over a stolen computer disc containing roughly 1,400 names of foreign account holders. Armed with this incriminating list, Germany immediately began cracking down on hundreds of its citizens who appeared guilty of tax fraud. The Germans also shared the list with tax authorities in other countries, creating a massive tax evasion scandal that quickly widened to include tax evasion investigations in Britain, Ireland, Sweden, Finland, Norway, the Netherlands, France, Austria, Italy, Greece,

Spain, Canada, Australia, New Zealand, and the United States. Although far more serious than the comical unintended Swiss invasion of 2007, the scandal brought Liechtenstein and the wealth that may surreptitiously cross its borders once again into the full media spotlight. Germany, for its part, indignantly called for a crackdown on bank practices that shelter assets of foreign citizens from tax liability in their home countries, thereby launching an intemperate war of words between Berlin and Vaduz. Other countries soon chimed in, with France notably announcing plans to make it an aim of its presidency of the EU to force tougher rules on Liechtenstein and other tax havens.

The reaction from Liechtenstein was swift. Crown Prince Alois responded with a public display of indignation over the fact that the Germans had acquired their information through an act of cross-border espionage. The information had been stolen, and the methods by which the Germans had obtained it were both morally and legally questionable. In a veiled reference to Germany's past history as an aggressor nation, the crown prince was quoted as declaring Liechtenstein to be ". . . a small country, dependent on friendly, neighborly relations," before pointedly adding, "But we are also a sovereign state and we do not—we hope—live in an era when might makes right."[11] On a less stirring but unquestionably firm note, government officials and spokespeople for LGT Group defended the integrity of the principality's "offshore" banking practices, pointing out that it is the responsibility of investors, not Liechtenstein, to meet the tax requirements of their home countries, and that Liechtenstein does nothing to encourage clients to cheat on their taxes. At the same time, though, notes of conciliation were also offered. Liechtenstein promised to review the principality's laws on trusts and foundations, which are the financial services most likely to be utilized for purposes of tax evasion. LGT officials also took pains to emphasize the fact that its trust subsidiary, from which the list of clients was stolen, accounted for only a small and diminishing share of its overall financial activities.[12]

The flow of money across borders plays a major role in defining modern Liechtenstein as an economic enterprise. This may well have been already in play long ago as a simple function of how the principality came into existence, first as a political investment, but ultimately as a base for the far-flung interests and dealings of the ruling family. The discrete handling of other people's money has certainly been a prominent feature of the country's existence since the 1920s. The current storm over Liechtenstein as a space of banking privacy embedded in an otherwise increasingly integrated and cooperative European regulatory landscape will eventually pass, most likely with some gesture of accommodation between the principality and its critics, but also with a steadfast refusal on the part of Liechtenstein to compromise very far on its secretive financial and legal traditions. The sheltering of money is an integral part of what the country is all about. The international prominence of this activity gives added meaning to its borders, a fact often reflected by the expensive cars with foreign plates typically parked in front of bank buildings in Vaduz. To equate the place with the privileged power of money is a relatively easy thing to do. Indeed, in a recent ploy to attract corporate conferences, Liechtenstein offered clients the opportunity to "rent a state." In addition to the privilege of flying their corporate flag in the capital, takers were offered exclusive access to virtually everything from accommodations, conference venues, special events and activities, and officials (short of the prince himself)—and even one of the princely castles.[13]

National Identity

One recent effect of the tax haven scandal was to generate an outpouring of seldom seen patriotic sentiment among the citizenry. Amid a general wave of popular indignation, one of the local papers, *Liechtensteiner Vaterlands*, is reported to have observed, "We're not a very patriotic people, but under pressure from Germany, everyone is banding together."[14] The fact that the country is not normally very demonstrative about its national identity is not all that surprising. Given its extremely small size, sovereign entanglements with the fortunes of an autocratic family dynasty, history of external political and economic integration with neighboring areas and countries, and reputation for loose financial interests and dealings with the outside world, it is somewhat difficult to imagine an overtly nationalistic culture.

In fact, strong but complex identities do exist. If nothing else, there is the need to feel something other than Swiss, Austrian, or German.[15] The true ethnic nationals are locally known as Liechtensteiners. For the most part, they are descended from the old-stock families that have lived there for generations. Their traditional language is Alemannic, a dialect of German speech native to the area. They are also predominantly Roman Catholic and conservative in their views.[16] Strong local identities also exist. The country is divided administratively into two regions—the Oberland and the Unterland—which coincide territorially with the two old fiefdoms of Vaduz and Schellenberg, from which the principality emerged. The Oberland (County of Vaduz) comprises the upper country overlooking the valley of the Upper Rhine, while the Unterland (Lordship of Schellenberg) stretches along the low-lying river terraces. The distinction between the two has always been preserved (they are commonly seen as having distinctive cultural traits), and even today the government is required to divide its four councilors equally between representatives of each.[17] Careful representation of the two regions is also observed in the makeup of the country's twenty-five-member parliament (*Landtag*), which by law consists of 15 representatives from the Oberland and 10 from the Unterland. Within the two regions, the Principality is organized territorially into 11 municipalities (*Gemeinden*). These administrative units are direct descendants of the old feudal village communes, replete in many cases with boundaries so convoluted as to create exclaves and enclaves within neighboring municipalities.

On the other hand, foreign influences abound. More than a third of the resident population today is foreign born, a condition that is largely due to the need to import skilled workers to help staff the country's burgeoning financial and industrial sectors. Moreover, on any given day large numbers of foreign workers—nearly fourteen thousand by the latest estimates—commute into the principality from nearby areas of Switzerland, Austria, and Germany.[18] Cross-border labor movements have always been a feature of economic life in Liechtenstein. People have long crossed freely back and forth over the borders in search of seasonal work. In the past, however, the direction of these flows was more often out than in, given the fact that Liechtenstein was, economically speaking, a backwater area and therefore more likely to be an exporter of labor. This has clearly changed. While the vast majority of today's outsiders are German speaking and therefore culturally akin to the local population, they are still noticeably outsiders. The fact that nearly two-thirds of the country's labor force now consists of foreign-born residents and commuters is difficult to ignore, and in fact there has been a backlash on the part of ethnic Liechtensteiners who are increasingly vocal about their fears of being overwhelmed by outsiders.[19]

The issue of belonging, or citizenship, has always been a sensitive subject. Local concerns about outsiders are reflected in the peculiarly intimate process by which citizenship is attained. In Liechtenstein, the decision lies with the most local authority, the commune. The standard procedure is that after five years of permanent residence, an applicant's request to become a naturalized citizen is brought before a meeting of the commune assembly, where it is voted up or down by secret citizen ballot. The de facto requirement, then, rests on one's ability to live among one's neighbors for a period of years and eventually win their acceptance. Only after local acceptance has been achieved is the decision referred to the parliament and the prince for final approval. This can be culturally and socially challenging for would-be applicants, as well as expensive, and has given the principality a reputation for exclusiveness. Indeed, until the law was changed in 1996, citizenship could be passed down only by birth through the male line, and citizenship through marriage still requires twelve years of permanent residence in addition to three years of marriage. The Council of Europe's Commission on Racism and Intolerance has declared the conditions for granting citizenship in Liechtenstein "too restrictive."[20]

Central to conceptions of identity in the broadest sense is the relationship between the princely ruling family and its subjects. The prince, after all, was initially an outsider, as were the representatives he sent to govern his princely territory. Although the local population swore fealty to him through his representatives—in the case of the Unterland in the village of Bendern in 1699, and in the case of the Oberland in the town of Vaduz in 1712—tensions were in place from the very beginning. Indeed, at the time of swearing of fealty, the locals were adamant that their ancient rights and privileges be acknowledged and respected for all time. And, later, in negotiations between subjects and prince over successive constitutions for the principality, the protection of local rights remained a bone of contention. Thus, for example, all attempts on the part of the prince in these negotiations to bring an end to the distinction between Oberland and Unterland were steadfastly resisted. A princely absolute veto power over laws passed by the parliament was only grudgingly accepted at first, and later was curtailed under the Constitution of 1921, which clearly vested power in both the prince and the people. In the interests of balance, the Constitution of 1921 also prohibited the prince from dissolving the parliament without a referendum and obligated him to form democratically constituted governments. This gradual reconciliation of the rights of subjects with those of the sovereign prince, much of which took place over the course of the nineteenth century and culminated in the Constitution of 1921, eventually fostered in Liechtenstein a sense of popular national identity that fused the ideas of place and monarchy into a kind of symbiotic balance.

Indeed, it would be misleading to say that no national sentiment or spirit exists. Something of the sort, which focused on a romantically intertwined narrative of place, history, and monarchy, was clearly already in place by the end of the nineteenth century. As early as 1847, a popular history of the principality had been published that helped to instill a sense of pride.[21] A national anthem had been written by the late 1950s.[22] Subsequent histories made much of the people's love of freedom, bravery in the face of adversity, pride in their institutions, and accomplishments. The independent pride of the people is perhaps best exemplified by the political movement that led up to the 1921 Constitution, in which advocates of local rights, working under the slogan "Liechtenstein for Liechtensteiners," ensured that the new constitution would reserve appointment to government offices to native Liechtensteiners. Organizations and associations also exist that celebrate through publications and exhibits what they see as the unique natural, cultural, and artistic attributes of the principality.[23] Perhaps, above all, there is a strong identification with the

FIGURE 9.2
Liechtenstein Border Marker. Presse- und Informationsamt, Vaduz.

ruling monarchy, to which the country owes its very existence, and in no few instances its survival (figure 9.2).

Age-old tensions, nonetheless, lie beneath the surface. The most recent example of this occurred in 2003 when Prince Hans-Adam II called for a referendum on a proposal that would significantly expand his powers. The prince's proposal called for a revision of the 1921 Constitution that would grant him the unilateral right to dismiss the government, increase his influence over the appointment of judges, excuse himself from the authority of the principality's constitutional court, and allow him to veto new laws passed by the parliament by simply refusing to take action on them during the six-month period following their passage. In return, the citizens were offered the possibility of a no-confidence vote on their monarch through a referendum, in which case the male members of the princely family would decide whether to replace him with another member of the family. The whole affair quickly escalated into quite a flap because at the first hint of opposition, the prince let it be known that if he failed to get his way he might just move his residence from Liechtenstein to his holdings in Austria. This threat came on top of everyone's memory of a petulant princely remark made on an earlier occasion in which he threatened to sell the castle to "Bill Gates or anyone else who can afford it" and carry on his affairs from his estates in Austria.[24] For the first time in generations, the people of the principality found themselves being treated by their monarch as though they were chattel living on a feudal estate. To add more discomfort to the situation, rumblings soon emerged from the political affairs committee of the Council of Europe Parliamentary Assembly questioning whether Liechtenstein could remain a member of the council if the referendum passed because that would mean that the country would no longer be a democracy.

While most of the citizenry were put off by the prince's demands, their affection for the monarchy and the sense that the identity of the place and the prince's continued presence there were inextricably intertwined seem to carry the day (after all, the country has his name on it). The referendum passed by a resounding majority of 64.3 percent of the votes cast. The turnout was 87.7 percent of eligible voters.[25] With this victory, Hans-Adam II succeeded in moving his country in the opposite direction to that of Europe's other hereditary constitutional monarchies. He had added to his powers in an age when most other monarchs have seen their powers reduced. In the summer of 2003, the Council of Europe made good on its threat to review whether Liechtenstein could remain a member of the organization. The delegation sent to the country to investigate did not recommend rescinding the country's membership, but it did advise that the Council begin monitoring democratic processes there. At about the same time, Prince Hans-Adam II announced his intention to step down in one year's time and transfer power to his son, Crown Prince Alois. The transfer of official duties took place in August of 2004. At that time, Hans-Adam retained his role as chief of state, but no longer as ruling prince.

Conclusion

Do borders matter? In the case of Liechtenstein they clearly do, but it is also clear that the meaning of the country's borders has varied and continues to do so, depending on what may be at issue. Since the Peace of 1815, the country's borders have marked the limits of sovereign authority as exercised by the princely ruling house of Liechtenstein and have enjoyed international recognition as the territorial definition of a sovereign and independent state. For most of that time, however, the country has been in economic union and close political association with one of its neighbors: first with Austria for a period of sixty-seven years, and then with Switzerland for a period now approaching nine decades. These alignments with its neighbors have meant that for nearly all of its sovereign history, at least one of its borders has been essentially open, while the other has been controlled for custom purposes, not by Liechtenstein itself, but by one of its neighbors on their mutual behalf. Although officially real, the country's borders have been at least partially violable at all times and subject to considerable cross-border economic, cultural, and administrative influences.

From another perspective, Liechtenstein's borders have assumed profound meaning when it comes to the international movement and seclusion of individual wealth. The country has long cultivated a reputation as a tax haven, providing offshore banking and financial services to moneyed interests around the world. In this sense, its borders are both violable and closed—violable in that they are open to the unrestricted cross-border flow of funds and closed in that once inside, funds are sheltered within what might be regarded as a space of privacy. This explains the outrage at the methods used by Germany to gain privileged information about the holders of trusts accounts in Liechtenstein. From Liechtenstein's perspective, Germany's cross-border espionage was an affront to the country's sovereignty as well as a morally reprehensible activity. The borders of Liechtenstein, like those of some other microstates, are unique in that they enclose a small but privileged financial space, the existence of which may be seen by other states as out of step with an increasingly more integrative and globalizing world.

For the citizens of Liechtenstein, the historic borders of the country also help to separate them from their neighbors and define them as a people. Those who trace their roots back for generations—the true Liechtensteiners—can look toward traditions that are related to language, religion, folk, and material culture long associated with the valleys and mountains of their ancestral homeland. But even here, specific localities—Oberland as opposed to Unterland, and one commune as opposed to another—can offer an even more intimate sense of identity. Borders are also important in that a combination of open borders and prosperity has led to the recent influx of large numbers of outsiders, which in turn has aroused among insiders a troubling sense of cultural swamping. Certainly not to be forgotten in the quest for a national consciousness is the common and long-standing connection with the ruling family that lends its name to the territory. The mere physical presence of the princely family within the borders of the principality is a force that pulls people together—even to the point of propelling them to accept what might otherwise be seen as outrageously undemocratic demands by their sovereign.

As a land-locked microstate deep in the heart of Europe, Liechtenstein cannot help but experience unique border dynamics inherent in its minuscule size, history, and location. Tucked between three larger German-speaking states, locked into a close but unequal relationship with its Swiss neighbors, and drawn inexorably into an increasingly integrated European community and globalizing world economy, the country must work hard to maintain its own distinctive persona. Its borders matter, not so much in their role as static, fixed barriers, but in the way that their special meanings and functions make Liechtenstein what it is.

10

Misiones Province, Argentina
How Borders Shape Political Identity

Eric D. Carter

I N THE TOWN OF PUERTO IGUAZÚ, in Misiones province, Argentina, there is a peculiar tourist attraction: a park built around a boundary marker. Here, you can enjoy a rare view of three different countries at the same time, what Argentines call the *triple frontera*, or triple frontier. Below you is the Iguazú River, emerging from a deep gorge, joining with the mighty Paraná River— these are the physical features that separate Brazil, Paraguay, and Argentina. The boundary markers for Argentina (painted blue and white), Brazil (green and yellow), and Paraguay (red, white, and blue) complete the geopolitical symmetry of the scene: three stout obelisks, displaying national colors, against the shared backdrop of churning brown water, red volcanic soil, and verdant green forest.

Around nine in the morning, tour buses begin to arrive. Groups of travelers, mostly Argentines, greet the unusual site. This is a sideshow in a larger tour, which will take them to the region's most famous attraction, Iguazú Falls, just twenty kilometers (twelve miles) to the southeast. The visitors pose in groups to have their pictures taken. Many, no doubt, are reenacting the scene of countless photos taken by family and friends through the years.[1] Taking snapshots here is a patriotic ritual, commemorating their presence at the edge of Argentine territory—almost literally the edge, as the precipice below attests. The viewing pleasures soon exhausted, the groups scatter to the tourist market, where, in addition to local handicrafts, travelers may purchase bags of yerba maté, the national beverage and the archetypical product of Misiones province (yerba maté is available at any supermarket, corner store, or gas station). Is a package purchased here endowed with supercharged nationalist meaning? A few feet away, an undeniably patriotic monument receives few visitors. An austere plaque in black steel commemorates Argentina's demoralizing war with the United Kingdom over the Malvinas, or Falkland Islands, in 1982. As with all war monuments, the plaque may be seen as either a testament to, or an argument for, national unity. Its placement here is deeply symbolic: tiny, remote, tropical Misiones stands with the Malvinas, its territorial antipode in the cold, rough South Atlantic, united only by a nationalist dream that continues to unfold.

This chapter focuses on the issues of nationalism, borders, and identity in Misiones province, Argentina. Unlike most of the other case studies in this volume, the boundaries of Misiones are formed almost entirely by "natural" features: the Iguazú, Paraná, and Uruguay rivers, along with four other smaller watercourses draining the volcanic uplands in the heart of the province (figure 10.1). Indeed, less than 5 percent of its 1,200 kilometer (746 mile) boundary is demarcated by artificial survey lines.[2] Nevertheless, the boundaries defining Misiones are anything but natural. For one, any combination of physical features in the region, including other rivers, mountain ranges, or drainage divides, could potentially have become the boundaries of present-day Misiones. More importantly, the unusual shape of the province is really the product of historical events. Moreover, boundaries on the ground do not merely delimit a political unit called Misiones or simply contain a community that identifies with Misiones—the "Misioneros." As the tourist attraction of the triple frontier demonstrates, boundaries have played a central role in the way that Misioneros see themselves and represent their identity to the rest of Argentina and the world.

Through a discussion of the rich cultural and political history of Misiones, this chapter explores a number of issues in political geography. First, it shows how a selective reading, reshaping, and repetition of local history serves as a foundation for a coherent cultural and political identity.[3] The province's foundational narratives are characteristically geographical and uphold an implicit argument for Misiones as a natural, inevitable, and bounded political entity. Clashing with this ideal of coherence, however, is the recurring theme of Misiones's vulnerability, which derives from the province's geographic situation and unusual, protruding shape. Ironically, a perception of territorial exposure and permeability helps to stimulate a unified identity. Memories of assaults, incursions, and dismemberments by neighboring polities—including the Portuguese empire, the independent states of Brazil and Paraguay, the adjoining province of Corrientes in Argentina, and even (somewhat paradoxically) the Argentine state—are a part of the province's heritage and proof of its resilience.

FIGURE 10.1
Map of Misiones Province, Argentina, and Surrounding Region. Cory Johnson of XNR.

This chapter also explores the double tension of localized identity. Over time, Misioneros have developed a coherent identity in opposition to two sets of "others."[4] On the one hand, an important process of nationalization has occurred. Misioneros have tended to define themselves as Argentine and adopt elements of Argentine culture to distinguish themselves from Paraguay and Brazil. In keeping with nationalist ideology, these countries have been frequently denigrated as uncivilized, bellicose, or culturally inferior. At the same time, Misioneros have worked to construct a unique identity for their small territory *in opposition to* the rest of Argentina, especially in resistance to the hegemony of the national core region of the Pampas centered in Buenos

Aires.[5] Today, Misiones plays the role of a peripheral exotic territory within the Argentine national imagination, a role often embraced by the Misioneros themselves.

The next section describes the historical foundations of Misiones identity, starting with the religious communities that gave the province its name: the Jesuit missions. The following section turns to a discussion of the tensions of constructing a coherent Misionero identity within the framework of Argentine nationalism during the nineteenth and twentieth centuries. The last section examines the geopolitical dimensions, ambiguities, and contradictions of borderland identities in contemporary Misiones.

From Earthly Paradise to Empty Space

The Misiones identity coalesces around a common history. The trajectory of this story, which has accumulated cultural significance through repetition, represents a variation on the Garden of Eden story central to Western culture: a story of rise, fall, and redemption.[6] Jesuit priests, who ruled the Spanish colonial territory known as Las Misiones ("the missions") for over 150 years, and Guaraní Indians are the protagonists of this story. Together, they built an "earthly paradise" out of the threatening wilderness, yet venal, worldly interests destroyed their endeavor. In this standard history, Misiones degenerated into a state of anarchy and savagery following the Jesuits' expulsion. This return to wilderness, however, set the stage for the redemption of Misiones in the late nineteenth century: a strong state (Argentina) would restore social and spatial order, and a new class of people (European colonists) would return the "light of civilization" to the wilderness.

The era of Jesuit missionary activity in the region (1609–1767) is unique in the colonial history of South America due to the special political role granted to this religious order. By the late 1500s, the Spanish crown had become frustrated by its inability to govern the upper Río de la Plata basin (figure 10.2). The Spanish could not subjugate the indigenous populations east of Asunción, while colonial possessions were threatened by Portuguese expansionism inland from coastal settlements. As a result, in 1609, the Spanish crown entrusted the Jesuits with the governance of the region. Over the next few decades, Jesuit priests concentrated Guaraní Indians from tiny, dispersed hamlets into a network of thirty nucleated settlements, known as *reducciones* or *misiones* (missions).[7] These were located in present-day Argentina, Brazil, and Paraguay. Explanations vary as to why the Guaraní acceded, without armed coercion, to live under the authority of the Jesuits. Older interpretations stress the attraction of Christianity, the charisma of the Jesuits, or the promise of

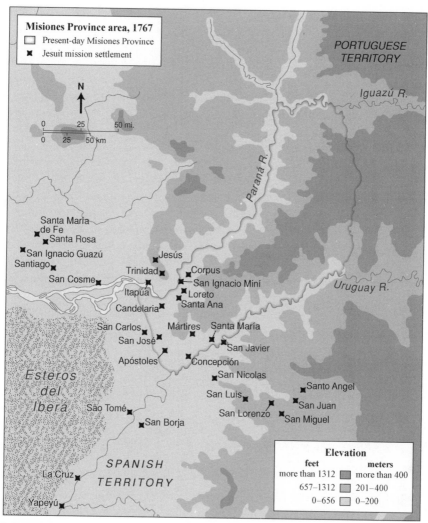

FIGURE 10.2
Historical Map of Río de la Plata Basin Highlighting Jesuit Missions. Cory Johnson of XNR.

material goods. More recently, it has been suggested that the Guaraní, faced with slave raids from the east or the prospect of indentured servitude under Spanish conquistadors, chose mission life as the least objectionable option.[8]

These missions are often portrayed as model communal societies; as one contemporary tourist brochure puts it, the reducciones "left a legacy of a civilizing experience, unprecedented in the whole world."[9] The utopian spirit of the missions has also been popularized in a well-known feature film, *The Mission* (1986). The historical record indicates that the missions were productive, mostly self-sufficient, and linked to extensive trading networks. Residents of the missions grew a variety of crops in individual subsistence plots and larger, communal plantations, including vegetables, citrus trees, tobacco, maize, and cotton. The Jesuits also innovated the domestication of an important plant native to the area, the yerba maté bush (*Ilex paraguayensis*), whose leaves are used to make a kind of green tea. Yerba maté became the missions' leading cash crop and the key to their expanding wealth. Through the Jesuits, the Guaraní also learned to raise livestock and excelled at crafts such as carpentry, masonry, stonecutting, and metalworking. As the *reducciones* grew, many came to resemble small cities. In 1680, the thirty Jesuit missions had a population five times larger than that of the colonial district of Buenos Aires. By 1732, the Guaraní population of the *reducciones* numbered over 140,000.[10]

However, it was the very success of the Jesuits' missionary enterprise that laid the foundations for its downfall. Spanish colonists and civil authorities had grown envious of the Jesuits' prosperity. For this and other reasons, in 1767 King Carlos III of Spain ordered the expulsion of the Jesuits from the New World colonies and the "confiscation of their assets."[11] The Jesuit experiment had come to an abrupt conclusion.

In the aftermath of the Jesuits' expulsion, the social order of the missions gradually dissolved, and their territories were divided among new authorities. Without Jesuit leadership, the *reducciones* lost their social purpose, while their productivity declined, partially as a result of broad-scale changes in the colonial economy. The conditions of mission life deteriorated as epidemic diseases and poor nutrition led to higher mortality. Many of the Guaraní fled into the hills to escape new, more onerous forms of subordination, while others settled into Spanish towns. As a result, the missions rapidly declined from almost 89,000 inhabitants in 1768 to just 38,000 in 1802.[12]

Complicating matters further, "a long period of administrative confusion occurred following the departure of the Jesuits," and "the area reverted to the wilderness it had once been prior to the arrival of the Spanish."[13] A succession of wars, lasting for decades, dismembered the old mission territory, fomented political chaos, and accelerated the region's demographic collapse. From 1810 to 1870, Misiones was governed, invaded, or occupied, in part or in whole, by the Spanish and Portuguese empires; the newly independent states of Brazil, Paraguay, and Uruguay; the Confederación Oriental del Paraná, a confederation of provinces separated from the authority of Buenos Aires; the province of Corrientes; and, eventually, the national state of Argentina.[14] Argentina consolidated its sovereignty over Misiones with the conclusion of the bloody War of the Triple Alliance (1864–1870), in which Brazil, Uruguay, and Argentina united to bring humiliating defeat to Paraguay. When all was said and done, the old Jesuit territory had been "divided among neighboring countries [Paraguay, Brazil, and Uruguay] and within Argentina, absorbed by the province of Corrientes."[15]

The story of the Jesuit missions is essential in the historical narrative of Misiones. For one, a few of the old mission pueblos, including Corpus and San Ignacio on the Paraná River, would persist and provide historical continuity through the continuous nucleated settlement of those sites. The ruins of the missions themselves, in particular the best-preserved relics at San Ignacio Miní, are important symbols of the Misionero identity. Their majestic architecture evokes a glorious past, consecrated by UNESCO as World Heritage Sites. Second, the prior existence of a "greater" Misiones, once extending into present-day Paraguay and Brazil but reduced through bellicose dismemberment, also underscores claims of territorial continuity in the heart of Misiones.

Finally, placing the Jesuits in the role of founders of Misiones helps to develop a claim for the moral righteousness of this territory. In the common history, Jesuit Misiones is portrayed as an earthly paradise characterized by harmony in two sets of relationships: between man and nature, and between Europeans and indigenous peoples. The "civilized Indian" is a paradigm of identity for the region. For example, a stylized Guaraní serves as the icon for the province's major newspaper, *El Territorio*.[16] This is a land seemingly free of the taint of original sin, that is, the mark of colonial conquest and brutality. The post-Jesuit return to wilderness has been exaggerated since Misiones was not completely depopulated and its economy did not grind completely to a halt.[17] But the projection of Misiones as "empty space" created a tabula rasa for the second conquest of Misiones, this time by an ambitious, modern nation-state intent on opening up the territory to colonization and economic development. Emissaries from Buenos Aires to the northeastern frontier would label Misiones the "Argentine Eden," even as they created the blueprint for its transformation through farming, forestry, and industry.[18]

Incorporation into the Nation-State

The outcome of the War of the Triple Alliance established geopolitical stability in the upper Río de la Plata basin, thus facilitating the development of Misiones. In a rapidly growing and politically unified Argentina, Misiones assumed the role of a frontier region awaiting full integration into the nation-state. During the second half of the nineteenth century, frontiers played a special role in the formation of Argentine national identity.[19] Leading political elites viewed the state's territorial expansion not as aggression but as the necessary, inevitable, and long-awaited penetration of civilization into sparsely populated and underutilized "barbaric" lands.[20] Their "program for taming the land" included "railroads, better river transportation, new seaports, private ownership of land, and foreign investment."[21] A program for invigorating the racial stock of Argentina went hand in hand with economic development. The national government vigorously encouraged the immigration of Europeans, who were viewed as racially superior to the country's "gauchos, Indians, and mixed-bloods."[22]

This Argentinean analogue to the contemporary North American spirit of manifest destiny colored discussions of the future of Misiones following the War of the Triple Alliance. Politicians and Argentine travelers to the region portrayed Misiones as an untamed wilderness or "desert" (in the sense of "unpopulated" or "deserted" rather than "dry land").[23] The "Indians have disappeared," wrote one traveler, Alejo Peyret, in 1881.[24] Other travelers reported that the few inhabitants they found were unfit for the modern world. The land, according to Rafael Hernández, was occupied by "anthropophagus [man-eating] Indians, some of them even with tails."[25] In widely read reports to Buenos Aires, journalists characterized the Misioneros as a polyglot, primitive lot, scarcely a part of the Argentine nation.[26] As Hernández reported, "It is easier for us to get along with Europeans than with this fraction of compatriots."[27]

Such reports of a sparsely populated wilderness blessed with lush vegetation, warm climates, fertile soils, and natural resources gave weight to arguments for the nationalization and colonization of Misiones. Only the national government would have the means of organizing such an endeavor, and, it was argued, only Europeans had the requisite energy, thrift, diligence, and capacity for planning to realize the productive potential of the land.[28] A continuing perception of the territorial ambitions of neighboring Brazil made colonization not merely a question of economics but also one of national security.[29]

The increasingly powerful national state believed that Misiones should fall under its domain for the sake of development and security. In an 1881 letter to the national Senate, President Julio A. Roca justified the government's eminent domain over Misiones:

> The ancient and flourishing populations of Misiones, today are nothing but ruins and wilderness. Only wild nature reigns there in all its splendor. . . . In that vast expanse, which in the past was an active center of work and culture, today there are neither churches nor schools; not a single new industry has been introduced; not a single, stable nucleus of population exists that is capable of sustaining itself and multiplying itself on the land it occupies; thus the most

powerful seeds of wealth remain inevitably lost, and the natural products of such rich soil are entirely abandoned to isolated efforts, which may satisfy the need for individual gain, but can do nothing to promote the general welfare.[30]

However, the province of Corrientes, which insisted on its jurisdiction over the area, tried to prevent nationalization. After debate over vexing questions of federalism, the Congress voted to create the national territory of Misiones under direct rule from Buenos Aires.[31]

A few years later, after the Argentine state peaceably settled a final boundary dispute with Brazil, the stage was set for rapid agricultural colonization, urban growth, and economic development.[32] In the early twentieth century, Misiones attracted immigrants from across Europe as well as from neighboring countries. Making use of federal public domain that remained unsurveyed after the Corrientes land grab, the Argentine government created agricultural colonies, enticing colonists with free land along with other support and services.

The establishment of these agricultural colonies profoundly shaped the province's cultural landscape, most notably through the creation of ethnically distinctive communities. The first of these colonies, Apóstoles, was established in 1898 on land that had once been the site of a Jesuit *reducción* of the same name. Colonized by farmers from Galicia, a region that is today shared by Poland and the Ukraine, Apóstoles continues to maintain its ethnic heritage in its local institutions, especially churches.[33] Most of the farmers in Apóstoles, as in much of the rest of Misiones territory, went into the cultivation of yerba maté.[34]

Later, private colonization endeavors created ethnic enclaves. One of the earliest private colonies, Eldorado, was administered and populated by German immigrants. Adolfo Schwelm, the founder of the colony, chose this name due to its connection with the legend of El Dorado, which had enticed Spanish conquerors to seek their fortune in South America some four hundred years before. According to the publicity designed to attract colonists, this "earthly paradise" in Misiones did not offer gold, but rather a "land of milk and honey"—climate and soils suitable for year-round production of a wide array of crops.[35] As geographer Robert C. Eidt demonstrated in his classic study of frontier settlement in Misiones, German colonies not only impacted local culture but also left an unmistakable imprint on the provincial landscape due to their linear settlement pattern, known as the *waldhufendorf* system.[36] Today, towns such as Eldorado, Puerto Rico, and Montecarlo, with their business districts stretching along a single avenue, retain the telltale signs of the German influence on local settlement.

Through these colonization efforts, the ethnic landscape of Misiones had been transformed by the mid-twentieth century. From 1920 to 1947, the population of Misiones grew by 390 percent, to almost 250,000. At the end of this period, about 38 percent of the population was foreign born.[37] Although welcomed at first, the intensity of immigration led to social and political fissures. In the 1930s, the territorial government worried that immigrants, particularly Germans, were adapting poorly to Argentine society. Official reports attributed the slow assimilation of German migrants to the insularity of the agricultural colonies, where they could conserve "their habits, their language, their systems," and pass these down to generations born in Argentina.[38]

Adding to this preoccupation over delayed assimilation, political change in Germany was having an impact in Argentina. Nazification of German communities in Argentina accelerated. By 1938, for example, the vast majority of German-language schools in the country "were more or less loyal to a conservative German nationalism, if not to Hitlerism."[39] A survey of about two dozen German-language schools in Misiones territory suggested that they were not only inculcating principles of national socialism but also receiving funding from the Third Reich itself.[40] The perception of a Nazi threat turned Misiones into "an ideological and cultural battleground and a strategic concern to the Argentine government."[41] Echoing the words of Rafael Hernández some fifty years before, "Argentine officials visiting these towns reported they scarcely felt themselves to be on Argentine soil at all."[42] Once again, but under very different circumstances, envoys from the heart of Argentina found the territory of Misiones to be fragmented, its culture incoherent.

Economic development, public education, and a historically minded project of identity construction worked to counter such ethnic fragmentation. The continual improvement of the Misiones road system united dispersed rural communities, and the region became further integrated into the growing Argentine consumer market. Meanwhile, public schools taught the Spanish language and tried to promote a shared cultural history.[43]

In order for Misiones to become a full-fledged province, however, it needed a coherent political and cultural identity framed within Argentine nationalism yet unique enough to justify political autonomy. In the 1940s, local historians played a crucial role in constructing such an identity.[44] In an illustrative case of the "invention of tradition," historians marshaled the Jesuits, Guaraní, and other historical personalities for this project.[45] One major historian, Aníbal Cambas, asserted that Misiones, as a political entity, was "older than the Argentine nation" itself, since it had been called an autonomous province in colonial times.[46] Cambas and his colleagues reframed provincial status as a restoration of the natural political rights of Misiones, rather than a plea to a higher authority for a new administrative designation. Elements of Misionero tradition were recovered or invented in folktales, poems, songs, pageants, and fairs. The school curriculum began to reflect socialization not only to Argentine nationalism but also to the Misionero identity.[47] With the historical basis of an autonomous Misiones established, it became a province in 1953.

Boundaries, Territory, and the Geopolitics of Identity

Now a province, Misiones continued its economic development, demographic expansion, and territorial consolidation. Land conversion for agriculture and forestry continued apace as national highways provided direct links to national markets.[48] The province's southern plains, central uplands, and Paraná River valley became densely settled agrarian and urban landscapes. No longer empty space, Misiones assumed a more substantial place in the national imagination as the home of a patchwork of European ethnic enclaves and as the purveyor of warm-climate agricultural products, such as tung trees (whose seeds are processed into wood varnishes), tea, citrus fruit, and especially yerba maté. This green tea, the national beverage, became so identified with Misiones that maps of the province were often used as logos on yerba maté packages (figure 10.3).[49] Misiones also became a tourist playground, thanks to its warm climate, veneer of wilderness, and exotic animals. Iguazú Falls, Argentina's second national park, is the main attraction along with the Jesuit missions.

Recent events and reinterpretations have created fissures in the standard conceptions of Misiones identity. Probably the most important innovation in this area is a continuous reappraisal of the foundational myths of Misiones, in particular the role of indigenous peoples. As discussed above, Misiones history is generally seen to begin with the arrival of the Jesuits, with a consequent erasure of premissionary societies and polities. In the historical construction of Misiones identity, some Guaraní have been used as heroic figures, for example, as freedom fighters in the wars of independence from Spain.[50] Yet such portrayals represent an unfortunate tendency in nationalist myth making throughout Latin America: romanticizing Indians ensconced safely in the glorious past while marginalizing or obscuring indigenous peoples in the present.[51] By the 1980s, an international community of scholars, mainly Argentine, Paraguayan, and Brazilian anthropologists and historians, had begun to reappraise the history of the Jesuit missions and the contemporary status of the Guaraní people.[52]

Debates in the scholarly realm passed into the political arena. In 1979, the National University of Misiones conducted a revealing census of indigenous peoples in the province.[53] In 1987, the legislature of Misiones passed the *Ley del Aborigen* (Law of the Aborigines), which acknowledged the cultural autonomy and territorial rights of Mbya Guaraní Indians in the province.[54]

FIGURE 10.3
Gallery of Yerba Maté Bags Featuring Logo Maps of Misiones Province. These, along with many other yerba maté brands, are on display at the Museo Histórico Arqueológico in Montecarlo, Misiones province. Photo by Eric Carter.

Carlos Santacruz, the Radical Party politician introducing the bill, argued that the time had come for "a radical historical revisionism" to acknowledge a history of "deculturation" of the Guaraní that the Jesuits helped to create.[55] Opponents of the law appealed to the coherence of Misionero identity and the need for assimilation. One local politician argued, "In Argentina, there is only one people, the Argentine, and in Misiones only one people, the *misionero*; legislating for the Guaraní we create an ethnic minority, set apart from the national society."[56] While the province's Law of the Aborigines has not produced major social changes, mere recognition of the Mbya Guaraní communities serves to undermine important elements of the conventional wisdom of the Misioneros' identity narrative. In addition, a reform of the national constitution in 1994 formalized the status of indigenous groups throughout Argentina, further increasing the Guaranís' political visibility.[57]

There is a countervailing force to the fragmenting or pluralizing tendencies of identity construction and reconstruction. Ironically, it is the acute awareness of the geopolitical *vulnerability* of Misiones that helps maintain a coherent identity. As we have seen, Misiones has been framed within a geopolitical discourse for a long time. Commonplace metaphors, drawing on cartography and anatomy, create an everyday language of Misiones' vulnerability where it is "boxed in" (*arrinconada*), a "political gulf," an "appendage," an "arm," and so on.[58] These metaphors reify the territory by treating it as a thing with essential characteristics, not as a socially constructed process.[59] These metaphors also underscore the physical attachment of Misiones to the rest of Argentina, which requires cultural, political, and economic connections for the persistence of boundary stability.

While the idea of living on the national frontier has long informed everyday culture in Misiones, the effect of geopolitics on the region reached its apex in the mid-1970s under Argentina's last military government. The country's armed forces had long strategized to counter Brazilian territorial expansion, and Misiones was seen as a pathway to Brazil's projected control of the Río de la Plata basin. The province was a soft point for invasion, a "vulnerable salient" into foreign territory.[60] The construction of the massive Itaipú Dam on the Paraná River about twenty kilometers (twelve miles) upstream from Puerto Iguazú heightened anxiety over Brazil's control of the hydroelectric potential of the basin. It also provoked Argentina's military government to build the Yacyretá Dam, a joint project with Paraguay, as a geopolitical response.[61] The dictatorship also prioritized the paving of militarily strategic highways in Misiones while neglecting the improvement of commercially important roads in the heart of the province.[62]

In this tense atmosphere, anxieties over cultural nationalism resurfaced. Raúl Rey Balmaceda, a geographer sympathetic to the military regime, articulated concerns over the vulnerability of Argentine culture at the margins of the national territory, particularly in Misiones. In his view, national borders were the "epidermis" of the national organism, while national identity "radiated" from the heart or core of the country, in the Pampas, where the vitality of *argentinidad* was the strongest, thanks to the conservation of traditional elements of national identity. All of the borders were far from this core, and *argentinidad* reached them only in weak doses. Without this "traditional heritage," these more "recently populated" areas, such as Misiones, were weakly nationalized. As a result, the borders were "defenseless against influences coming from the outside."[63] He argued that the diffusion of Brazilian (and

Paraguayan) culture was leading to a deterioration of national identity, citing the common use in Misiones of *portuñol*, a hybrid of Portuguese and Spanish, as a key example.

This paranoid geopolitical rhetoric has faced scholarly challenge and has mostly faded in the popular imagination over the past twenty-five years.[64] Everyday anxieties over Misiones's permeable borders, however, have not disappeared. Fears of unrestrained cross-border traffic periodically resurface, and characters in these commonplace migrations serve a useful purpose in the reproduction of Misionero identity.[65] It is usually Paraguay that serves as the foil or important "other" in the construction of a common identity for Misiones.[66] One key example is the group of female Paraguayan merchants known as *paseras*, who cross the Paraná River from Encarnación, Paraguay, to Posadas, the capital of Misiones, on a daily basis. As Lidia Schiavoni demonstrates, the *paseras* have always represented the discomforting permeability of the international border and the ambiguities of identity in the borderlands.[67] Citizens of Posadas frequent the market stalls where the *paseras* sell their wares, and the city government has continuously developed the marketplace in an effort to formalize and regulate the cross-border commerce. Yet, at the same time, the market strikes a dissonant chord, containing the presence of ethnic "others" who are marked by difference. Over the years, newspaper articles, city government reports, and the everyday discourse of citizens of Posadas have reviled the *paseras* as "dirty," "barefoot," and "poorly dressed," and their marketplace as "unsanitary," "disorderly," and full of "contraband" items. Many of the government efforts to regulate the cross-border trade have been couched in the language of hygiene and sanitation to portray the *paseras* as a source of contamination from without. Indeed, rules to force the congregation of the *paseras* into their market "enclave" near the river may be seen as a type of quarantine to limit the exposure of the city at large to this contaminating influence.[68] Other attacks on the *paseras* focus on the deterioration of the city's public space by calling their presence a reminder of the "old village" that it was, not the orderly, modern city it has become.[69]

More recent international political developments have further complicated the symbolic meaning of boundaries in the Misiones region. First, the insular and sometimes aggressive geopolitics of the 1970s gave way to concerted efforts to promote regional-scale integration. By the early 1990s, Argentina, Brazil, Paraguay, and Uruguay formed a regional trading bloc known as Mercosur, or the Common Market of the Southern Cone. Mercosur has led to a new territorialization or rescaling of identity, with Misiones and the triple frontier area laying claim to the label "the heart of Mercosur" (figure 10.4).[70] Coinciding with the start of Mercosur, a new "friendship bridge" between Posadas and Encarnación was completed in 1990. Politicians from both coun-

FIGURE 10.4
Map of "Triple Frontier" Zone. Cory Johnson of XNR.

tries claimed that the bridge symbolized "the end of borders," international unity, and a new, transnational identity. Guaraní and Jesuit histories were reappropriated, for example, in local newspapers, to now substantiate the claim that the Posadas and Encarnación constituted a borderland community that "had always been integrated" culturally and economically.[71]

The attempted reterritorialization through market integration coincides with a new "securitization" of the triple frontier zone, which includes the urban centers of Puerto Iguazú, Foz de Iguaçu, and Ciudad del Este (in Argentina, Brazil, and Paraguay, respectively). For decades, energetic commerce has characterized the triple frontier as consumers and merchants take advantage of price differentials related to cross-border differences in exchange rates, taxes, and customs duties.[72] Since September 11, 2001, the global media and powerful governments have characterized the region as a sanctuary for Islamic terrorists, who are said to thrive in the anarchic atmosphere created by porous borders and constant interchange of people, goods, and capital.[73] In a *New York Times* article published two weeks after the attack on the World

Trade Center, a Brazilian federal police official said of the triple frontier:
"This is one of the world's great centers of lawlessness. . . . Every criminal
activity that you can possibly think of flourishes here, from drug and arms
trafficking to money laundering, counterfeiting, carjacking, contraband and
prostitution."[74] Suspicion of the area was further enhanced when U.S. soldiers
discovered a poster of Iguazú Falls in an Al Qaeda operative's house in Kabul,
Afghanistan. Substantial Arab communities in Foz de Iguaçu and Ciudad del
Este have been the targets of police investigations, harassment, and deportation. The U.S. FBI, CIA, Treasury Department, and Pentagon, and possibly
even Israel's intelligence agency, Mossad, have been involved with local intelligence gathering and aided antiterror task forces.[75] While no one doubts the
persistence of illegal activity in the region, claims about the triple frontier's
role in a global terrorist network remain mostly unproven.[76]

Conclusion

As recent media representations of the triple frontier region suggest, boundaries continue to play a major role in the way that Misiones is viewed by the
rest of the world. For Misioneros, the idea of their province as a coherent,
bounded, and indeed "natural" territory is crucial for sustaining a political
and cultural identity. Yet this short review of Misiones's historical geography
reveals that the province's borders are not natural but rather the product
of history. Moreover, the construction of a common Misiones identity has
depended on the selective reading and reinterpretation of history. As a history with a foregone conclusion supporting the existence of an autonomous
political entity known as Misiones, places, events, and historical figures are
marshaled to advance a singular and directed political argument. As the narrative becomes standardized, other everyday political occurrences, such as
the assertion of Guaraní autonomy, the persistence of itinerant Paraguayan
merchants, or illicit activities around the triple frontier, threaten the stability
of core values and beliefs.

However, this is not to say that the history of Misiones is somehow false.
Rather, this chapter demonstrates how national identities, and even regional
or provincial identities, depend on the construction of a common history and
the internalizing of bounded political spaces. As political boundaries become
naturalized, evidence of their construction fades, and their role as highly
charged and deeply symbolic spaces becomes second nature to people on both
sides of the border. In this respect, Misiones is not unique.

Misiones presents an interesting case, insofar as territorial vulnerability
is a constant refrain in its identity narrative. Recognition of historical dis-

memberment of the larger territory governed by the Jesuits during colonial times offers some poignancy to this master narrative. Perceptions of vulnerability from without have helped solidify a sense of cultural cohesion. Today, anxieties over the triple frontier could be interpreted as a continuation of the long-standing discourse of the province's susceptibility to external dangers. Although it is sometimes viewed as an emergent transnational zone, we could also view the triple frontier *not* as an emergent transnational space where national boundaries are obliterated, but rather as a place where the meaning, symbolism, and importance of those boundaries becomes even more acute.[77]

Nevertheless, in the future, transnational organizations and alliances in civil society are likely to become more prominent. Many of these are commercial in nature, whether connected with Mercosur or not, while other efforts involve transnational environmental movements to protect the regions' forests, wildlife, and aquifers.[78] To some degree, Misionero involvement with such efforts reflects the double tension of their identity: at once Argentine (nationalist) yet also quite distinct from the rest of Argentina (localist). Misiones tends to represent itself as unique due to late political consolidation, a tropical environment, and its role as a tourist center. Yet at times it also claims to be the most Argentine of provinces, having forged a coherent identity out of multiple ethnicities. Surprisingly perhaps, international linkages help facilitate the development of a unique local identity. Indeed, as the Argentine anthropologist Alejandro Grimson has argued, Misiones is quite dependent economically on the persistence of international borders, which offer inherent commercial opportunities. Thus a desire to maintain strong international boundaries need not imply an aggressive or adversarial stance against Paraguay or Brazil. Rather, it may simply be an expression of the (economic) benefits that Misioneros gain from the existence of those borders.[79]

In this borderland region, far from the center of national life, it is not surprising that Misiones's political identity is full of tensions and contradictions. Whether or not the border is natural may be beside the point—the border is a *social reality* that will continue to play a vivid, central role in the lives of Misioneros.[80]

11

Point Roberts, Washington

Boundary Problems of an American Exclave

Julian V. Minghi

A LITTLE OVER FIFTY YEARS ago, I arrived in the Pacific Northwest to start graduate work at the University of Washington after completing an honors geography degree from Durham University in the United Kingdom. Eighteen months later, in the summer of 1959, as I was defending my MA thesis and about to begin the PhD program, I received a summer job with Whatcom County in Bellingham, ninety miles north of Seattle. The planning commission there hired three University of Washington graduate students to document in detail the situation regarding contemporary residential and commercial development on Point Roberts. Although a very small unincorporated part of the county, totaling only 12.7 square kilometers (5 square miles), Point Roberts was of growing international importance due to the designation of the forty-ninth parallel as the boundary between United States and British territory a century earlier. This international boundary divided Point Roberts from the Canadian Fraser Delta region and meant that this slice of American territory could be reached by land only after passing through Canada. As a result, Point Roberts can be considered an American exclave (figure 11.1). Often regarded as "a geopolitical oddity," a study of Point Roberts highlights many of the general problems associated with exclaves around the world.[1] As shall be seen, these problems weave a complex web over Point Roberts, caught between the discontiguous "mother" country (the United States) and the adjacent interceding country (Canada).[2]

The rapid growth of the Vancouver metropolitan area during the 1950s, and especially its greatly improved road access to the south, triggered a host of new problems on Point Roberts. Residential and commercial developers

FIGURE 11.1
Point Roberts—American Exclave. Cory Johnson of XNR.

sought to take advantage of the differences in American and Canadian law on either side of the boundary. Concerned by these developments, the U.S. State Department pressured the state of Washington to investigate the situation. The actual impetus for this action emanated from the Delta municipality across the border in Canada, which complained about the growing cross-border problems resulting from uncontrolled development on Point Roberts. These complaints, passed on to the U.S. State Department by the government of British Columbia and Canada's Foreign Affairs ministry, generated this "up and down" Delta-Victoria-Ottawa-Washington, D.C.-Olympia-Bellingham hierarchical chain reaction.

Much of this growth on Point Roberts could be attributed to Canadians purchasing land from the local farmer-fisher population for summer cottages. Yet few of these sales were registered with the county government, and building permits were seldom obtained. The permanent population, officially less than three hundred, had clearly grown to more than double this number. During the peak summer months, there were several thousand people staying on the point, creating public health problems due to the inadequate sanitation facilities and water supply. Canadians accounted for virtually all this population growth. In addition, the difference in legal drinking ages during this period between the state of Washington (eighteen) and the province of British Columbia (twenty-one) led to massive southward traffic flows, especially on weekends, as youthful Canadian drinkers frequented several Point Roberts taverns established in response to this demand. One of these taverns was said to be the largest in the entire state of Washington! The lone deputy county sheriff assigned to Point Roberts could not possibly hope to control the resultant brawls and traffic accidents. On the Canadian side of the border, the adjoining residential suburbs in the municipality of Delta experienced a sharp rise in traffic and associated accidents.

Efforts to document the situation on Point Roberts during the summer of 1959 were not appreciated by those wishing to continue these lucrative real-estate transactions, mainly local American landowners and Canadian developers. Yet there seemed to be support among some of the new Canadian cottage owners who hoped our report would somehow lead to improvements concerning local water supplies, sewage disposal, local law enforcement, and other public services. Indeed, over the next decade, the study provided the basis for a series of proactive policies attempting to alleviate these problems.[3]

Although the study had ended, I kept an active interest in the development of Point Roberts through the 1960s, both as part of my dissertation on the U.S.-Canadian boundary and because I joined the faculty at the University of British Columbia in 1964.[4] Building on my interests in the teaching of political geography, I worked with Roger Kasperson in 1967–1968 to develop a "boundary dispute" role-playing simulation set on Point Roberts as one of the activities making up the political geography unit of the High School Geography Project (HSGP), a National Science Foundation–funded project of the Association of American Geographers.[5] Point Roberts provided a wonderful milieu for studying borderland problems, and no great imagination was needed to take an extra step beyond the existing problems and actually simulate a border dispute between Canada and the United States.

Despite some good intentions on both sides of the border, the real problems of Point Roberts did not abate, as evidenced by findings from an opinion survey of Point Roberts residents in March 1971. The survey is discussed later in this chapter.[6] Hence, in April 1971, Canada and the United States sent a joint letter to the International Joint Commission instructing it to investigate the Point Roberts situation. Established by the two countries in 1909, the IJC works to resolve any problems arising along the eight thousand kilometer (five thousand mile) United States-Canadian boundary (this figure includes the Alaska/Canada border). On December 18, 1971, the IJC held a public hearing on Point Roberts to hear testimony from a variety of state and local government officials, service providers, and concerned boundary dwellers about the point's problems.[7] Thus life had caught up with fiction!

Although the appearance of the western U.S.-Canadian border, a straight line running from Minnesota to the Pacific Ocean, might lead one to assume that it was demarcated on some objective and logical basis, the story of this border's creation was marked by a great deal of contingency and chance. Although the relatively free cross-border movement of people, goods, and services, epitomized by the implementation of the North American Free Trade Agreement in 1994, might seem to indicate a border of increasing irrelevance, a closer examination demonstrated that this border, including the small stretch separating Point Roberts from Canada, continues to have a very real impact in our increasingly globalized world. This chapter begins by examining the process that led to the demarcation of the U.S.-Canadian border and the consequences resulting from the unintended creation of the Point Roberts exclave. The chapter then attempts to ascertain the degree to which the original classroom simulation pertaining to Point Roberts's boundary problems matched the actual IJC hearing in 1971. The chapter then follows developments over the past forty-plus years, especially efforts to revamp security and border control measures in the wake of the September 11, 2001, terrorist attacks. Although basically a historical study at the micro scale, the changing dynamic surrounding Point Roberts's border helps illustrate some of the larger-scale problems pertaining to exclaves in general and the Canadian-American borderland in particular.

Creating the Border

The formation of the U.S.-Canadian border began with the 1783 Treaty of Paris, which established the independence of the American colonies and their boundaries with the rest of British-controlled (Canadian) territory. Although this and subsequent agreements largely resolved the eastern boundary from the Atlantic Ocean through the Great Lakes, much of the territory to the north and west remained unexplored. As Spanish, French, and Russian influence in North America declined, it became clear that Britain and the United States would be the main competitors for the region, although neither the Americans nor the British had much information concerning the northwestern portions of the continent. The British Mackenzie expedition of 1793 and the journey of Lewis and Clark a decade later greatly increased knowledge about the region and set off decades of exploration, economic competition, partial settlement, and political confrontation between the two powers. Britain's Hudson's Bay Company and the American Fur Company played central roles as they competed for territorial control to further their fur-trading activities throughout the region.

To help further define their western border, the British and Americans agreed in 1818 to use the forty-ninth parallel running west from the Lake of the Woods in Minnesota to the crest of the Rocky Mountains as the new international boundary through the interior of the continent. But rather than following this line to the Pacific Ocean, this treaty called for British and American "joint occupancy" for the territory centered on modern-day British Columbia, Washington, and Oregon. By avoiding any clear national claim of sovereignty to the region, the treaty was intended to further exploitation by the fur companies rather than pave the way for settlement. Yet as the fur trade declined and settlers began spreading through the area in the early 1830s, pressure increased to clarify territorial sovereignty in the region.

The situation came to a head in the 1840s. American demands were epitomized by the slogan of "Fifty-Four Forty or Fight," which called for pushing the U.S. border north beyond the fifty-fourth parallel. This would essentially remove Britain from the Pacific Coast by taking all the territory south of Russian Alaska. On the other hand, Britain was interested in securing access to the interior through the Columbia River and hence wanted it adopted as the international divide, which would have left British Columbia and much of Washington on the British side. Luckily, the two governments chose compromise over confrontation. In the Treaty of Washington of 1846, also known as the Oregon Treaty, Britain and the United States agreed to extend their boundary westward along the forty-ninth parallel from the Rocky Mountains, where it had reached in 1818, to the Pacific Ocean.

Although the forty-ninth parallel had been designated as the border, it took several surveys, which were subject to considerable azimuth error at the time, and nearly two decades to confirm that Point Roberts was definitely south of the line and cut off from the rest of American territory. Given the continuing hostility between the neighboring states and the point's seemingly strategic location relative to the Strait of Georgia, the United States decided to designate the point a military reserve and hence not open to settlement. In 1871, after a decade of dispute over which channel the boundary would follow through the Georgia Strait to the Pacific, including competing military occupations of the main island of San Juan, both sides agreed to arbitration by the new German emperor. In his decision, which favored the United States, with the most westerly channel as the boundary and giving America sovereignty over the

San Juan Islands, Kaiser Wilhelm also specifically affirmed the U.S. possession of Point Roberts, once and for all.

In an entertaining narrative on the history of Point Roberts, Richard Clark has recorded the sometimes colorful events associated with its unique status of indefinite sovereignty during the last half of the nineteenth century.[8] Despite its military reserve status, the point's isolation attracted criminality and those seeking to evade law enforcement officers. By the late 1890s, several families of Icelandic origin had established residence on the point. After a few years in the Winnipeg area, these families, ironically, traveled through Canada on the Canadian Pacific Railway to find this ideal empty farming and fishing location. After the U.S. War Department sent an official to investigate this "squatter" situation, the designation as a military reserve was terminated. This allowed the new residents to get official title to their land and served to give Point Roberts a more normal status as an unincorporated, if discontiguous, community in Whatcom County.[9]

Minimal links with the sovereign power suited these independent, rural settlers. By 1960, there were about 270 permanent residents, the vast majority being Americans citizens of Icelandic descent. Scheduled public boat service between the point and Bellingham had been discontinued as uneconomic in the early 1950s, so middle- and high-school children were bussed daily about forty kilometers (twenty-five miles) through Canada to reach Blaine, Washington. Normal public services were minimal but not a major problem, while commercial and other necessary activities involved occasional cross-boundary trips into Canada and/or through Canada to the U.S. mainland. Only in the late 1950s, with improvements in Vancouver's access south toward the U.S. border with the opening of the Deas Island Tunnel and Freeway to link with the terminus of U.S. Interstate 5 at Blaine, did the situation of Point Roberts change dramatically (figure 11.2). Suddenly, urban Canadians in search of reasonably priced beach property for a summer cottage could pass rapidly through the Fraser Delta region, with its strict planning codes to protect agriculture against private shoreline development, to find what they wanted on Point Roberts. By 1969, Point Roberts counted 288 "permanent" residents (anyone living there for more than six months in a year) but was invaded in the summer months by as many as 3,500 temporary residents. Of the 1,600 property owners, more than 86 percent were Canadian.[10] In a study conducted at the behest of Washington State's U.S. congressman, Lloyd Meeds, Drew Pettus also found that the state and federal services for Point Roberts were extremely limited, while Whatcom County found that the costs of services, such as road maintenance and law enforcement, far exceeded tax revenues and were hence hardly justified, especially when the majority benefiting were not U.S. citizens. Based on these findings, Pettus speculated that there was general dissatisfaction

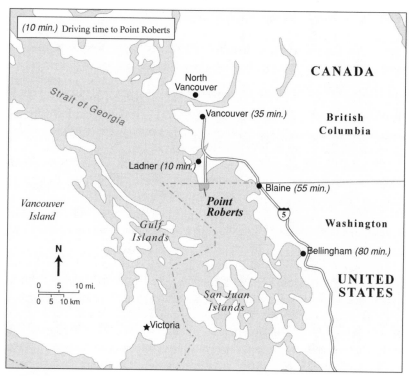

FIGURE 11.2
Driving Times to/from Point Roberts. Cory Johnson of XNR.

with community life and a feeling of distrust and discontent with local administration among both American and Canadian residents.[11]

Simulating a Border Dispute

As mentioned above, I worked with Robert Kasperson to develop a political geography component for the High School Geography Project for the Association of American Geographers during the late 1960s. The centerpiece of this unit was a role-playing classroom activity involving boundary disputes. Given my familiarity with Point Roberts, it was an obvious choice for a simulated dispute between the United States and Canada. The following provides a brief overview of how this border dispute simulation played out in the classroom.

The boundary dispute begins with a radio bulletin interrupting regular programming from Ottawa in which the Canadian prime minister dramatically announces the launching of a full investigation of the situation on Point Roberts, charging that the boundary separating the point from British Columbia is without historical or legal justification. Thirty separate role profiles and suggestions for students were developed for the entire weeklong activity. Four roles were assigned to each of the Canadian and American negotiating teams, four roles for local Point Roberts residents, and a flexible number of roles as private American and Canadian citizens. The role profiles provided a personal background on each, often indicating the biases one could expect when opinions about the future of Point Roberts were given.

Four roles, two from each country, were developed for the International Joint Commission and unsurprisingly were modeled on the actual IJC membership as it stood in the late 1960s. Emphasis was placed on their camaraderie in working on different problems together and their tradition of acting more as a unit than as national spokespersons. There were also three roles for members of an arbitration commission, from Mexico, Japan, and India, with profiles suggesting cultural and Cold War biases that could come into play. The critical role of moderator is assigned to a student with leadership abilities as this student has the responsibility to maintain orderly discussion throughout the activity. Finally, the roles for editor and reporter were created for the local newspaper *The Pointer*, giving the point a virtual newspaper a generation ahead of reality as it was not until the mid-1990s that a new monthly newspaper, *The All Point Bulletin (APB)*, actually began publication.

After introducing the problem and preliminary discussions on the first day, hearings begin on day two with citizens giving testimony to the negotiating teams and to the IJC. The Canadian negotiating team and then the American team make their case on days three and four, and on day five the arbitration commission takes testimony and the IJC presents a report. On day six, the activity ends with the negotiating teams reaching agreement on a settlement or, if deadlocked, with the IJC making a recommendation. If this is not possible, the arbitration commission settles the dispute. The final solution and summaries of all daily activity are reported in *The Pointer*.

The teacher's guide points out that there may be several solutions of differing degrees of acceptability to each party. While simulating the boundary dispute in school trials before publication and in university undergraduate courses since, I found that the most common solution was a decision to "internationalize" the point, either as an international park or a university. Simply awarding the point to Canada was a close second, while retaining the status quo was far less popular. In most cases the moderator, normally a top student, had a powerful influence on the direction discussions took toward a solution.

A Real Border Dispute—The IJC Hearing, December 1971

The one-day hearing of December 18, 1971, at The Breakers Tavern focused on the problems identified in the original American-Canadian letter to the IJC, which stated that the residents of Point Roberts and others were confronted by a variety of problems caused by "isolation from the rest of the U.S. by the international boundary."[12] Specifically, the problems identified included customs regulations, employment in Canada and on the point, health and medical services, electricity and telephone services, and law enforcement. Testimony was sought from the local, state/provincial, and federal levels of government on both sides of the boundary. Four of the six commissioners were present, two from each country. The chair, Christian Herter, announced the six names of those making up the International Point Roberts Board, which would eventually make recommendations on Point Roberts to the IJC. This board seemed similar to the two simulated negotiating teams, although its members did not participate directly in the hearings.

Whatcom County commissioner Frank Roberts, whose district included the point, stated at the outset that American sovereignty over Point Roberts was nonnegotiable in any possible solution. There had been some recent informal discussions about the possibility of swapping Canadian sovereignty over a strip of land near the base of the Alaskan panhandle to the United States in return for Canadian control over Point Roberts. Surprisingly, this statement was not seriously challenged for the rest of the hearings. The desire of Canadian officials to retain the goodwill of Americans as they sought solutions to the Point Roberts dilemma seemed to prevent any open discussion of a possible change in sovereignty. Indeed, such a solution was seen as "unthinkable" by the next witness, the Canadian federal member of parliament for the constituency immediately adjacent to the Point (Burnaby, Richmond, and Delta), Tom Goode. Indeed, he also found an "internationalization" solution, whether as park or university, to be without precedent, unacceptable, and inequitable. The idea of creating an international park had certainly been discussed openly in the press at that time but was never formally proposed. More recently, in the mid-1990s, the IJC actually revived the idea and advanced it as a proposal. This, however, met with little or no support from any of the interested parties. Members of the British Columbia legislative assembly for the adjacent constituency of Delta, Robert Wenman, on the other hand, felt that all possible solutions should be considered and that, given the future increase in population pressure from British Columbia, it would probably be desirable for the point to become Canadian, although there was no follow-up to this speculation. The mayor and administrator of Delta municipality were adamant that they needed close involvement in any solution since they were absorbing the greatest negative impact from Point Roberts.

Joint testimony and follow-up discussion from an American and a Canadian representing the Point Roberts Community Association, a binational group of 425 property owners (87 percent of whom were Canadian) take up fully one-third of the hearing document but, in actuality, took up less time than government officials' testimony and also came very late in the day. This grassroots view of the problems concerning health care, electricity, water supply, customs and immigration, sewage disposal, schooling, and law enforcement brought home the reality of the situation's complexities and the difficulty of achieving a solution. A rival group, the Point Roberts Voters Association (100 percent American) wanted changes in Canadian law regarding employment, medical care, and so on, that, it hoped, would attract a large number of Americans to move to Point Roberts to work in Canada. Clearly, the dwindling American segment of the population feared ever-increasing Canadian control over local decisions and hence sought to reverse the trend. Other major statements came from officials of the electricity supplier, Puget Sound Power and Light, and of the telephone company, B.C. Telephone Co. Toward the end of the day, testimony was taken from six individuals, a mix of U.S. and Canadian borderland residents, each with a particular complaint or request for change concerning the point.

The Simulation versus the Reality

Aside from the fact that in reality there was no real international dispute over the boundary and hence an international arbitration commission plays no part, the IJC is common to both, and its members did, as suggested in the simulation, tend to act as good friends and as a unit rather than as two Americans against two Canadians. In a sense, the witnesses testifying in 1971 bear a close resemblance to those playing simulated roles as the private citizens and the two negotiating teams. Perhaps the greatest contrast comes with the minimal role played in reality by "concerned citizens" as those actually giving testimony were drawn largely from the different levels of government or those charged with providing services to the point. Given the unique international nature of the problems being discussed, it was hardly surprising that the actual will of individuals among the local population, reflecting narrow and conflicting self-interest, was given such low priority by the IJC. The simplification necessary to allow for a successful role-playing classroom activity imposed a serious constraint on the ability to project the complexity of the real problems facing the point and hence on thoroughly understanding the impact of any given solution. Even if the importance of the point's exclave status was minimized in materials provided to the students, selecting such a unique location for a boundary dispute activity raised collateral problems, further complicating the process of finding a fair solution. In the real world, there was no influential moderator.

In March 1971, using students in a field project of a political geography class at the University of British Columbia, I organized a survey of Point Roberts residents, the results of which were published a year later.[13] The aim was to test the validity of theories about systems stress, or unusually high pressure on the existing infrastructure caused by the unique situation, concerning exclaves and discontiguity based on research by Merritt and Robinson.[14] Three common elements were recognized about exclaves: problems of integration with the mother country (the United States) compared with the adjacent country (Canada); problems of increased stress beyond normal levels due to density and small size; and problems of internal integration. This last-named set of problems is often dependent on the laws of the mother country pertaining to the settlement and activities of citizens of the adjacent country. In the case of Point Roberts, these problems are particularly relevant to the status of the Canadian residents. On the other hand, economic and social proximity to the adjacent country can lead to a tendency toward a reduced sense of belonging to the mother country. Indeed, Americans on Point Roberts are certainly more attuned to Canadian habits and idiosyncrasies. Noncontiguity clearly imposes higher costs of administering and serving the exclave without any possibility of defraying these costs through the tax base. Despite the expanding Canadian population, the tax base remained too narrow to meet the ever-expanding costs of public spending. Its size compounds the problems of a narrow economic base and dependence on the adjacent state for some services, such as the water supply. In addition, the international boundary curtails journey-to-work patterns, further undermining the economic base. The resulting inadequate or nonexistent services place stress on the exclave.

Given the sharp divide between American and Canadian residents, it is not surprising that a common sense of community is slow to develop and that a low level of integration persists. Hostility within the Point Roberts community was reflected in the presentations made by local residents at the December 1971 IJC hearing. Our survey showed that employment and shopping links among the point's residents were far stronger with British Columbia than with Washington. Survey results concerning newspaper readership and other external linkages showed an overall Canadian dominance but with national biases remaining between the two populations. There was a general feeling of dissatisfaction with the quality of services provided, but Canadians were the most dissatisfied.

A Border Opening and Closing

While the basic facts on the ground remain the same, the past forty years have witnessed some important changes. Perhaps the most striking change has been the slow but steady development of a borderland community straddling the Point Roberts-Delta boundary (figure 11.3). The old lines of conflict defined largely by American versus Canadian nationality are now blurred by an increasingly proactive community of interest, with support for policies leading to a generally beneficial outcome for the entire Point Roberts population. The total official resident population in 1970 had grown to 662, only 18 percent of whom were American. It had almost doubled to 1,308 by 2000, although the "housing count" was 1,820 with 67 percent of the units vacant, indicating a continuing rise in the Canadian segment of the population (estimated at 70

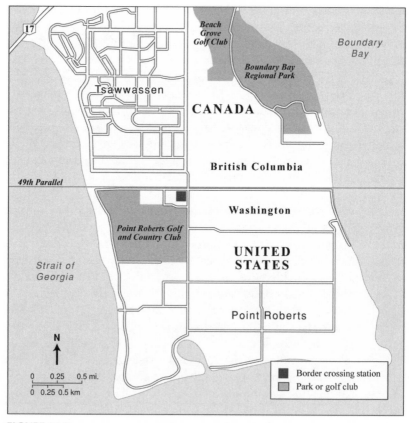

FIGURE 11.3
Point Roberts Close Up. Cory Johnson of XNR.

percent), both permanent and temporary. The Point Roberts Registered Voters Association, once the voice of the U.S. population only, now boasts more than four hundred members and is a mix of both nationalities.

The epitome of this change is found in the establishment of the new monthly newspaper *The All Point Bulletin* in 1995. Identifying itself as "The Community Newspaper of Point Roberts, WA and Delta, BC," the *Bulletin* claims a circulation of eight thousand. As the Canadian segment of the point's permanent population enters its third generation, evidence from the *Bulletin*'s content indicates that a more locally based identity emerged that has more common points of view with the U.S. population. Also, as the functioning of the borderland regime became stabilized and routine, shared common interests with the adjoining Delta population emerged. Soon a grassroots borderland viewpoint was being articulated in seeking compatible policies from the upper levels of the political hierarchy in ways that were nonexistent in past decades. The newspaper, for example, takes pride in leading the successful fight against the proposal from the IJC to turn Point Roberts into an international park.

Part of the explanation for these changes may rest with the fact that one of the major problems that previously beset the population on both sides of the border resolved itself in the past few decades. The nocturnal migration of Canadian youth seeking alcoholic beverages in Point Roberts taverns due to the difference in legal drinking age has stopped. Ironically, the national drinking age is now universally twenty-one years in the United States but has been reduced to nineteen in British Columbia. Indeed, the infamous Breakers Tavern, site of the IJC hearing in 1971, closed its doors permanently a decade ago.

Under these improving circumstances, the main concern seems to have shifted away from a "United States-versus-Canada" basis to a more shared frustration over the increased barrier effect of the boundary since September 11, 2001. Until recently, crossing the border in and out of Point Roberts was seldom a problem. There were three crossing points, with a few Canadian and U.S. border officials on duty for restricted hours and a mostly unfenced border in between. Hence the border remained fairly open with few restrictions to movement across it. Increased security measures since 9/11 have brought significant changes to the Point Roberts Canadian border. There is now only one crossing point, which is manned round the clock, and a substantial fence has been erected along the entire length of the border.

A recent issue of the *Bulletin* gives more evidence of this trend. Under the headline "More Local Border Control Wanted," a report from the February 2008 annual meeting of the International Mobility and Trade Corridor quoted participants as discussing how the changing border security measures might work for everyone. U.S. Consul General in Vancouver, Lewis Lukens, predicted shorter lines at crossing points as Washington and British Columbia introduced new enhanced driver licenses in the hope that these would substitute for passports.[15] Representatives from the U.S. Customs and Border Protection (CBP) and Whatcom County were being invited to the next meeting of the Point Roberts Registered Voters Association so that they could be questioned on issues concerning the easing of border-crossing red tape.

In a somewhat successful attempt to soften the impact of increased border security since 9/11, the two federal governments have introduced the Nexus program, which allows frequent and routine border crossers to apply for privileged status. This allows them to pass through special lanes, minimizing delays at the Blaine border crossing. Problems have, however, plagued the Nexus program. Applications take months to process and can be turned down arbitrarily without any possibility of appeal. Just one "illegal" item found aboard a vehicle, such as an errant orange inadvertently left from a past supermarket purchase, can lead to permanent elimination from the program under its "zero-tolerance" policy. While this program seems to present Point Roberts residents routinely traveling by road to the United States with a distinct advantage in avoiding delays, it has become most unpopular because of its arbitrariness, inconsistency, and insensitivity. Indeed, in May 2008 a website was set up specifically to collect "Nexus horror stories" from abused users.[16]

Another *Bulletin* story reports on new problems for Canadian weekend residents. The local postmaster announced that mailboxes with a three-day accumulation would be cleared out, the mail returned to the post office, held for ten days, and then returned to the sender.[17] An angry letter to the editor from a Canadian with a Delta address but claiming to be a Point Roberts property owner for eighteen years, questioned this new policy as "totally unreasonable" and claimed it would lead to chaos at the post office.[18] In yet another problem with the U.S. mail, beginning April 4, 2008, the Canadian Border Services Agency (CBSA) began requiring the daily USPS van carrying mail from the Blaine sorting office to Point Roberts to use the commercial lanes and to have a full manifest listing all items carried instead of passing through the passenger lanes it had been using for decades without a manifest. The USPS announced that the extra time required to prepare a manifest and to cross the border using the always slow and crowded commercial crossing point would delay distribution of mail on Point Roberts until the next day.[19]

Increasingly, the permanent population of Point Roberts is aging, and as the retirement segment expands, the complexity of the Canadian-American realities of everyday life seems of declining importance to these less mobile and point-rooted folk. They find the more rural and less frenetic pace of life with a minimum of government services to be quite satisfactory and indeed preferable to living on the British Columbian lower mainland or elsewhere in Whatcom County. Not surprisingly, it has recently been noted that this particular quality has been reflected in the point's increasing attraction as a wildlife refuge for a variety of animal species of the lower mainland as they find a suitable habitat in this still-forested and less-populated sanctuary.[20]

Conclusions

On Point Roberts, Americans have accepted that their future is tied to Canadians and Canada. Conversely, Canadian residents now realize that their unique identity must reflect the reality of continuing American sovereignty and thus differentiate them from other British Columbians, as residents in the United States. One has to admire the enterprise of the local chamber of commerce, which in discussing crime and security on its website, pointed out that the point is a de facto "gated community" given the around-the-clock presence of U.S. and Canadian immigration and customs officers at the only entry point! In answering the question "Is there a police department?" the chamber states "not exactly" but goes on to point out that normally two deputy sheriffs are available at the headquarters in Bellingham (seventy to eighty minutes away by car) and that this represents one of the highest ratios of police to public for any community in Whatcom County. To avoid travel through Canada, criminals arrested for serious offenses are normally transported to Bellingham by the county sheriff's helicopter or by U.S. Coast Guard cutter, depending on weather conditions and availability, placing an enormous cost burden on the county. The "Sheriff's Report," regularly appearing in the *Bulletin*, indicates there are one or two such prisoner transports per month. Also, an equal number of suspected crime perpetrators avoid arrest by reentering Canada before the crime is reported. Obviously, the "gated community" idea does not work so well in reverse.

Forty years ago Clark suggested that Point Roberts could be viewed in four different contexts: as a Canadian visa community, as a Canadian squatter community, as an American/Canadian retirement community, and as a Canadian dormitory community.[21] Today, it remains all four, but the squatter and dormitory aspects are decreasing with a greater emphasis on the more clearly legal visa and retirement lifestyles. Perhaps the most sobering conclusion one can reach as a result of this assessment of the problems, simulated and real, facing Point Roberts almost fifty years ago, is that no matter how dire a situation seems to be in a borderland, the best solution may not be sudden, controversial change in sovereignty or regulations but rather a muddling through that allows for goodwill and a borderland community identity to germinate, grow, and somehow make a going concern of the abnormal.

All the evidence pointed toward this trend until a few years ago. One suspects that a generalization can be made about borderland communities evolving in this manner. In this case, the original problems of fifty years ago were due to conflicts of interest between American and Canadian local populations placed in this analogous situation. Now, the problems are based more on national policies on both sides of the border that seem in conflict with the best interests of the border dwellers. The impact of 9/11 and the consequent obsession with borderland security under the U.S. Homeland Security apparatus have now rudely interrupted this positive evolution. Indeed, there is clear evidence that the borderland community identity has diminished under the stress of losing grassroots control to solve problems informally as they arise. The level of frustration and anger has also been elevated recently, as evidenced at the 2008 annual meeting of the Point Roberts Voters Association in March. As reported in the *Bulletin*, the local U.S. Customs and Border Protection director, who had been invited to attend, raised a good deal of resentment. When responding to complaints about needless delays in crossing the border, he solemnly stated: "We are the sheepdog and like it or not we have to protect your lives. Sheep may be wary of the sheepdog but happy to have him around when the wolf shows up."[22] The current preoccupation of the American federal government to harden the U.S.-Canadian border in response to the September 11, 2001, terrorist attacks has clearly complicated the daily lives of the people living on this unique American exclave, Point Roberts.

12

Conclusion

Borders in a Changing Global Context

Alexander C. Diener and Joshua Hagen

DURING THE PARTITION OF THE Ottoman Empire following World War I, Winston Churchill, then British colonial secretary, allegedly claimed that he created the borders for the British mandate of Transjordan, roughly modern-day Jordan, "with the stroke of a pen one Sunday afternoon in Cairo." The oddly geometric outline of Jordanian borders, especially its jagged eastern edge, gave rise to speculation that Churchill had hiccupped while drawing this portion (figure 12.1). The result was the sharp point of Saudi territory wedged deep into Jordan, sometimes known as "Winston's Hiccup."[1]

While Churchill probably exaggerated his importance and the hiccup incident is highly suspect, the anecdotes surrounding the creation of Jordan's "odd" border highlight how recent and arbitrary much of the modern political map is, regardless of how normal, logical, or natural portions of it may appear. As stable political institutions with functional boundaries, states, even those considered "old," usually date to some point in the past two centuries. Cultures are certainly older, and ethnic communities may be traced into prehistory, but the states and borders that form the basic organizational units of the contemporary international system are relatively modern. It is not surprising that the borders of postcolonial regions of Africa, Asia, Latin America, or the Middle East often stemmed from rather arbitrary pen strokes of men gathered around maps. It is, however, important to recognize that no political border is more natural or real than another. Rather, all borders are human constructions and as such derive their function and meaning from the people they divide.

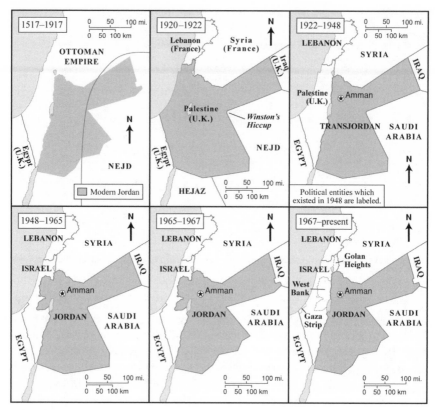

FIGURE 12.1
"Winston's Hiccup" along the Jordanian-Saudi Border. Cory Johnson of XNR.

This book began by pointing out the sense of sanctity or permanence the general public often associates with international borders. The chapters that followed portrayed the complex histories and contingent events that shaped some of the oddest-looking borders and how those dividers of geopolitical space have affected lives even to this day. We would like to conclude the book by addressing why international borders have held such a seemingly immutable quality and why they remain an integral topic of study for the future.

Modern societies are permeated by notions and practices of territoriality at a variety of scales. From individual land ownership to attachments to national homelands, human territoriality can be regarded as a "powerful geographic strategy to control people and things by controlling area."[2] Indeed, state borders seem to be examples of human territoriality writ large. As noted by James Anderson and Liam O'Dowd:

Ultimately, the significance of borders derives from the importance of territoriality as an organizing principle of political and social life. The functions and meanings of borders have always been inherently ambiguous and contradictory; and these characteristics seem to take on new salience with claims about emerging "borderless worlds" and the "space of places" giving way to the "space of flows."[3]

Looking to history, contemporary students of geopolitics are compelled to consider that power has not always been tied to state-centered territories. As outlined in the introduction, the decline of divine-right leadership and its replacement by representative government, along with urbanization inspired by industrialization and the dissemination of "enlightenment values," challenged the structured social hierarchies of Europe. This challenge ultimately required a new conception of territory. Frontiers were no longer valued or even tolerated, as the land area of the continent was divided up between equivalent units of sovereignty and national loyalty.

This period was crucial in establishing states and their territories as pools of power from which a new global, sociospatial order would emerge. Borders gained greater significance than ever before because of their practical role in ensnaring people within what John Agnew calls the "territorial trap." This concept derives from three interrelated assumptions. The first is that states have exclusive power within their territories (i.e., sovereignty). This first assumption leads to the second, namely that domestic (internal) and foreign (external) affairs represent fundamentally different realms of political and social activity, each with its own separate rules. Finally, the boundaries of the state define the boundaries of the society (the former acts as a container for the latter).[4]

These assumptions are compared with a "trap" since they serve to limit thinking to an intuitional fixity for international borders. They reinforced one another to emphasize a state-centered view of power and placed the delimitation of space occupied by states beyond history.[5] In essence, during the nineteenth century when economic and social practices emerged almost exclusively in relation to the state, the territorial trap was sprung and projected a normative value to state-scale institutions. Businesses, trade unions, representative politics, sports, military, education, and art were considered most efficient and pragmatic in relation to the states that housed them. A sense that they *should* be state centered was advanced through methodological nationalism within the new social sciences.[6] Economics, sociology, and political science were "all founded to provide intellectual services to the modern state" and in turn support the idea that local communities would give way to national societies. In essence, the state became educator of the populace, framing and shaping identity to fit the new religion of the nation.

Often drawing from a particular ethnic history, nationalized elites not only projected the national society into a primordial past but also, whether factual or not, portrayed its evolution within the framework of its occupied or desired territory. The "homeland" came to be viewed as a divinely sanctioned stage upon which a national drama would play out. Proof of its validity lay in the post-Westphalian geopolitical reality that as nationalization occurred in one territory, a neighbor's security was most readily obtained through its own nationalization. In this process, other spatial political organizing principles were plowed under, leaving only the ideal of the nation-state with functional legitimacy. Indeed, Anthony Smith argued that "representing space as state territoriality also serves to put statehood outside of time, because of the strong tendency to associate space with stasis or changelessness, and thus impose an intellectual stability on the world that would otherwise be difficult."[7] This territorial stability has served as a guarantor of sociospatial order. Looking to Aristotle and Machiavelli, one could posit it also propagates a social order in which elites structure access to power.

It is clear that new communication and transportation technologies have, in conjunction with political changes over the past two decades, altered the meaning of national territories. Conceptualized as the "most active sites of territorial complexes," borders constitute the physical and institutional forefront of this transition.[8] Catalysts of the alleged shift from states as the primary units of global spatial organization have come from a variety of sources. Declining significance of military might along with the expansion of global markets, cyberspace, and transnational capitalism (multinational companies) have, according to some, lessened the need for bounded spaces.

Indeed, the emergence of alternative modes of governance (international governmental organizations and nongovernmental organizations) in conjunction with the theory of "democratic peace" points to a more cooperative international system, where borders may be seen as more hindrance than help. However, not unlike the obsolescence of walled cities, where technology and new paradigms of sociopolitical organization rendered the walls unnecessary and even encumbrances to modernization, a new territorial form will undoubtedly replace the old. Even where de-territorialization is occurring, re-territorialization will follow. Its form may differ from that which preceded it, but its function is not likely to stray too far.

John Herz once theorized that state borders would cease to serve as security barriers following the advent of nuclear weapons.[9] With the security equation changed, he argued states would give way to regional blocs, in some ways not unlike those foreseen in Samuel Huntington's clash of civilizations thesis.[10] In both of these hypothetical and highly debated scenarios, a new scale of territoriality is predicted to emerge and replace the old. Yet even these dramatic changes would not entail a perpetual de-territorialization any more than did the historical evolution of city-states or empires to nation-states. Rather, these periods of transition represent a complex renegotiation of spatiality.

We see today, and are likely to continue to witness, contradictory processes pertaining to borders. Where NAFTA breaks down barriers to transstate trade and interaction, the post-9/11 security environment curtails cross-border movement, requiring documentation as never before and even raising the prospect of a physical barrier across the perimeter of the southwestern United States. Where cyberspace facilitates instantaneous contact across space, access to the diversity of world cultures, and the unprecedented emancipation of thought, it also serves as a pulpit of xenophobia, an outlet for propaganda, and a forum for various types of oppression. During this stage of shifting spatiality, borders conspicuously embody such contradictory and multifaceted roles.

> They are at once gateways and barriers to the "outside world," protective and imprisoning, areas of opportunity and/or insecurity, zones of contact and/or conflict, of co-operation and/or competition, of ambivalent identities and/or aggressive assertion of difference. These apparent dichotomies may alternate with time and place, but—more interestingly—they can co-exist simultaneously in the same people, some of whom have to regularly deal not with one state but two.[11]

As the previous quotation suggests, corporeal mobilities have played a powerful role in altering the meaning of borders.

While borders continue to serve to order our lives, they also perpetuate difference and "othering" along with belonging and identity. Perhaps more prevalently today than at any point in history, we understand the transportable and multiscalar nature of territory and thus the multilayered role of borders in a variety of social settings. David Newman states:

> Our understanding of territories and borders is less rigid and less deterministic than in the past. Territory and borders have their own internal dynamics, causing change in their own right as much as they are simply the physical outcome of decision making. They are as much perceived in our mental maps and images as they are visible manifestations of concrete walls and barbed-wire fences.[12]

The "oddity" of a distant border may be reproduced in the urban environs of a global city like London or New York. Concentrations of Pakistanis may enact territoriality over their neighborhood and exclude fellow British citizens of Indian extraction. In such cases, borders in the landscape emerge from the identities carried within individuals and groups. They are expressions of identity and representations of power that can be inclusive or exclusive and serve as bridges or barriers. They compel ethical considerations: For whom are they constructed? By whom? What end do they serve?

The lived experience of borders reminds us that their opacity is as important as their transparency, that sites of transition can become sites of contestation, and vice versa. Borders, we argue, will not anachronize. They require further study both from the top down and from the bottom up, from the state scale and from the local scale. Borders are perhaps the most obvious political geographic entity in the lives of human beings. As such, they are worthy of in-depth study and consideration as to the effect they have on our lives. This book in no way represents a comprehensive treatment of borders or even of "odd" international borders. Yet by drawing upon the fields of world history, international relations, political sociology, political anthropology, and international law, we hope it inspires further studies in political geography and the power humans wield to both physically and metaphorically shape our very bordered world.

Notes

Chapter 1: Introduction: Borders, Identity, and Geopolitics

1. See Melissa Jordine, *The Dispute over Gibraltar* (New York: Chelsea House, 2007).

2. Robert MacPhail, "King Stirs Up Hornets' Nest with Trip to Disputed Towns," *The Times*, 5 November 2007, 37; Victoria Burnett, "Morocco Angry at Royal Visit to Enclaves," *New York Times*, 6 November 2007, A14.

3. Peter Gold, *Europe or Africa? A Contemporary Study of the Spanish North African Enclaves of Ceuta and Melilla* (Liverpool: Liverpool University Press, 2000).

4. Martin Ira Glassner and Chuck Fahrer, *Political Geography*, 3rd ed. (New York: Wiley, 2004), 84.

5. Julia Lovell, *The Great Wall: China Against the World 1000 BC–AD 2000* (New York: Grove Press, 2006), 16.

6. Alejandro Colás, *Empire* (Cambridge: Polity Press, 2007), 39.

7. Simon Schama, *A History of Britain: At the Edge of the World? 3000 BC–AD 1603* (New York: Hyperion, 2000), 34. See also Christopher Whittaker, *Frontiers of the Roman Empire: A Social and Economic Study* (Baltimore: Johns Hopkins University Press, 1994); Derek Williams, *The Reach of Rome: A History of the Roman Imperial Frontier 1st–5th Centuries AD* (New York: St. Martin's, 1997); Stephen Mitchell, *A History of the Later Roman Empire* (Malden, Mass.: Blackwell, 2007), 81–86, 338–43.

8. See Bruce Batten, "Frontiers and Boundaries in Pre-Modern Japan," *Journal of Historical Geography* 25, no. 2 (1999): 166–82; Firoozeh Kashani-Sabet, *Frontier Fictions: Shaping the Iranian Nation, 1804–1946* (Princeton: Princeton University Press, 1999); Malcolm Todd, *The Early Germans* (Malden, Mass.: Blackwell, 2004); Timothy Gregory, *A History of Byzantium* (Malden, Mass.: Blackwell, 2005); Kathryn Ebel, "Representations of the Frontier in Ottoman Town Views of the Sixteenth Century," *Imago Mundi* 60, no. 1 (2008): 1–22.

9. See Allen Buchanan and Margaret Moore, eds., *States, Nations and Borders: The Ethics of Making Boundaries* (Cambridge: Cambridge University Press, 2003).

10. Jacques Le Goff, *The Birth of Europe*, trans. Janet Lloyd (Malden, Mass.: Blackwell, 2005), 4. See also Walter Pohl, Ian Wood, and Helmut Reimitz, eds., *The Transformation of Frontiers from Late Antiquity to the Carolingians* (Boston: Brill, 2001); Florin Curta, ed., *Borders, Barriers, and Ethnogenesis: Frontiers in Late Antiquity and the Middle Ages* (Turnhout, Belgium: Berpols, 2005).

11. See Malcolm Anderson, *Frontiers: Territory and State Formation in the Modern World* (Cambridge: Polity Press, 1996); Alexander Murphy, "The Sovereign State System as Political-Territorial Ideal: Historical and Contemporary Considerations," in *State Sovereignty as Social Construct*, ed. T. J. Biersteker and C. Weber (Cambridge: Cambridge University Press, 1996), 81–120.

12. See Norman J. G. Pounds, "The Origins of the Idea of Natural Frontiers in France," *Annals of the Association of American Geographers* 41, no. 2 (1951): 146–57; Norman J. G. Pounds, "France and 'Les Limites Naturelles' from the Seventeenth to the Twentieth Centuries," *Annals of the Association of American Geographers* 44, no. 1 (1954): 51–62; Peter Sahlins, "Natural Frontiers Revisited: France's Boundaries Since the Seventeenth Century," *American Historical Review* 95, no. 5 (1990): 1423–52; Michael Heffernan, "History, Geography and the French National Space: The Question of Alsace-Lorraine, 1914–18," *Space & Polity* 5, no. 1 (2001): 27–48.

13. See Mark Bassin, "Imperialism and the Nation-State in Friedrich Ratzel's Political Geography," *Progress in Human Geography* 11, no. 4 (1987): 473–95; F. Farinelli, "Friedrich Ratzel and the Nature of (Political) Geography," *Political Geography* 19, no. 8 (2000): 943–55.

14. C. B. Fawcett, *Frontiers: A Study in Political Geography* (Oxford: Clarendon Press, 1918), 62. See also Thomas Holdrich, *Political Frontiers and Boundary Making* (London: Macmillan, 1916); Charles Homer Haskins and Robert Howard Lord, *Some Problems of the Peace Conference* (Cambridge, Mass.: Harvard University Press, 1922); Hugh Dalton, *Towards the Peace of Nations: A Study of International Politics* (London: George Routledge, 1928).

15. Richard Hartshorne, "A Survey of the Boundary Problems of Europe," in *Geographic Aspects of International Relations*, ed. Charles Colby (Chicago: University of Chicago Press, 1938), 164.

16. See Richard Hartshorne, "Suggestions on the Terminology of Political Boundaries," *Annals of the Association of American Geographers* 26, no. 1 (1936): 56–57; Samuel Boggs, *International Boundaries: A Study of Boundary Functions and Problems* (New York: Columbia University Press, 1940); Stephen Jones, "The Description of International Boundaries," *Annals of the Association of American Geographers* 33, no. 2 (1943): 99–117.

17. J. R. V. Prescott, *The Geography of Frontiers and Boundaries* (London: Hutchinson University Library, 1965), 29. See also Stephen Jones, "Boundary Concepts in the Setting of Place and Time," *Annals of the Association of American Geographers* 49, no. 3 (1959): 241–55; Julian Minghi, "Boundary Studies in Political Geography," *Annals of the Association of American Geographers* 53, no. 3 (1963): 407–28.

18. W. A. Douglas Jackson, "Whither Political Geography?" *Annals of the Association of American Geographers* 48, no. 2 (1958): 178.

19. Norman J. G. Pounds, *Political Geography* (New York: McGraw-Hill, 1963), 19.

20. Ladis Kristof, "The Nature of Frontiers and Boundaries," *Annals of the Association of American Geographers* 49, no. 3 (1959): 278.

21. Kenichi Ohmae, *The End of the Nation State: The Rise of the Regional Economies* (New York: Free Press, 1995), 11.

22. See Kenichi Omae, *The Borderless World: Power and Strategy in the Interlinked Economy* (New York: HarperBusiness, 1990); Richard O'Brien, *Global Financial Integration: The End of Geography* (New York: Council on Foreign Relations Press, 1992); Jean-Marie Guéhenno, *The End of the Nation-State* (Minneapolis: University of Minnesota Press, 1995); Manuel Castells, *The Rise of the Network Society* (Malden, Mass.: Blackwell, 1996).

23. Peter Taylor, "The State as Container: Territoriality in the Modern World-System," *Progress in Human Geography* 18, no. 2 (1994): 151–62; Anssi Paasi, "Boundaries as Social Processes: Territoriality in the World of Flows," *Geopolitics* 3, no. 1 (1998): 69–88.

24. See David Newman and Anssi Paasi, "Fences and Neighbours in the Postmodern World: Boundary Narratives in Political Geography," *Progress in Human Geography* 22, no. 2 (1998): 186–207; Vladimir Kolossov, "Border Studies: Changing Perspectives and Theoretical Approaches," *Geopolitics* 10, no. 4 (2005): 606–32; David Newman, "The Lines That Continue to Separate Us: Borders in our 'Borderless' World," *Progress in Human Geography* 30, no. 2 (2006): 143–61; Alexander C. Diener and Joshua Hagen, "Theorizing Borders in a 'Borderless World': Globalization, Territory and Scale," *Geography Compass* 3, no. 3 (2009): 1196–1216.

25. David Newman, "Borders and Bordering: Towards an Interdisciplinary Dialogue," *European Journal of Social Theory* 9, no. 2 (1996): 181. See also Gearóid Ó Tuathail, "Borderless Worlds? Problematising Discourses of Deterritorialisation," *Geopolitics* 4, no. 2 (1999): 139–54; Gerald Blake, "State Limits in the Early Twenty-First Century: Observations on Form and Function," *Geopolitics* 5, no. 1 (2000): 1–18; Peter Andreas and Thomas Biersteker, *The Rebordering of North America: Integration and Exclusion in a New Security Context* (New York: Routledge, 2003); Jason Ackleson, "Constructing Security on the U.S.-Mexico Border," *Political Geography* 24, no. 2 (2004): 165–84.

26. David Thelan, "Rethinking History and the Nation-State: Mexico and the United States," *Journal of American History* 86, no. 2 (1999): 441.

27. See Olive Schofield and Gerald Blake, eds., *The Razor's Edge: International Boundaries and Political Geography* (New York: Kluver Law International, 2002); Joan Anderson and Egbert Wever, "Borders, Border Regions and Economic Integration: One World, Ready or Not," *Journal of Borderland Studies* 18, no. 1 (2004): 27–38; Colin Flint, ed., *The Geography of War and Peace: From Death Camps to Diplomats* (Oxford: Oxford University Press, 2005); Henk van Houtum, Olivier Kramsch, and Wolfgang Zierhofe, eds., *B/ordering Space* (Aldershot, U.K.: Ashgate, 2005); Miles

Kahler and Barbara Walter, eds., *Territoriality and Conflict in an Era of Globalization* (Cambridge: Cambridge University Press, 2006).

28. Sami Moisio, "Redrawing the Map of Europe: Spatial Formation of the EU's Eastern Dimension," *Geography Compass* 1, no. 1 (2007): 99. See also David Kaplan and Jouni Häkli, eds., *Boundaries and Place: European Borderlands in Geographical Context* (Lanham, Md.: Rowman & Littlefield, 2002); Oliver Kessler and Jan Helmig, "Of Systems, Boundaries, and Regionalisation," *Geopolitics* 12, no. 4 (2007): 570–85; Merje Kuus, "Something Old, Something New: Eastness in European Union Enlargement," *Journal of International Relations and Development* 10, no. 2 (2007): 150–67.

29. See Peter Sahlins, *Boundaries: The Making of France and Spain in the Pyrenees* (Berkeley and Los Angeles: University of California Press, 1989); Thomas Wilson and Hastings Donnan, eds., *Border Identities: Nation and State at International Frontiers* (Cambridge: Cambridge University Press, 1998); Jan Buursink, "The Binational Reality of Border-Crossing Cities," *GeoJournal* 54, no. 1 (2001): 7–19; Ulf Matthiesen and Hans-Joachim Bürkner, "Antagonistic Structures in Border Areas: Local Milieux and Local Politics in the Polish-German Twin City Gubin/Guben," *GeoJournal* 54, no. 1 (2001): 43–50; Glen Sparrow, "San Diego-Tijuana: Not Quite a Binational City or Region," *GeoJournal* 54, no. 1 (2001): 73–83.

30. James Anderson and Liam O'Dowd, "Borders, Border Regions and Territoriality: Contradictory Meanings, Changing Significance," *Regional Studies* 33, no. 7 (1999): 603.

Chapter 2: The Border Enclaves of India and Bangladesh: The Forgotten Lands

This chapter is based in part on work supported by the U.S. National Science Foundation under grant No. 0602206 and the American Institute of Bangladesh Studies. Thanks to Robert Kaiser and the book's editors, Alexander Diener and Joshua Hagen, for commenting on earlier drafts of this chapter. Any errors that remain are mine.

1. The data for this chapter is based on interviews and focus groups conducted in the fall of 2006 in and around several Indian enclaves inside Bangladesh. The Bangladeshi enclaves in India were not visited. Therefore, the chapter focuses on the experiences of the residents of the 102 Indian enclaves in Bangladesh. See table 2.1 for the total numbers of enclaves. Brendan Whyte, *Waiting for the Esquimo: An Historical and Documentary Study of the Cooch Behar Enclaves of India and Bangladesh* (Melbourne: University of Melbourne, 2002).

2. Formal censuses have not been conducted in the enclaves since the early 1950s, and estimates of the total population range from 50,000 to 300,000 people. Brendan Whyte, who has done an exhaustive study of the enclaves, estimates the population to be roughly 100,000 people. "A Poll Meaningless for Some Indians," *Statesman*, 1 October 1999, A1.

3. Whyte, *Waiting for the Esquimo.*

4. Nitish Sengupta, *History of the Bengali Speaking People* (New Delhi: UBS Publishers, 2001).

5. Pranab Kumar Bhattacharyya, *The Kingdom of Kamata Koch Behar in Historical Perspective* (Calcutta: Ratna Prakashan, 2000).

6. Whyte, *Waiting for the Esquimo.*

7. Sengupta, *Bengali Speaking People.*

8. Adrian Sever, *Documents and Speeches on the Indian Princely States* (Delhi: B. R. Publishing, 1985).

9. Bhattacharyya, *Kingdom of Kamata Koch Behar.*

10. Ram Prasad Vyas, *British Policy Towards Princely States of India* (Jodhpur: Twenty-First Century Publishers, 1990).

11. Whyte, *Waiting for the Esquimo.*

12. Ian Barrow, *Making History, Drawing Territory: British Mapping in India c. 1756–1905* (New Delhi: Oxford University Press, 2003); Nicholas Dirks, "Guiltless Spoliation, Picturesque Beauty, Colonial Knowledge, and Colin Mackenzie's Survey of India," in *Perceptions of South Asia's Visual Past,* ed. Catherine Asher and Thomas Metcalf (New Delhi: American Institute of Indian Studies, 1994), 211–32; Matthew Edney, *Mapping an Empire: The Geographical Construction of British India 1765–1843* (Chicago: University of Chicago Press, 1997); Patricia Seed, *Ceremonies of Possession in Europe's Conquest of the New World, 1492–1640* (New York: Cambridge University Press, 1995).

13. Whyte, *Waiting for the Esquimo.*

14. Whyte, *Waiting for the Esquimo.*

15. T. Y. Tan and Gayendra Kudaisya, *The Aftermath of Partition in South Asia* (New York: Routledge, 2000).

16. The 1947 partition created only two countries in the former British colonial holdings. Pakistan consisted of two halves that were not contiguous, and in 1971 the eastern half of Pakistan broke away to form the independent country of Bangladesh.

17. Total population figures from the 1941 census are as follows: Dinajpur (9.1% Tribal, 40.2% Hindu, 50.7% Muslim); Rangpur (0.9% Tribal, 27.8% Hindu, 71.3% Muslim); Jalpaiguri (26.4% Tribal; 50.6% Hindu, 23.0% Muslim); Cooch Behar (0.6% Tribal; 61.6% Hindu; 37.8% Muslim). Percentages of Muslims are given because that is the category that was used to make decisions. In the partition process "Tribal" groups, now more commonly called Adivasis [aboriginal], were often lumped in with Hindus, inflating their numbers. Many scholars have argued that even beyond the issue of categorizing Adivasis as Hindus, in the early twentieth century it was misleading to place people in Bengal into the binary categories of Hindu and Muslim at all because there were many syncretistic beliefs and practices that blurred these lines. Shiba Prasad Chatterjee, *The Partition of Bengal: A Geographical Study with Maps and Diagrams* (Calcutta: D. R. Mitra Press, 1947); Census of India (Delhi: Manager of Publications, 1941); Rafiuddin Ahmed, *The Bengal Muslims, 1871–1906: A Quest for Identity* (Delhi: Oxford University Press, 1981); Rafiuddin Ahmed, ed., *Understanding the Bengal Muslims: Interpretative Essays* (New Delhi: Oxford University Press, 2001); Reece Jones, "Whose Homeland? Territoriality and Religious Nationalism in Pre-Partition Bengal," *South Asia Research* 26, no. 2 (2006): 115–31; Reece Jones,

"Sacred Cows and Thumping Drums: Claiming Territory as 'Zones of Tradition' in British India," *Area* 39, no. 1 (2007): 55–65; Reece Jones, "Searching for the Greatest Bengali: The BBC and Shifting Identity Categories in South Asia," *National Identities* 10, no. 2 (2008): 149–65.

18. Sumit Ganguly, *Conflict Unending: India and Pakistan Tensions Since 1947* (New York: Columbia University Press, 2002).

19. Willem Van Schendel, "Stateless in South Asia: The Making of the India-Bangladesh Enclaves," *Journal of Asian Studies* 61, no. 1 (2002): 115–47; Willem Van Schendel, *The Bengal Borderlands: Beyond State and Nation in South Asia* (London: Anthem Press, 2005).

20. Ritu Menon and Kamla Bhasin, *Borders and Boundaries: Women in India's Partition* (New Brunswick, N.J.: Rutgers University Press, 1998); Ganguly, *Conflict Unending*.

21. Whyte, *Waiting for the Esquimo*; "Indian Enclave People Want to Become Bangladeshi," *Independent*, 28 April 2003, A1.

22. A union is the smallest level of local government in Bangladesh.

23. Whyte, *Waiting for the Esquimo*.

24. In this chapter, I use *home country* to refer to the country that the enclave officially belongs to and *host country* to refer to the country that surrounds the enclave.

25. Whyte, *Waiting for the Esquimo*.

26. Rounaq Jahan, *Pakistan: Failure in National Integration* (New York: Columbia University Press, 1972).

27. Ekram Kabir, *Border Fencing: A Major Irritant in Indo-Bangla Relations* (Dhaka: News Network, 2005).

28. The name of the corridor, *Tin Bigha*, comes from the size of the corridor. A *bigha* is a unit of land that is substantially smaller than an acre. *Tin* means "three" in Bengali.

29. Kabir, *Border Fencing*.

30. Whyte, *Waiting for the Esquimo*.

31. "India and Bangladesh; No Light For the Corridor," *Economist*, 13 June 1992, 33; "Hindus Protest Transfer," *Washington Post*, 27 June 1992, A14.

32. "Hindus Protest Transfer."

33. "Bangladesh, India Joint Team Assesses Possible Enclave Exchange," *Prothom Alo*, 30 May 2007.

34. Whyte, *Waiting for the Esquimo*.

35. "Indo-Bangla Officials Visit Enclaves," *Statesman*, 30 May 2007, A3.

36. "Landlocked People's Plight," *Statesman*, 13 April 2006, A1; "Bangladesh, India Joint Team."

37. Bangladesh is 83 percent Muslim. Census data for the enclaves are unavailable; however, enclave leaders estimated that the enclaves are 99 percent Muslim. During my time in the enclaves, with the help of enclave leaders, I was able to find only one Hindu family.

38. D. Sarkar, "Indian Chitmahals are a Haven for Terrorists," *Times of India*, 16 January 2001, A1. I visited the Dahala Khagrabari enclave and saw no evidence of insurgent camps.

Chapter 3: The Uzbekistan-Kyrgyzstan Boundary: Stalin's Cartography, Post-Soviet Geography

Research for this chapter was made possible by the Economic and Social Research Council for funding my doctoral research and by the British Academy for providing me with a Small Research Grant in 2004 to conduct postdoctoral work on "The impact of the Ferghana Valley boundary closures on border communities" (SG:38394). I would like to express my gratitude to both organizations. Some previously published material has been used here with the permission of the publishers. This material is drawn from two of my previous articles: "The Critical Geopolitics of the Uzbekistan-Kyrgyzstan Ferghana Valley Boundary Dispute, 1999–2000," *Political Geography* 23, no. 6 (2004): 731–64, copyright Elsevier; and "For Ethnography in Political Geography: Experiencing and Re-imagining Ferghana Valley Boundary Closures," *Political Geography* 25, no. 6 (2006): 622–40, copyright Elsevier.

1. Interviews, two anonymous inhabitants, Barak village, August 12, 2004. For a more detailed analysis of one such journey in another part of the Ferghana Valley borderlands, see Madeleine Reeves, "Travels in the Margins of the State: Everyday Geography in the Ferghana Valley Borderlands," in *Everyday Life in Central Asia: Past and Present*, ed. Jeff Sahadeo and Russell Zanca (Bloomington: Indiana University Press, 2007).

2. *Jer Talash.* Unpublished research document on border and land disputes in the Osh viloyat, prepared by an anonymous Kyrgyz journalist, 2000.

3. R. Legvold, "Great Power Stakes in Central Asia," in *Thinking Strategically: The Major Powers, Kazakhstan, and the Central Asian Security Nexus*, ed. R. Legvold (Cambridge, Mass.: American Academy of Arts and Sciences, 2003), 12.

4. Douglas Northrop, *Veiled Empire: Gender and Power in Stalinist Central Asia* (New York: Cornell University Press, 2004), 17.

5. John Agnew and Stuart Corbridge, *Mastering Space: Hegemony, Territory and International Political Economy* (London: Routledge, 1995).

6. Svat Soucek, *A History of Inner Asia* (Cambridge: Cambridge University Press, 2000), chapters 15 and 16.

7. Joseph Stalin, "'The Nation," in *Nationalism*, ed. John Hutchinson and Anthony Smith (Oxford: Oxford University Press, 1994), 20.

8. Paul Bergne, *The Birth of Tajikistan* (London: I. B. Tauris, 2007), 40–41.

9. Graham Smith, "The Soviet State and Nationalities Policy," in *The Nationalities Question in the Post-Soviet States*, ed. Graham Smith (London: Longman, 1996).

10. Soucek, *A History of Inner Asia*; Bergne, *The Birth of Tajikistan*.

11. Bergne, *The Birth of Tajikistan*.

12. Francine Hirsch, *Empire of Nations: Ethnographic Knowledge and the Making of the Soviet Union* (London: Cornell University Press, 2005), 184.

13. Hirsch, *Empire of Nations*.

14. Arslan Koichiev, "Ethno-Territorial Claims in the Ferghana Valley during the Process of National Delimitation, 1924–7," in *Central Asia: Aspects of Transition*, ed. Tom Everett-Heath (London: RoutledgeCurzon, 2003), 54.

15. Koichiev, *Ethno-Territorial Claims*, 55–56.

16. Koichiev, *Ethno-Territorial Claims*, 55.

17. Interview with Azim Karashev, member of bilateral Kyrgyzstan-Uzbekistan border demarcation committee, Osh, 6 December 2000.

18. Brendan Whyte, "Enclaves around the World," unpublished research paper.

19. *Jer Talash*.

20. Alexandre Bennigsen and Marie Broxup, *The Islamic Threat to the Soviet State* (London: Croom Helm, 1983), 132.

21. Martha Brill Olcott, "Ceremony and Substance: The Illusion of Unity in Central Asia," in *Central Asia and the World: Kazakhstan, Uzbekistan, Tajikistan, Kyrgyzstan, and Turkmenistan*, ed. Michael Mandelbaum (New York: Council on Foreign Relations, 1994), 39–41.

22. Ulugbek Babakulov, "Kyrgyz-Uzbek Border Tensions," *Reporting Central Asia* (London: Institute for War and Peace Reporting, 2002), http://www.iwpr.net (16 June 2002).

23. David Newman, "Boundaries," in *A Companion to Political Geography*, ed. John Agnew, Katharyne Mitchell, and Gerard Toal (Oxford: Blackwell, 2003).

24. Material from this and the subsequent section is drawn from the author's article "The Critical Geopolitics of the Uzbekistan-Kyrgyzstan Ferghana Valley Boundary Dispute, 1999–2000," *Political Geography* 23, no. 6 (2004): 731–64, and is used with permission.

25. For example, New York–based Human Rights Watch. See "Human Rights Abuse in Uzbekistan," Human Rights Watch, New York, September 2001.

26. "Katta fitnaning bir xalqasi," *Halq So'zi* 179, no. 2217 (9 September 1999), 1; "Narkobiznes—terrorning moliyaviy rahnamosi," *Halq So'zi* 190, no. 2228 (24 September 1999), 1.

27. Anssi Paasi, "Boundaries as Social Processes: Territoriality in the World of Flows," in *Boundaries, Territory and Postmodernity*, ed. David Newman (London: Frank Cass, 1999), 75.

28. Material from this and the subsequent section is drawn from the author's article "The Critical Geopolitics of the Uzbekistan-Kyrgyzstan Ferghana Valley Boundary Dispute, 1999–2000," *Political Geography* 23, no. 6 (2004): 731–64, and is used with permission.

29. Gearóid Ó Tuathail, *Critical Geopolitics: The Politics of Writing Global Space* (London: Routledge, 1996), 1.

30. A small break in the fence had been left to allow people to cross, but people told the author that the Uzbekistani soldiers had said that they were planning to demolish a lone house at this break and complete the barricade. Six years later, in April 2006, the threatened completion had still not materialized.

31. Names of individuals have been changed throughout.

32. Northrop, *Veiled Empire*, 48.

33. "Kyrgyz Opposition Holds 'Public Trial' of Leaders for Violent Clash," RFE/RL Newsline 12, no. 53, Part I (18 March 2008) (Prague: Radio Free Europe/Radio Liberty).

34. Necati Polat, *Boundary Issues in Central Asia* (Ardsley: Transnational Publishers, 2002), 51.

35. C. K. Alamanov, *Kyrgyztandyn Mamlakettik Chegarasynyn Kalyntanyshy (The Formation of Kyrgyzstan's State Boundary)* (Bishkek: Friedrich Ebert Siftung, 2005), 75.

36. "Kyrgyz Report Progress in Border Talks with Uzbekistan," RFE/RL Newsline 10, no. 219, Part I (29 November 2006) (Prague: Radio Free Europe/Radio Liberty).

37. Neville Maxwell, "How the Sino-Russian Boundary Conflict Was Finally Settled: From Nerchinsk 1689 to Vladivostok 2005 via Zhenbao Island 1969," *Critical Asian Studies* 39, no. 2 (2007): 229–53.

38. Polat, *Boundary Issues in Central Asia*.

39. Märta Johanson, *Self-Determination and Borders: The Obligation to Show Consideration for the Interests of Others* (Åbo, Finland: Åbo Akademi University Press, 2004).

Chapter 4: The Wakhan Corridor: Endgame of the Great Game

1. Francis E. Younghusband, *The Heart of a Continent: A Narrative of Travels in Manchuria, across the Gobi Desert, through the Himalayas, the Pamirs, and Chitral, 1884–1894* (London: John Murray, 1896).

2. M. Nazif Shahrani, *The Kirghiz and Wakhi of Afghanistan: Adaptation to Closed Frontiers and War* (Seattle: University of Washington Press, 1979); Younghusband, *The Heart of a Continent*.

3. John Wood, *A Journey to the Source of the River Oxus* (London: John Murray, 1872).

4. Two sources give the area of the Wakhan Corridor at roughly the same size. Johannes Humlum, in *La géographie de l'Afghanistan* (Copenhagen: Gyldendal, 1959), puts the number at roughly 10,000 square kilometers, and Anthony Fitzherbert and Charudutt Mishra, *Afghanistan Wakhan Mission Technical Report*, David Jensen, report coordination (Geneva: United Nations Environmental Programme, Food and Agriculture Organization, 2003), puts it at approximately 10,300 square kilometers. The only number that appears as a "definite" number is 8,936 square kilometers in Sabine Felmy and Hermann Kreutzmann's "Wakhan Woluswali in Badakhshan: Observations and Reflections from Afghanistan's Periphery," *Erdkunde* 58, no. 2 (2004): 97–117. The elevation information is taken from Felmy and Kreutzmann, "Wakhan Woluswali in Badakhshan"; Shahrani, *The Kirghiz and Wakhi*.

5. Humlum, *La géographie de l'Afghanistan*.

6. Shahrani, *The Kirghiz and Wakhi*; M. Aurel Stein, *Ruins of Desert Cathay: Personal Narrative of Explorations in Central Asia and Westernmost China* (London: Macmillan and Co., 1912).

7. Wakhan Development Project, "Wakhan District," 2002, http://www
.wakhandev.org.uk/ (23 February 2008).

8. M. Asimov, ed., *Tadzhikskaia Sovetskaia Sotsialisticheskaia Respublika* (Dushanbe: Glavnaia Nauchnaia Redaktsiia Tadzhikskoi Sovetskoi Entsiklopedii, 1984);
Felmy and Kreutzmann, "Wakhan Woluswali in Badakhshan"; Hermann Kreutzmann,
"Ethnic Minorities and Marginality in the Pamirian Knot: Survival of Wakhi and Kirghiz in a Harsh Environment and Global Contexts," *The Geographical Journal* 169, no.
3 (2003): 215–35; Wood, *A Journey to the Source.*

9. Shahrani, *The Kirghiz and Wakhi*; see also M. Aurel Stein, "Innermost Asia:
Its Geography as a Factor of History," *The Geographical Journal* 65, no. 5 (1925):
377–402.

10. Wood, *A Journey to the Source.*

11. M. Aurel Stein, *Innermost Asia: Detailed Report of Explorations in Central Asia,
Kan-su and Eastern Iran* (Oxford: Clarendon Press, 1928).

12. Kreutzmann, "Ethnic Minorities."

13. Stein, *Ruins of Desert Cathay*; Stein, "Innermost Asia."

14. B. Kushkaki, *Rahnuma-i Qataghan wa Badakhshan* (Kabul: Ministry of Defense
Press, 1923) as reported in Shahrani, *The Kirghiz and Wakhi.*

15. Shahrani, *The Kirghiz and Wakhi.*

16. Fitzherbert and Mishra, *Afghanistan Wakhan Mission.*

17. Lord George Curzon, *Frontiers* (Oxford: Clarendon Press, 1907). See also C.
Collin Davies, *The Problem of the North-West Frontier, 1890–1908* (Cambridge: Cam-
bridge University Press, 1932); David Dilks, *Curzon in India in Two Volumes* (New
York: Taplinger Publishing Company, 1969).

18. George de Lacy Evans, *On the Designs of Russia* (London: John Murray, 1828).

19. George de Lacy Evans, *On the Practicability of an Invasion of British India*
(London: J. M. Richardson, 1829); John MacNeill, *The Progress and Present Position
of Russia in the East* (London: RoutledgeCurzon, 2004 [1854]); Theo F. Rodenbough,
Afghanistan and the Anglo-Russian Dispute (New York: G. P. Putnam's Sons, 1885);
An Indian Officer, *Russia's March towards India* (London: Sampson Low, Marston &
Company, 1894); Léon Lecestre, ed., *Lettres Inédites de Napoléon Ier* (Paris: E. Plon,
Nourrit et Cie, Imprimeurs-Éditeurs, 1897); Christopher Herold, *Bonaparte in Egypt*
(New York: Harper & Row, 1962); Henry R. Huttenbach, "The Origins of Russian
Imperialism," in *Russian Imperialism from Ivan the Great to the Revolution*, ed. Taras
Hunczak (New Brunswick, N.J.: Rutgers University Press, 1974); M. E. Yapp, *Strate-
gies of British India: Britain, Iran and Afghanistan 1798–1850* (Oxford: Clarendon
Press, 1980); Milan Hauner, *India in Axis Strategy: Germany, Japan and Indian Na-
tionalists in the Second World War* (Stuttgart: Klett-Cotta, 1981).

20. Delmar Morgan, "Progress of Russian Explorations in Turkistan," *Proceedings
of the Royal Geographical Society of London* 14, no. 3 (1870): 229–35.

21. A term used by Indian Communists to describe British overreaction to Russian
advances both during the Great Game and during the Cold War. See K. S. Menon, *The
"Russian Bogey" and British Aggression in India and Beyond* (Calcutta: Eastern Trading
Company, 1957).

22. The Russians had "forward school" thinkers as well who advocated bold moves into Central Asia to ward off any incursions by the British north of the Amu Darya (that now forms part of the border between Afghanistan on one side and Tajikistan and Uzbekistan on the other). Although rarely officially sanctioned by the government in Saint Petersburg, successful reconnoitering or acquisition of new territory was quietly rewarded, while failure was met with official wrath to show the court and foreign diplomats that Russia did not have ulterior aims in Central Asia. See Peter Hopkirk, *The Great Game: The Struggle for Empire in Central Asia* (New York: Kodansha International, 1992).

23. Richard Isaac Bruce, *The Forward Policy and Its Results or Thirty-Five Years' Work amongst the Tribes on Our North-Western Frontier of India* (London: Longmans, Green, and Co., 1900); Davies, *The Problem*; Hopkirk, *The Great Game*; Gerald Morgan, *Anglo-Russian Rivalry in Central Asia: 1810–1895* (London: Frank Cass, 1981).

24. Davies, *The Problem*.

25. Curzon, *Frontiers*; Yapp, *Strategies*.

26. Edward Ingram, *In Defense of British India: Great Britain in the Middle East, 1775–1842* (London: Frank Cass, 1984).

27. Ingram, *In Defense*.

28. Karl E. Meyer and Shareen Blair Brysac, *Tournament of Shadows: The Great Game and the Race for Empire in Central Asia* (Washington, D.C.: Counterpoint, 1999).

29. Hopkirk, *The Great Game*.

30. Lady Elizabeth Butler immortalized this event in 1879 in the famous painting called "Remnants of an Army" now in the Tate Collection. After this debacle, the forts at Kandahar and Jalalabad were abandoned "by way of" Kabul, where they were successful in freeing the hostages and, as an act of vengeance against the city, decided to tear down the great covered bazaar of Kabul, a task that took them two days to complete before they retired from Afghanistan. See Hopkirk, *The Great Game*.

31. Speculation of routes of Russian invasion was rife in British India at this time. Two of the more highly ranked speculators were General Rodenbough, who conjectured four ways to enter India, all of which went through Herat (Rodenbough, *Afghanistan and the Anglo-Russian Dispute*), and Major-General C. M. MacGregor, who laid out "calmly and dispassionately" five ways in which Russia could invade India (C. M. MacGregor, *The Defence of India: A Strategical Study* [Simla: Government Central Branch Press, 1884]).

32. Louis E. Frechtling, "Anglo-Russian Rivalry in Eastern Turkistan, 1863–1881," *Journal of the Royal Central Asian Society* 26, no. 3 (1939): 471–89; MacGregor, *Defence of India*; Morgan, *Anglo-Russian Rivalry*.

33. H. W. C. Davis, *The Great Game in Asia (1800–1844)* (London: Humphrey Milford, Oxford University Press, 1927).

34. See, as major examples, H. Sutherland Edwards, *Russian Projects against India: From the Czar Peter to General Skobeleff* (London: Remington & Co. Publishers, 1885); Fernand Hue, *Les Russes et les Anglais dans L'Afghanistan* (Paris: E. Dentu, Libraire-Éditeur, 1885); MacGregor, *Defence of India*; George B. Malleson, *The Russo-Afghan*

Question and the Invasion of India (London: George Routledge and Sons, 1885); Charles Marvin, *Russia's Power of Seizing Herat, and Concentrating an Army There to Threaten India* (London: W. H. Allen & Co., 1884); Rodenbough, *Afghanistan and the Anglo-Russian Dispute*; Hugo Stumm, *Russia in Central Asia: Historical Sketch of Russia's Progress in the East up to 1873, and of the Incidents Which Led to the Campaign against Khiva* (London: Harrison and Sons, 1885); Arminius Vambéry, *The Coming Struggle for India: Being an Account of the Encroachments of Russia in Central Asia, and of the Difficulties Sure to Arise Therefrom to England* (London: Cassell & Company, 1885).

35. There were numerous headlines in the British press from mid-March through July 1885 (well documented in other publications) about the possibility of war between England and Russia. This situation was so serious that it rocked the London Stock Exchange and caused the stock market to become "greatly depressed and at one time there was a panic" ("Effect on the Money Markets," *New York Times*, 9 April 1885, 1). However, the American press was little different in its assessment of war, especially the *New York Times* as witnessed by the following: "Moving toward Herat," *New York Times*, 14 April 1885, 1; "The Impending Conflict," *New York Times*, 17 April 1885, 1; "A Conflict Inevitable," *New York Times*, 24 April 1885, 1. See also Rogers Platt Churchill, *The Anglo-Russian Convention of 1907* (Cedar Rapids: The Torch Press, 1939); Barbara Jelavich, *A Century of Russian Foreign Policy 1814–1914* (Philadelphia: Lippincott, 1964).

36. Francis Henry Skrine and Edward Denison Ross, *The Heart of Asia* (New York: Arno Press, 1973).

37. The part of the border between Afghanistan and Russia constituting the Amu Darya would also remain contentious into the Soviet period. Imperial Russia complained frequently that Afghanistan overused the tributary rivers of the Amu Darya that originated in Afghanistan (An Indian Officer, *Russia's March*), and the exact placement of the border caused tension between the Soviets and Afghans. However, in 1946 an agreement between the USSR and Afghanistan defined the boundary as the thalweg of the river. See William K. Fraser-Tytler, *Afghanistan: A Study of Political Developments in Central and Southern Asia* (London: Oxford University Press, 1967).

38. Edwards, *Russian Projects*; Hopkirk, *The Great Game*; Hue, *Les Russes et les Anglais*.

39. George Curzon, *The Pamirs and the Source of the Oxus* (London: Royal Geographic Society, 1896).

40. Francis E. Younghusband, *The Northern Frontier of Kashmir* (Delhi: Oriental Publishers, 1973 [1890]).

41. Percy Sykes, *A History of Afghanistan, Volume II* (London: Macmillan & Co., 1940); Asghar H. Bilgrami, *Afghanistan and British India: 1793–1907* (New Delhi: Sterling Publishers, 1972); Hopkirk, *The Great Game*; Anthony Verrier, *Francis Younghusband and the Great Game* (London: Jonathan Cape, 1991); Younghusband, *The Heart of a Continent*.

42. William Barton, *India's North-West Frontier* (London: John Murray, 1939).

43. H. C. Thomson, *The Chitral Campaign: A Narrative of Events in Chitral, Swat, and Bajour* (London: William Heinemann, 1895); Edward F. Knight, *Where Three*

Empires Meet: A Narrative of Recent Travel in Kashmir, Western Tibet, Gilgit, and the Adjoining Countries (London: Longmans, Green, and Co., 1897).

44. Younghusband, *The Northern Frontier.*

45. Actually, Chitral was to remain worrisome for some time. In 1898, while on a "shooting expedition" (often a cover for private citizens to do covert reconnaissance) in the Pamirs, Captain Ralph Cobbold of the 60th Rifles learned of "very complete plans" to take Chitral if the British left, apparently showing that the Russians viewed the newly drawn border as only temporary. See Hopkirk, *The Great Game*; Thomson, *The Chitral Campaign.*

46. For Rodenbough (*Afghanistan and the Anglo-Russian Dispute*) it was Herat, and for de Lacy Evans (*On the Practicability*) it was Kabul; however, the call for action came from "An Indian Officer" (*Russia's March*).

47. Verrier, *Francis Younghusband.*

48. William Habberton, *Anglo-Russian Relations concerning Afghanistan 1837–1907* (Urbana: University of Illinois, 1937); Pavel N. Luknitsky, *Soviet Tajikistan* (Moscow: Foreign Languages Publishing House, 1954); Lawrence Krader, *Peoples of Central Asia* (Bloomington: Indiana University Publications, 1966); René Grousset, *The Empire of the Steppes: A History of Central Asia* (New Brunswick, N.J.: Rutgers University Press, 1970); Curzon, *The Pamirs*; Stein, *Innermost Asia*; Wood, *A Journey to the Source.*

49. "Agreement between the Governments of Great Britain and Russia with Regard to the Spheres of Influence of the Two Countries in the Region of the Pamirs" as published in Habberton, *Anglo-Russian Relations.*

50. Churchill, *The Anglo-Russian Convention*; Davies, *The Problem.*

51. Geoffrey Wheeler, *The Modern History of Soviet Central Asia* (New York: Praeger, 1964).

52. Jelavich, *A Century of Russian Foreign Policy.*

53. Fraser-Tytler, *Afghanistan*; Morgan, *Anglo-Russian Rivalry.*

54. Sykes, *A History of Afghanistan.*

55. Churchill, *The Anglo-Russian Convention*; Louis Dupree, *Afghanistan* (Oxford: Oxford University Press, 1997).

56. Dupree, *Afghanistan.*

57. Felmy and Kreutzmann, "Wakhan Woluswali in Badakhshan."

58. Curzon, *Frontiers*; Dupree, *Afghanistan*; Morgan, *Anglo-Russian Rivalry.*

59. Churchill, *The Anglo-Russian Convention*; Fraser-Tytler, *Afghanistan.*

60. Krader, *Peoples of Central Asia*; Luknitsky, *Soviet Tajikistan.*

61. Skrine and Ross, *The Heart of Asia.*

62. Dupree, *Afghanistan*; Fraser-Tytler, *Afghanistan*; Shahrani, *The Kirghiz and Wakhi.*

63. Shahrani, *The Kirghiz and Wakhi*; M. Nazif Shahrani, "Afghanistan's Kirghiz in Turkey," *Cultural Survival Quarterly* 8, no. 1 (1984): 31–34; Felmy and Kreutzmann, "Wakhan Woluswali in Badakhshan"; Kreutzmann, "Ethnic Minorities;" Hermann Kreutzmann, "The Significance of Geopolitical Issues for Development of Mountainous Areas of Central Asia" (paper presented at the Strategies for Development and Food Security in Mountainous Areas of Central Asia International Workshop, 2005), http://www .akdn.org/publications/2005_akf_mountains_paper2_english.pdf (9 February 2008).

64. Olivier Roy, "Is the Conflict in Tajikistan a Model for Conflicts throughout Central Asia?" in *Tajikistan: The Trials of Independence*, ed. Mohammad-Reza Djalili, Frédéric Grare, and Shirin Akiner (New York: St. Martin's Press, 1997); Shahrbanou Tadjbakhsh, "Causes and Consequences of the Civil War," *Central Asia Monitor* no. 1 (1993): 10–14; Julien Thöni, *The Tajik Conflict: The Dialectic between Internal Fragmentation and External Vulnerability, 1991–1994* (Geneva: Programme for Strategic and International Security Studies, Occasional Paper No. 3, 1994); Astrid von Borcke, *Der tadschikische Bürgerkrieg: Lokale Tragödie oder geopolitische Herausforderung?* (Köln: Bundesinstitut für ostwissenschaftliche und internatonale Studien, 1995).

65. William C. Rowe, *On the Edge of Empires: The Hisor Valley of Tajikistan* (PhD dissertation, University of Texas at Austin, 2002).

66. Nick Coleman, "Tajik Leader, Aga Khan Open Afghanistan Bridge," *Agence France-Presse* 31 October 2006, as reported in *Ismaili Mail*, http://ismailimail.wordpress.com/2006/10/31/tajik-leader-aga-khan-open-afghanistan-bridge/ (8 January 2008).

67. Felmy and Kreutzmann, "Wakhan Woluswali in Badakhshan."

68. Felmy and Kreutzmann, "Wakhan Woluswali in Badakhshan."

69. Felmy and Kreutzmann, "Wakhan Woluswali in Badakhshan."

70. Wakhan Development Project, "Wakhan District."

71. Kreutzmann, "Ethnic Minorities"; Wakhan Development Project, "Wakhan District."

72. Henk van Houtum and Ton van Naerssen, "Bordering, Ordering, and Othering," *Tijdschrift voor Economische en Sociale Geografie* 93, no. 2 (2002): 125–36; Allen Buchanan and Margaret Moore, *States, Nations, and Borders: The Ethics of Making Boundaries* (Cambridge: Cambridge University Press, 2003); Thomas Lunden, *On the Boundary: About Humans at the End of Territory* (Stockholm: Södertörns Högskola, 2004); Henk van Houtum, Olivier Kramsch, and Wolfgang Zierhofer, *B/ordering Space* (Aldershot: Ashgate, 2005); David Newman, "The Lines That Continue to Separate Us: Borders in Our 'Borderless' World," *Progress in Human Geography* 30, no. 2 (2006): 143–61.

73. Daphne Berdahl, *Where the World Ended: Re-Unification and Identity in the German Borderland* (Berkeley: University of California Press, 1999); Felmy and Kreutzmann, "Wakhan Woluswali in Badakhshan"; Newman, "The Lines."

Chapter 5: The Caprivi Strip of Namibia: Shifting Sovereignty and the Negotiation of Boundaries

1. *CIA World Factbook*, https://www.cia.gov/library/publications/the-world-factbook/geos/wa.html (11 March 2008).

2. Maria Fisch, *The Caprivi Strip during the German Colonial Period, 1890–1914 [with a Chapter on the Boundary Dispute up to the Present]* (Windhoek: Out of Africa Publishers, 1999), 51.

3. Raymond G. Gordon Jr., ed., *Ethnologue: Languages of the World*, 15th ed. (Dallas, Tex.: SIL International, 2005), http://www.ethnologue.com/ (11 March 2008).

4. Pierre Englebert, *Should I Stay or Should I Go? Compliance and Defiance in National Integration in Barotseland and Casamance*, unpublished manuscript, December

2004, http://www.politics.pomona.edu/penglebert/Compliance%20and%20Defiance
-afrika%20spectrum.pdf, 50 (11 March 2008).

5. Anglo-Portuguese Treaty (Article I), 1886.

6. Anglo-German Treaty, 1890.

7. See Horst Drechsler, *Let Us Die Fighting: The Struggle of the Herero and Nama
against German Imperialism (1884–1915)* (London: Zed Press, 1980).

8. Fisch, *The Caprivi Strip*, 15.

9. Fisch, *The Caprivi Strip*, 16–17.

10. The settlement was named in honor of Bruno von Schuckmann, governor of
German South-West Africa and the one who had appointed Streitwolf as the first
administrator of the Caprivi Strip.

11. Fisch, *The Caprivi Strip*, 140–143.

12. Fisch, *The Caprivi Strip*, 141.

13. *The Essential Facts about the League of Nations*, Secretariat, Information Section
(Geneva, 1938).

14. Legal Assistance Centre, *NAMLEX: Index to the Laws of Namibia, 2004 Update*,
(Windhoek), 1–4, http://www.lac.org.na/Pdf/namlex2004.pdf (11 March 2008).

15. SA Proclamations 12 of 1922 and 23 of 1922.

16. SA Proclamation 196 of 1929.

17. SA Eastern Caprivi Zipfel Administration Proclamation 26 of 1929.

18. SA Eastern Caprivi Zipfel Administration Proclamation 147 of 1939.

19. Fisch, *The Caprivi Strip*, 14.

20. South-West Africa Constitution Amendment Act 95 of 1977.

21. The conflict in Angola finally ended in 2002 with the death of Savimbi in an
ambush, bringing peace to the Angolan frontier of the Caprivi Strip.

22. Maria Fisch, *The Secessionist Movement in the Caprivi: A Historical Perspective*
(Windhoek: Namibia Scientific Society, 1999), 18.

23. Fisch, *The Secessionist Movement*, 15.

24. Fisch, *The Secessionist Movement*, 22.

25. The Zambian government had defeated a separatist movement in neighboring
Barotseland by 1997, eliminating one possible source of external support. The death
of Savimbi in 2002 ended another potential ally.

26. Bridget Weidlich, "Caprivi Strip Proclaimed Park," *The Namibian* (Windhoek), 23 November 2007, http://allafrica.com/stories/printable/200711230655.html
(11 March 2008).

Chapter 6: The Renaissance of a Border That Never Died:
The Green Line between Israel and the West Bank

1. Previous studies of the Green Line, on which part of this chapter is based,
include: D. Newman, "The Functional Presence of an 'Erased' Boundary: The Re-
emergence of the 'Green Line,'" in *World Boundaries: The Middle East and North
Africa*, ed. C. H. Schofield and R. N. Schofield (London: Routledge, 1993), 71–98; D.
Newman, *Boundaries in Flux: The Green Line Boundary between Israel and the West*

Bank—*Past, Present and Future*, Monograph Series, *Boundary and Territory Briefings*, no. 7, International Boundaries Research Unit (Durham, U.K.: University of Durham, 1995); M. Brawer, "The Making of an Israeli-Palestinian Boundary," in *The Razor's Edge: International Boundaries and Political Geography*, ed. C. Schofield, D. Newman, A. Drysdale, and J. Brown (London: Kluwer Law International, 2002), 473–92; G. Falah, "The Green Line Revisited: October 2000," in *The Razor's Edge: International Boundaries and Political Geography*, ed. C. Schofield, D. Newman, A. Drysdale, and J. Brown (London: Kluwer Law International, 2002), 493–512.

2. For an overview of the evolution of Israel's borders, see M. Brawer, *The Borders of Israel* (in Hebrew) (Yavneh Press, 1987); G. Biger, *The Boundaries of Modern Palestine, 1840–1947* (London: Routledge, 2004); G. Biger, "The Boundaries of Israel—Palestine, Past, Present and Future: A Critical Geographical View," *Israel Studies* 13, no. 1 (2008): 68–93.

3. For a cartographic overview of the different partition proposals, see M. Gilbert, *Atlas of the Arab-Israeli Conflict* (London: Routledge, 2002).

4. Report of the UN Special Commission on Palestine—UNSCOP—1947.

5. Across from the Jordanian port of Aqaba, the Israeli port and resort town of Elat has evolved during the past sixty years, while the Egyptian resort of Taba is directly south of Elat in what has become a triborder area. In addition, Saudi Arabia lies less than fifteen kilometers to the south on the Jordanian side of the peninsula.

6. For a thorough analysis of the origins of the Palestinian refugee problem, see B. Morris, *The Birth of the Palestinian Refugee Problem, 1947–1949* (Cambridge: Cambridge University Press, 1989); B. Morris, *The Birth of the Palestinian Refugee Problem Revisited* (Cambridge: Cambridge University Press, 2004).

7. Professor Moshe Brawer had carried out Arab village surveys in 1947–1948. Following the opening of the border in 1967, he returned to carry out new social and economic surveys. His findings are discussed in Brawer, *The Borders of Israel.*

8. For a fascinating account of the problems encountered in implementing the Green Line, see Brawer, *The Borders of Israel.*

9. B. Morris, *Israel's Border Wars 1949–1956: Arab Infiltration, Israeli Retaliation, and the Countdown to the Suez War* (Oxford: Clarendon Press, 1993).

10. Ghazi Falah, "Dynamics and Patterns of the Shrinking of Arab Lands in Palestine," *Political Geography* 22, no. 2 (2003): 179–209.

11. A. Kellerman, *Society and Settlement: Jewish Land of Israel in the Twentieth Century* (Albany: State University of New York Press, 1993); B. Kimmerling, *Zionism and Territory* (Berkeley: University of California Press, 1983); D. Newman, "The Role of Civilian and Military Presence as Strategies of Territorial Control: The Arab-Israel Conflict," *Political Geography Quarterly* 8, no. 3 (1989): 215–27.

12. J. Portugali, "Nomad Labour: Theory and Practice in the Israeli-Palestinian Case," *Transactions of the Institute of British Geographers* 14, no. 2 (1989): 207–20; M. Semyonov and N. Lewin-Epstein, *Hewers of Wood and Drawers of Water: Noncitizen Arabs in the Israeli Labor Market* (Ithaca, N.Y.: Cornell University Press, 1987).

13. See D. Newman, "The Territorial Politics of Exurbanisation: Reflections on Thirty Years of Jewish Settlement in the West Bank," *Israel Affairs* 3, no. 1 (1996): 61–85; D. Newman, "From 'hitnachalut' to 'hitnatkut': The Impact of Gush Emunim and

the Settlement Movement on Israeli Society," *Israel Studies* 10, no. 3 (2005): 192–224; E. Weizman, *Hollow Land: Israel's Architecture of Occupation* (London: Verso Publishers, 2007); I. Zertal and A. Eldar, *Lords of the Land: The War over Israel's Settlements in the Occupied Territories, 1967–2007* (New York: Nation Books, 2007).

14. D. Newman, "A Green Line in the Sand," *New York Times,* 9 January 2007, 17.

15. It has been argued that this constitutes de facto annexation, regardless of whether any attempt at de jure changes in the status of the region have been attempted by the government.

16. Newman, "The Functional Presence."

17. Shalom Reichman, "Policy Reduces the World to Essentials: A Reflection on the Jewish Settlement Process in the West Bank since 1967," in *Planning in Turbulence,* ed. D. Morley and A. Shachar (Jerusalem: Magnes Press, 1987); David Newman, "Colonization as Suburbanization: The Politics of the Land Market at the Frontier," in *City of Collision,* ed. P. Misselwitz et al. (Basel, Switzerland: Birkhäuser Publishers, 2006), 113–20.

18. Newman, "Colonization as Suburbanization."

19. Of the entire length of the separation barrier, only 7 percent is wall, while the rest is fence. Nevertheless, the media images of the barrier have tended to focus on the grotesqueness of the wall sections and their impact on the local residents.

20. There have been many analyses of the separation barrier/security fence-wall since its construction was started. For a diverse range of analyses, critiques, and rationales, see I. Kershner, *Barrier: The Seam of the Israeli-Palestinian Conflict* (New York: Palgrave Macmillan, 2005); D. Makovsky, *A Defensible Fence: Fighting Terror and Enabling a Two State Solution* (Washington, D.C.: Washington Institute for Near East Policy, 2004); Palestinian Environmental NGOs Network (PENGON), ed., *The Wall in Palestine: Facts, Testimonies, Analysis and Call to Action* (Jerusalem: PENGON, 2003); Israel Information Center, *Saving Lives: Israel's Security Fence* (Jerusalem: Ministry of Foreign Affairs, 2003).

21. International Court of Justice, Legal Consequences of the Construction of a Wall in the Occupied Palestinian Territory, 9 July 2004; Israel Supreme Court, Beit Sourik Village Council vs. 1. The Government of Israel: 2. Commander of the IDF Forces in the West Bank [February 29, 2004; March 11, 2004; March 17, 2004; March 31, 2004; April 16, 2004; April 21, 2004; May 2, 2004]; Israel High Court Ruling Docket H.C.J. 7957/04—International Legality of the Security Fence and Sections near Alfei Menashe—September 15, 2005.

22. This has raised the specter of Israeli neocolonialism following a withdrawal from the West Bank and is viewed with suspicion and animosity on the part of the Palestinians.

23. The Oslo Accords are categorical in their statement that the West Bank and Gaza Strip are part of a single problem, and hence, a single solution. The validity of this has been brought into question with the rise to power of Hamas in the Gaza Strip and the resulting tensions between Hamas and the Palestinian Authority (Fatah).

24. In the 1990s, there had been a proposal by a Japanese consortium to construct an extraterritorial bridge linking the two areas, while there have also been proposals

for a sunken road that would not be directly controlled by Israel, as well as an improved rail link extending southward to the Gaza Strip from its present terminus in the Israeli city of Ashkelon.

25. G. Falah and D. Newman, "The Spatial Manifestation of Threat: Israelis and Palestinians Seek a 'Good' Border," *Political Geography* 14, no. 8 (1995): 689–706; D. Newman, "Creating the Fences of Territorial Separation: The Discourse of Israeli-Palestinian Conflict Resolution," *Geopolitics and International Boundaries* 2, no. 2 (1998): 1–35; D. Newman, "The Geopolitics of Peacemaking in Israel-Palestine," *Political Geography* 21, no. 5 (2002): 629–46.

26. See Herzliyah Conference, *Demarcating an Israel-Palestine Boundary: Principles and Professional Considerations* (Working Group of Geographers, EUROBorder Conf Project, January 2006).

27. J. McHugo, "Resolution 242: A Legal Reappraisal of the Right Wing Israeli Interpretation of the Withdrawal Phrase with Reference to the Conflict between Israel and the Palestinians," *ICLQ* 51 (2002): 851–82.

28. Israel Palestine Center for Research and Information, "A Political Statement for Israeli-Palestinian Peace," http://www.walkthegreenline.org/program_political _statment.html (6 August 2009).

Chapter 7: Locating Kurdistan: Contextualizing the Region's Ambiguous Boundaries

1. David Newman, "The Lines That Continue to Separate Us: Borders in Our 'Borderless' World," *Progress in Human Geography* 30, no. 2 (2006), 146. There are some areas, particularly in Iraqi Kurdistan, where signposts declare the entrance into Kurdistan.

2. Hakan Özoglu, *Kurdish Notables and the Ottoman State: Evolving Identities, Competing Loyalties, and Shifting Boundaries* (Albany: State University of New York, 2004), 1.

3. Maria O'Shea, "Between the Map and the Reality: Some Fundamental Myths of Kurdish Nationalism," *Peuples Mediterraneens* no. 68–69 (1994): 165–83; Mehrdad Izady, *A Concise Handbook: The Kurds* (Washington, D.C.: Taylor & Francis, 1992), 3.

4. Izady, *The Kurds*, 1; Denise Natali, *The Kurds and the State: Evolving National Identity in Iraq, Turkey, and Iran* (Syracuse, N.Y.: Syracuse University Press, 2005), xvii.

5. There are many dialects of Kurdish, including Kurmanji, which is common in northern Iraq and southeastern Turkey; and Sorani, which is common in eastern Iraq. Defining what is meant by the term *Kurd* is a difficult task. The politics of identity of Kurds and their internal differences have been the subject of several books and articles but is beyond the scope of this chapter. See, for example: Izady, *The Kurds*; David McDowall, *A Modern History of the Kurds* (New York: I. B. Tauris, 2000).

6. Izady, *The Kurds*, 34.

7. Izady, *The Kurds*, 23–49. Turkish and Mongolian raiders also swept through the region around 1250.

8. Natali, *Kurds and State*, 1.

9. Kendal Nezan, "The Kurds under the Ottoman Empire," in *A People without a Country*, ed. Gerard Chaliand (New York: Olive Branch Publishing, 1993), 14–15; McDowall, *Modern History of the Kurds*, 25.

10. Izady, *The Kurds*, 52.

11. The origin and time in which Kurdish nationalism grew is debated. Some claim the 1847 revolt lead by Bedirhan Pasha and/or the Shaykh Ubaydallah movement of 1880 was the origin, for example, Gerard Chaliand, *The Kurdish Tragedy* (London: Zed Books, 1992). Others claim Kurdish nationalism did not emerge until after World War I and the demise of the Ottoman Empire, for example, Hakan Özoglu, "'Nationalism' and Kurdish Notables in the Late Ottoman Republican Era," *International Journal of Middle East Studies* 33, no. 3 (2001): 393.

12. McDowall, *Modern History of the Kurds*, 53; David McDowall, "The Kurdish Question: A Historical Review," in *The Kurds: A Contemporary Overview*, ed. Philip Kreyenbroek and Stephan Sperl (New York: Routledge, 1992), 16.

13. Izady, *The Kurds*, 56.

14. Margaret MacMillan, *Peacemakers: The Paris Peace Conference of 1919 and Its Attempt to End War* (London: John Murray, 2001), 455–56.

15. Maria O'Shea, *Trapped between the Map and Reality* (New York: Routledge, 2004), 143.

16. Numerous Kurdish leaders and emirs attempted to become leader of a free Kurdistan, but none was entirely supported. Two of the more notable Kurdish organizations include the Society for the Advancement (Ascension) of Kurdistan, formed in 1918; and the Committee for the Independence of Kurdistan, formed in Cairo in 1919. Özoglu, "'Nationalism' and Kurdish Notables," 393; McDowall, *Modern History of the Kurds*, 121–25; Saad Eskander, "Britain's Policy in Southern Kurdistan: The Formation and the Termination of the First Kurdish Government, 1918–1919," *British Journal of Middle Eastern Studies* 27, no. 2 (2000): 142; Mordechai Nisan, *Minorities in the Middle East: A History of Struggle and Self Expression* (Jefferson, N.C.: McFarland & Company, 1991).

17. Özoglu, *Kurdish Notables*, 38–42.

18. Sherif Pasha, "Memorandum on the Claims of the Kurdish People, Paris, March 22, 1919," *The International Journal of Kurdish Studies* 15, no. 1–2 (2001): 136.

19. Sherif Pasha, "Claims of the Kurdish People," 131.

20. Sherif Pasha excluded Lake Van because this region was also claimed by the Armenian delegation, led by Bogos Nubar Pasha (see Özoglu, *Kurdish Notables*, 39; Kendal, "Kurds under the Ottoman Empire," 33). Though there was much contention between the two groups over the same territory, not to mention the Kurds' role in the Armenian genocide, the Kurds and Armenians compromised during postwar negotiations, and each agreed to recognize the other's claims. See Sherif Pasha, "Claims of the Kurdish People"; Paul Helmreich, *From Paris to Sèvres: The Partition of the Ottoman Empire at the Peace Conference of 1919–1920* (Columbus: Ohio State University Press, 1974), 205.

21. Özoglu, *Kurdish Notables*, 95. In his March 20, 1920, demands submitted to Richard Webb, the British high commissioner in Istanbul, Emin wrote that "Kurdish lands consist of the Ottoman vilayets of Diyarbakir, Harput, Bitlis, Van and Mosul and the sanjak of Urfa" (as in Özoglu, *Kurdish Notables*, 40).

22. O'Shea, *Between the Map and Reality*, 139.

23. Özoglu, *Kurdish Notables*, 39.

24. Anatolia is the peninsula of Turkey in Asia also referred to as Asia Minor. It is bounded by the Black Sea to its north and the Mediterranean to its south and east.

25. Özoglu, "'Nationalism' and Kurdish Notables," 2. In addition to granting part of Anatolia to the Kurds, the Treaty of Sèvres also granted portions of the peninsula to Italy, France, and Greece.

26. Martin Van Bruinessen, *Agha, Shaikh, and State: The Social and Political Structures of Kurdistan* (London: Zed Books, 1992), 25–33; MacMillan, *Peacemakers*, 465.

27. Robert Olson, *The Emergence of Kurdish Nationalism and the Sheikh Said Rebellion, 1880–1925* (Austin: University of Texas Press, 1989); Van Bruinessen, *Agha, Shaikh, and State*. This rebellion was at least in part invoked as a reaction to the secularizing policies of the new Turkish leadership.

28. McDowall, "Kurdish Question," 18.

29. Van Bruinessen, *Agha, Shaikh, and State*, 28–29.

30. Carole O'Leary, "The Kurds of Iraq: Recent History, Future Prospects," *Middle East Review of International Affairs* 6, no. 4 (2002): 18.

31. Though politically divided, autonomous Iraqi Kurdistan was peaceful until May 1994, when disputes between the PUK and the KDP erupted into a brief civil war. There has also been conflict between Iraqi Kurds and the PKK of Turkey.

32. Parag Khanna, "Waving Goodbye to Hegemony," *New York Times Magazine*, section MM, January 27, 2008, 34.

33. Deborah J. Gerner and Jillian Schwedler, "Trends and Prospects," in *Understanding the Contemporary Middle East*, ed. Deborah J. Gerner and Jillian Schwedler (Boulder, Colo.: Lynne Reinner Publishers, 1992), 432; Jeffrey Goldberg, "After Iraq," *The Atlantic* (January/February 2008): 69–79; Ralph Peters, "Blood Borders: How a Better Middle East Would Look," *Armed Forces Journal* (June 2006): 1–3.

34. Michael Gunter, "A De Facto Kurdish State in Northern Iraq," *Third World Quarterly* 14, no. 2 (1993): 300; Goldberg, "After Iraq"; Peters, "Blood Borders."

35. For detailed discussion of foreign policies in the region regarding Kurdistan, see Robert Olson, ed., *The Kurdish National Movement in the 1990s: Its Impact on Turkey and the Middle East* (Lexington, Ky.: University Press of Kentucky, 1996).

36. O'Shea, *Between the Map and Reality*, 5.

37. O'Shea, *Between the Map and Reality*, 165. For some cartographic examples, see F. R. Maunsell, "Kurdistan," *The Geographical Journal* 3, no. 2 (1894): 81–92. See Izady, *The Kurds*, 3–6, for details on early twentieth-century mapping of the region by British, Russians, Turks, and Persians. See Mark Sykes, "The Kurdish Tribes of the Ottoman Empire," *The Journal of the Royal Anthropological Institute of Great Britain and Ireland* 38 (1908): 451–86 for details on the "approximate distribution of Kurdish Tribes of the Ottoman Empire."

38. *National Geographic Atlas of the Middle East* (Washington, D.C.: National Geographic Society, 2003).

39. For example, see Karen Culcasi, "Cartographically Constructing Kurdistan within Geopolitical and Orientalist Discourses," *Political Geography* 25, no. 6 (2006): 680–706; *Goodes World Atlas*, 2nd ed. (Skokie, Ill.: Rand McNally, 2005).

40. O'Shea, *Between the Map and Reality*, 8.

41. O'Shea, "Between the Map and the Reality," 180.

42. See O'Shea, *Between the Map and Reality*, 165–232, for further discussion on maps made by various Kurdish groups.

43. Özoglu, *Kurdish Notables*, 1; Mary Ann Tétreault, "International Relations," in *Understanding the Contemporary Middle East*, ed. Deborah J. Gerner and Jillian Schwedler (Boulder, Colo.: Lynne Reinner Publishers, 2004), 150; O'Shea, *Between the Map and Reality*, ix; Abbas Vali, "The Kurds and their 'Others': Fragmented Identity and Fragmented Politics," *Comparative Studies of South Asia, Africa and the Middle East* 18, no. 2 (1998): 82–95.

44. Gunter, *Kurdish Predicament in Iraq*, 134. Gunter, "A De Facto Kurdish State," 309–12.

45. Carl Dahlman, "The Political Geography of Kurdistan," *Eurasian Geography and Economics* 43, no. 4 (2002): 273.

46. Gunter, "A De Facto Kurdish State," 304.

Chapter 8: Russia's Kaliningrad Exclave: Discontinuity as a Threat to Sovereignty

1. Evgeny Vinokurov, *The Theory of Exclaves* (Lanham, Md.: Lexington Books, 2007), 3.

2. See Norman Davies, *God's Playground: A History of Poland*, Vol. 1 (New York: Columbia University Press, 1982); Richard Krickus, *The Kaliningrad Question* (Lanham, Md.: Rowman & Littlefield, 2002).

3. See Norman Davies, *God's Playground: A History of Poland*, Vol. II (New York: Columbia University Press, 1982), 3–162; Christopher Clark, *Iron Kingdom: The Rise and Fall of Prussia, 1600–1947* (Cambridge, Mass.: Belknap Press of Harvard University Press, 2006).

4. Davies, *God's Playground*, Vol. II, 378.

5. Woodrow Wilson, "Address to a Joint Session of Congress on the Conditions of Peace, January 8th, 1918," *The American Presidency Project*, http://www.presidency.ucsb.edu/ws/index.php?pid=65405 (1 June 2007).

6. See Norman J. G. Pounds, "A Free and Secure Access to the Sea," *Annals of the Association of American Geographers* 49, no. 3 (September 1959): 256–68.

7. Davies, *God's Playground*, Vol. II, 378–392; Anna Cienciala, "The Battle of Danzig and the Polish Corridor at the Paris Peace Conference of 1919," in *The Reconstruction of Poland, 1914–1923*, ed. Paul Latawski (New York: St. Martin's, 1992),

71–94; George White, *Nation, State, and Territory: Origins, Evolutions, and Relationships*, Vol. I (Lanham, Md.: Rowman & Littlefield, 2004), 204–28.

8. Richard Blanke, *Orphans of Versailles: The Germans in Western Poland 1918–1939* (Lexington: University Press of Kentucky, 1993), 18.

9. Blanke, *Orphans*, 244.

10. Blanke, *Orphans*, 23.

11. Sally Marks, *The Illusion of Peace: International Relations in Europe, 1918–1933* (New York: Palgrave Macmillan, 2003), 13.

12. Hans Mommsen, *The Rise and Fall of Weimar Democracy* (Chapel Hill: University of North Carolina Press, 1996), 104.

13. For examples in English, see A. Proeller, *The Polish Corridor, East Prussia and the Peace* (London: Williams and Norgate, 1929); Werner Fuchs and Robert Sherwood Allan, *Poland's Policy of Expansion as Revealed by Polish Testimonies* (Berlin: Deutscher Ostmarken-Verein, 1932); Alex Schmidt, *The Preposterous Corridor: Polish Testimony against Germany's Mutilation* (Berlin: Edwin Runge, 1933).

14. Johann Fürst, *Der Widersinn des polnischen Korridors* (Berlin: Deutsche Rundschau, 1926); Schmidt, *The Preposterous Corridor*.

15. Arnold Zelle, *50 Korridorthesen: Abrechnung mit Polen* (Berlin: Volk und Reich, 1939); Friedrich Heiss, *Deutschland und der Korridor* (Berlin: Volk und Reich, 1939).

16. Davies, *God's Playground*, Vol. II, 404.

17. Robert Machray, *East Prussia: Menace to Poland and Peace* (Chicago: American Polish Council, 1943), 45. For other examples in English, see Stanislaw Slawski, *Poland's Access to the Sea and the Claims of East Prussia* (London: Eyre and Spottiswoode, 1925); Casimir Smogorzewski, *Poland, Germany and the Corridor* (London: Williams & Norgate, 1930); Henry Strasburger, *German Designs on Pomerania: An Analysis of Germany's Revisionistic Policy* (Toruń, Poland: Baltic Institute, 1933); Stanisław Srokowski, *East Prussia* (Toruń, Poland: Baltic Institute, 1934).

18. Roman Lutman, *The Truth about the "Corridor": Polish Pomerania: Ten Points* (Toruń, Poland: Baltic Institute, 1933), 34; *Zehn Thesen ueber Pommerellen* (Toruń, Poland: Baltic Institute, 1933), 20.

19. For example, Foreign Policy Service, "German-Polish Relations: Danzig–the Polish 'Corridor'–East Prussia–Upper Silesia," *Information Service* 3, no. 12 (August 1927): 169–84; Shepard Stone, "German-Polish Disputes: Danzig, the Polish Corridor and East Prussia," *Foreign Policy Reports* 9, no. 9 (July 1933): 94–104.

20. Robert Donald, *The Polish Corridor and the Consequences* (London: Thornton Butterworth, 1929), 269; E. W. Polson Newman, *Britain and the Baltic* (London: Methuen, 1930), 216; Emil Lengyel, *The Cauldron Boils* (London: Dial Press, 1932), 3.

21. George Bilainkin, *Within Two Years! Being the Narrative of a Journey to the Polish Corridor, the Tinder Box of Europe* (London: Marston, 1934); H. G. Wells, *The Shape of Things to Come: The Ultimate Revolution* (London: Hutchinson, 1933), 104–7.

22. Davies, *God's Playground*, Vol. II, 431–34; Richard Evans, *The Third Reich in Power* (New York: Penguin Press, 2005), 687–705.

23. Henryk Bagiński, *Poland's Freedom of the Sea*, 4th ed. (Kirkcaldy, U.K.: Allen Lithographic, 1944), 25; Casimir Smogorzewski, *East Prussia Must Disappear* (London: Free Europe, 1944), 44.

24. Krickus, *The Kaliningrad Question*, 27.

25. Robert Conquest, *Stalin: Breaker of Nations* (London: Phoenix, 1991), 266.

26. Tony Sharp, "The Russian Annexation of the Königsberg Area 1941–1945," *Survey* 23, no. 4 (1977–1978): 156.

27. The final protocol of the Potsdam Conference stated: "The conference has agreed in principle to the proposals of the Soviet Government concerning the ultimate transfer to the Soviet Union of the City of Königsberg and the area adjacent to it as described above subject to expert examination of the actual frontier. The President of the United States and the British Prime Minister have declared that they will support the proposal of the Conference at the forthcoming peace settlement." *Documents on Germany 1944–1961* (U.S. Government Printing Office, 1961), 37.

28. Joseph B. Schechtman, *Post War Population Transfers in Europe* (Philadelphia: University of Pennsylvania Press, 1962), 36.

29. Christopher Dobson, John Miller, and Ronald Payne, *The Cruelest Night* (Boston: Little, Brown, 1979), 16–17, 27.

30. Krickus, *The Kaliningrad Question*, 38.

31. Emil J. Guttzeit, *Ostpreussen in 1440 Bildern—Geschichtliche Darstellung* (Leer, Germany: Gerhard Rautenberg, n.d.); Priit Vesilind, "Kaliningrad: Coping with a German Past and a Russian Future," *National Geographic* 191, no. 3 (1997): 110–23.

32. Romuald J. Misiunas, "Rootless Russia: Kaliningrad—Status and Identity," *Diplomacy and Statecraft* 15, no. 2 (2004): 401.

33. Misiunas, "Rootless Russia," 395.

34. See Elke Knappe, "Der ländliche Raum des Gebietes Kaliningrad: Der Transformationsprozess in der Viehwirtschaft," *Europa Regional* 4, no. 3 (1996): 24–30; William R. Stanley, "Russia's Kaliningrad," *Pennsylvania Geographer* 39, no. 1 (2001): 29.

35. Krickus, *The Kaliningrad Question*, 22.

36. Gennady M. Fyodorov, "The Social and Economic Development of Kaliningrad," in *Kaliningrad: The European Amber Region*, ed. Pertti Joenniemi and Jan Prawitz (Aldershot, U.K.: Ashgate, 1998), 35.

37. Fyodor Kushnirsky, "Post Soviet Attempts to Establish Free Economic Zones," *Post Soviet Geography and Economics* 38, no. 3 (1997): 144–62.

38. Christian Wellman, "Recognising Borders: Coping with Historically Contested Territory," in *The Kaliningrad Challenge*, ed. Hanne-Margret Birckenbach and Christian Wellmann (Münster, Germany: Lit Verlag, 2003), 281.

39. Krickus, *The Kaliningrad Question*, 82.

40. Paul Holtom, "The Kaliningrad Test in Russian-EU Relations," *Perspectives on European Politics and Society* 6, no. 1 (2005): 32.

41. Holtom, "The Kaliningrad Test," 45.

42. Krickus, *The Kaliningrad Question*, 70.

43. Andrew Osborn, "Russia Opens Sea Route to Kaliningrad to Break 'Blockade,'" *The Independent*, 12 September 2006, 19.

44. Holtom, "The Kaliningrad Test," 40.

45. Yury Zverev, "Kaliningrad: Problems and Paths of Development," *Problems of Post Communism* 54, no. 2 (2007): 15, 21.

46. O. V. Kuznetsova and V. A. Mau, *Kaliningradskaya oblast: ot "nepotoplyaemogo avianostsa" k "nepotop-lyaemomu sborochnomu tsehu"* (*Kaliningrad Oblast: From the "Unsinkable Aircraft Carrier" to the "Unsinkable Assembly Shop"*) (Moscow: Russia in United Europe Committee, 2002); Paul Holtom, "Detached Regions and Their Role in Return to Empire: The Cases of East Prussia and Kaliningrad," in *Baltic Democracy at the Crossroads*, ed. Sten Berlund and Kjetil Duvold (Kristiansand, Norway: HøyskoleForlaget, 2003), 219–51; Christopher Browning and Pertti Joenniemi, "Contending Discourses of Marginality: The Case of Kaliningrad," *Geopolitics* 9, no. 3 (2004): 699–730; Sergei Prozorov, "The Narratives of Exclusion and Self-Exclusion in the Russian Conflict Discourse on EU-Russian Relations," *Political Geography* 26, no. 3 (2007): 309–29.

Chapter 9: Defining Liechtenstein: Sovereign Borders, Offshore Banking, and National Identity

1. The official quoted was Markus Amman, an interior ministry spokesperson. See Mark Oliver and agencies, "Liechtenstein: No Retaliation for Swiss 'Invasion,'" *Guardian*, 2 March 2007, http://www.guardian.co.uk/world/2007/mar/02/markoliver (11 March 2008).

2. Lindsay Hamilton, "Whoops! Swiss Accidentally Invade Liechtenstein," *ABC News*, 3 March 2007, http://abcnews.go.com/International/story?id=2921407&page=1 (11 March 2008); Roger Cohen, "A Wartime Scenario, Starring the Swiss," *International Herald Tribune*, 9 March 2007, http://www.iht.com/protected/articles/2007/03/09/news/globalist.php (11 March 2008); Peter Stamm, "Swiss Miss," *New York Times*, 10 March 2007, http://www.nytimes.com/2007/03/10/opinion/10stamm.html (11 March 2008).

3. Graham Martin, "The Principality of Liechtenstein—A Living Fossil from the Time of the Holy Roman Empire," *German Life and Letters* 42, no. 1 (1988): 72.

4. David Newman, "The Lines That Continue to Separate Us: Borders in Our Borderless World," *Progress in Human Geography* 30, no. 2 (2006): 143–61.

5. The narrative of Liechtenstein's establishment and subsequent development as a sovereign state is repeated in more or less the same form in all of the standard histories written about the principality. The description presented here follows the common outline and employs the commonly accepted historical facts recounted in these narratives. For some of the standard accounts available in English or English translation, see, for example, Pierre Raton, *Liechtenstein: History and Institutions of the Principality* (Vaduz: Liechtenstein-Verlag, 1970); Otto Seger, *A Survey of Liechtenstein History* (Vaduz: Press and Information Office of the Principality of Liechtenstein, 1984); and David Beattie, *Liechtenstein: A Modern History* (London: I. B. Tauris, 2004).

6. Beattie, *Liechtenstein*, 38–41.

7. In 1938, following his accession on the death of his great uncle Franz Joseph I, Liechtenstein's new ruling prince, Franz Joseph II, decided to leave Austria and take up permanent residence in Vaduz. The move was motivated, in part, to escape the

Nazis, who had previously taken a dim view of the fact that the old prince's wife was Jewish and who generally regarded the old aristocratic families with disdain.

8. Most of the interned Russians immigrated to Argentina in 1948. See Raton, *Liechtenstein*, 146.

9. Beattie, *Liechtenstein*, 137.

10. World Bank, "GNI per Capita 2006, Atlas Method and PPP," http://site resources.worldbank.org/DATASTATISTICS/Resources/GNIPC.pdf (11 March 2008).

11. Eric Pfanner and Mark Landler, "Tax Inquiry? Principality Is Offended," *New York Times*, 20 February, 2008, http://www.nytimes.com/2008/02/20/business/worldbusiness/20evasion.html?ex=1361163600&en=0e347c04aa77d059&ei=5088&partner=rssnyt&emc=rss (11 March 2008).

12. Haig Zimonian, "Liechtenstein Offers to Push Bank Reform," *Financial Times*, 5 March 2008, http://www.ft.com/cms/s/0/c52b3b8c-ea3d-11dc-b3c9-0000779fd2ac.html (11 March 2008).

13. Sarah Lyall, "Vaduz Journal; For Rent One Principality. Prince Not Included," *New York Times*, 25 March 2003, http://query.nytimes.com/gst/fullpage.html?res=9A01E6D91530F936A15750C0A9659C8B63 (11 March 2008).

14. Reported in "Saving a Banking Boom from Berlin," *Time*, 28 February 2008, http://www.time.com/time/world/article/0,8599,1717950,00.html (11 March 2008).

15. Martin, "The Principality of Liechtenstein," 87.

16. During World War I, there was even a proposal that the Pope might be given political sovereignty over Liechtenstein so that he would have a sovereign territorial base—the Vatican at that time lacking political independence of Italy—that would allow him to play a role in the postwar peace conference. See Beattie, *Liechtenstein*, 43–44.

17. The people of the Oberland are traditionally thought to be more frivolous in their outlook, while those of the Unterland are more serious or somber. Barbara Greene, *Liechtenstein: Valley of Peace* (Vaduz: Liechtenstein-Verlag, 1967), 100.

18. CIA, *The World Factbook*, "Liecthtenstein," 31 December 2001, https://www.cia.gov/library/publications/the-world-factbook/geos/ls.html#Econ (11 March 2008).

19. "Liechtenstein: How Does Liechtenstein Envision Its Future?" *Mondaq*, 27 February 2008, http://www.mondaq.com/article.asp?articleid=57740 (11 March 2008).

20. Council of Europe: European Commission against Racism and Intolerance, *Second Report on Liechtenstein, adopted 28 June 2002*, 15 April 2003, http://www.coe.int/t/e/human_rights/ecri/1-ecri/2-country-by-country_approach/Liechtenstein/Liechtenstein_CBC_2en.asp (11 March 2008).

21. Peter Kaiser, *Geschichte des Fürstenthums Liechtenstein* (Chur, Switzerland: Grubenmann, 1847; reprinted Nendeln, Liechtenstein: Krauss, 1974) was the first published history of the principality. Kaiser is the country's best-known historian, politician, and champion of the common people.

22. Martin, "The Principality of Liechtenstein," 82.

23. See, for example, Konrad Geithner et al., *Lichtenstein 1212–1995* (Vaduz: Stadtverwaltung Lichtenstein, 1996). See also, Norbert Jansen, ed., *Beiträge zur liechtensteinischen Identität*, Liechtensteiner Politische Schriften, Band 34 (Schaan: Verlag der Liechtensteiner Akademischen Gesellschaft, 2001).

24. Fiona Fleck, "Prince to People: I'll Sell Up to Bill Gates," *Telegraph.co.uk*, 19 June 2001, http://www.telegraph.co.uk/news/main.jhtml?xml=/news/2001/02/11/wlich11.xml (11 March 2008).

25. IFES (International Foundation for Election Systems), "Election Guide: Liechtenstein Referendum, Results for Provision 1, Constitutional Referendum—Princely Initiative," 14 March 2003, http://www.electionguide.org/results.php?ID=326 (11 March 2008).

Chapter 10: Misiones Province, Argentina:
How Borders Shape Political Identity

1. A web search reveals dozens of such photographs posted online through such photo-sharing sites as Flickr.com and Picasa web albums; Google Earth's "Panoramio" feature also includes many such standard panorama photos around Puerto Iguazú.

2. Robert C. Eidt, *Pioneer Settlement in Northeast Argentina* (Madison: University of Wisconsin Press, 1971); José A. Margalot, *Geografía De Misiones* (Buenos Aires: Cultural Argentina, 1971).

3. Such rhetoric in a historical narrative is often called a "teleology," and "nationalist teleologies" have been crucial in building national identities worldwide. See Benedict Anderson, *Imagined Communities: Reflections on the Origin and Spread of Nationalism* (London: Verso, 1983); Raymond B. Craib, *Cartographic Mexico: A History of State Fixations and Fugitive Landscapes* (Durham, N.C.: Duke University Press, 2004), 49; Peter C. Perdue, "Where Do Incorrect Political Ideas Come From? Writing the History of the Qing Empire and the Chinese Nation," in *The Teleology of the Modern Nation-State: Japan and China*, ed. Joshua A. Fogel (Philadelphia: University of Pennsylvania Press, 2005), 197; Virginia Tilley, *Seeing Indians: A Study of Race, Nation, and Power in El Salvador* (Albuquerque: University of New Mexico Press, 2005).

4. Of course, this concept derives from the pioneering work of postcolonial theorist Edward Said. For more on the "othering" process in the context of nationalism, see Philip Spencer and Howard Wollman, *Nationalism: A Critical Introduction* (London: Sage, 2002), 58. See also Jonathan Ree, "Internationality," *Radical Philosophy* 60 (1992): 1–13.

5. Carmen A. Ferradás, *Power in the Southern Cone Borderlands: An Anthropology of Development Practice* (Westport: Bergin & Garvey, 1998), 43.

6. Such Edenic myths have been especially important in South America for legitimizing conquest of native peoples and the expansion of national economic development into tropical frontier regions. See Kent H. Redford, "The Ecologically Noble Savage," *Cultural Survival Quarterly* 15, no. 1 (1991): 46–48; J. Timmons Roberts and Nikki Demetria Thanos, *Trouble in Paradise: Globalization and Environmental Crises in Latin America* (New York: Routledge, 2003); Suzana Sawyer, *Crude Chronicles: Indigenous Politics, Multinational Oil, and Neoliberalism in Ecuador* (Durham, N.C.: Duke University Press, 2004); Candace Slater, *Entangled Edens: Visions of the Amazon* (Berkeley: University of California Press, 2002).

7. Although these terms are sometimes used interchangeably, *reducciones* (singular, *reducción*) carries different (and more negative) connotations than *misiones*. From the root verb *reducir*, *reducción* implies subjugation, conversion (to Christianity), and civilization, as well as the literal translation, "reduction." Thus, *reducción* is a loaded term, its more negative connotations emphasized in critical historical reappraisals of the work of Christian missionaries in colonial Latin America.

8. Eidt, *Pioneer Settlement in Northeast Argentina*; Ernesto J. A. Maeder, *Misiones: Historia de la Tierra Prometida* (Buenos Aires: Eudeba, 2004).

9. Programa Misiones Jesuiticas, "Misiones Jesuitico Guaranies" (n.d.).

10. Eidt, *Pioneer Settlement in Northeast Argentina*; Maeder, *Misiones*.

11. Maeder, *Misiones*, 108.

12. Maeder, *Misiones*, 118.

13. Eidt, *Pioneer Settlement in Northeast Argentina*, 55. Here, Eidt, writing in the early 1970s, reproduces the conventional, romanticized narrative, specifically the moment of the "fall" that ushers in a "dark age" before the "rise" that would follow a century later. Of course, this narrative contains more than a grain of truth, but claims of the area returning to "wilderness" are perhaps overstated and ideologically loaded. The main point is that, regardless of the veracity of specific historical claims, such a narrative is instrumental in the construction of a myth (or identity story) of Misiones.

14. Alfredo S. C. Bolsi, *Misiones: Una Aproximación Geográfica al Problema de la Yerba Mate y Sus Efectos en la Ocupación del Espacio y el Poblamiento* (Resistencia: Instituto de Historia de la Facultad de Humanidades de la Universidad Nacional del Nordeste, 1986); Maeder, *Misiones*.

15. Maeder, *Misiones*, 131.

16. Alejandro Grimson, "El Puente Que Separó Dos Orillas. Notas Para Una Crítica Del Esencialismo De La Hermandad," in *Fronteras, Naciones e Identidades: La Periferia Como Centro*, ed. Alejandro Grimson (Buenos Aires: Ediciones Ciccus/La Crujía, 2000), 203.

17. Bolsi, *Misiones*.

18. Francisco Manzi, *Impresiones De Viaje: Breves Apuntes Sobre El Territorio De Misiones* (Corrientes: La Popular, 1910), 42, 111.

19. Nicolas Shumway, *The Invention of Argentina* (Berkeley: University of California Press, 1991).

20. Gastón Gordillo, *Landscapes of Devils: Tensions of Place and Memory in the Argentinean Chaco* (Durham, N.C.: Duke University Press, 2004); Shumway, *The Invention of Argentina*.

21. Shumway, *The Invention of Argentina*, 135.

22. Shumway, *The Invention of Argentina*, 144.

23. On the meaning of the "desert" in the conquest of indigenous groups in Argentina, see Gordillo, *Landscapes of Devils*, 46–54.

24. Alejo Peyret, *Cartas Sobre Misiones* (Buenos Aires: Imprenta de la Tribuna Nacional, 1881), 96.

25. Rafael Hernández, *Cartas Misioneras* (Buenos Aires: Editorial Universitaria de Buenos Aires, 1973 [1887]), 98, cited in Ferradás, *Power in the Southern Cone Borderlands*, 46.

26. Grimson, "El Puente Que Separó Dos Orillas."

27. Hernández, *Cartas Misioneras*, 30, cited in Ferradás, *Power in the Southern Cone Borderlands*, 46; Héctor Eduardo Jaquet, *Los Combates por la Invención de Misiones* (Posadas: Universidad Nacional de Misiones, 2005).

28. Grimson, "El Puente Que Separó Dos Orillas"; Peyret, *Cartas Sobre Misiones*.

29. Ferradás, *Power in the Southern Cone Borderlands*, 43.

30. Cámara de Senadores de la Nación, *Diario de Sesiones*, Vol. 1 (Buenos Aires: 1881), 593.

31. On the eve of transferring power, however, the government of Corrientes bestowed most of the territory to provincial elites. Over two million hectares (roughly five million acres) were thus allotted to just thirty-eight landowners. This land grab effectively delayed large-scale colonization efforts since the federal government inherited a limited public domain for subdivision into agricultural colonies. Maeder, *Misiones*; Eidt, *Pioneer Settlement in Northeast Argentina*; María Cecilia Gallero de Urfer, *La Inmigración y Colonización Alemana en Misiones* (Buenos Aires: Academia Nacional de la Historia, 2003).

32. In the settlement, arbitrated by the government of the United States, Argentina lost all of the disputed territory to Brazil. For details on the dispute and settlement, see Mary Wilhelmine Williams, "The Treaty of Tordesillas and the Argentine-Brazilian Boundary Settlement," *Hispanic American Historical Review* 5, no. 1 (1922): 3–23; Estanislao S. Zeballos, *Argument for the Argentine Republic upon the Question with Brazil in Regard to the Territory of Misiones* (Washington, D.C.: Gibson Bros., 1894).

33. Leopoldo J. Bartolomé, *Los Colonos de Apóstoles: Estrategias Adaptativas y Etnicidad en Una Colonia Eslava en Misiones* (Posadas: Universidad Nacional de Misiones, 2000), 35. See also Jean Shor and Franc Shor, "Argentina: Young Giant of the Far South," *National Geographic* 113, no. 3 (1958): 297–352. Somewhat confusingly, there is also a region in Spain known as Galicia, which was also a major source region for migrants to Argentina in the late nineteenth and early twentieth centuries.

34. Bolsi, *Misiones*; Eidt, *Pioneer Settlement in Northeast Argentina*; Carlos Reboratti, "Migraciones y Frontera Agraria: Argentina y Brasil en la Cuenca del Alto Paraná-Uruguay," *Desarrollo Económico* 19, no. 74 (1979): 189–209.

35. Gallero de Urfer, *La Inmigración y Colonización Alemana*, 4–5.

36. Eidt, *Pioneer Settlement in Northeast Argentina*.

37. Bolsi, *Misiones*, 130.

38. Gallero de Urfer, *La inmigración y colonización alemana*, 6.

39. Ronald C. Newton, *The "Nazi Menace" in Argentina, 1931–1947* (Stanford, Calif.: Stanford University Press, 1992), 74.

40. Gallero de Urfer, *La Inmigración y Colonización Alemana*, 6.

41. Newton, *The "Nazi Menace" in Argentina*, 81.

42. Newton, *The "Nazi Menace" in Argentina*, 83.

43. Eidt, *Pioneer Settlement in Northeast Argentina*; Bartolomé, *Los colonos de Apóstoles*; Marcelo Escolar, Silvina Quintero Palacios, and Carlos E. Reboratti, "Geographical Identity and Patriotic Representation in Argentina," in *Geography and National Identity*, ed. David J. M. Hooson (Cambridge: Blackwell, 1994).

44. Jaquet, *Los Combates por la Invención de Misiones*.

45. For the concept of "invention of tradition," see E. J. Hobsbawm and T. O. Ranger, *The Invention of Tradition* (Cambridge: Cambridge University Press, 1983).

46. Aníbal Cambas, *Historia Política e Institucional de Misiones: Los Derechos Misioneros ante la Historia y ante la Ley* (Posadas: Ediciones S.A.D.E.M., 1984 [1945]), 341.

47. Jaquet, *Los Combates por la Invención de Misiones*.

48. Eidt, *Pioneer Settlement in Northeast Argentina*.

49. This shows the importance of the Misiones "map-as-logo," not only in the sense that Thongchai Winichakul and Benedict Anderson have used it, to reinforce a political identity, but also as a brand identity for marketing. Anderson, *Imagined Communities*; Thongchai Winichakul, *Siam Mapped: A History of the Geo-Body of a Nation* (Honolulu: University of Hawaii Press, 1994). On the "'logoization' of national territory" on maps, see Sarah A. Radcliffe, "Frontiers and Popular Nationhood: Geographies of Identity in the 1995 Ecuador-Peru Border Dispute," *Political Geography* 17, no. 3 (1998): 273–93. For an innovative analysis of maps as logos, see Robert M. Edsall, "Iconic Maps in American Political Discourse," *Cartographica* 42, no. 4 (2007): 335–47.

50. Grimson, "El Puente Que Separó Dos Orillas"; Jaquet, *Los Combates por la Invención de Misiones*.

51. Craib, *Cartographic Mexico*; Tilley, *Seeing Indians*.

52. See, for example, Bartomeu Meliá, *El Guaraní—Conquistado y Reducido: Ensayos de Etnohistoria* (Asunción: Centro de Estudios Antropológicos, Universidad Católica, 1986).

53. AnaMaria Gorosito, *Censo Indígena Provincial 1979* (Posadas: Dirección de Asuntos Aborígenes y Universidad Nacional de Misiones, 1981).

54. Donatella Schmidt, "Do You Have an Opy? Politics and Identity among the Mbya-Guarani of Argentina and Eastern Paraguay." (PhD thesis, Indiana University, 1991).

55. Schmidt, "Do You Have an Opy?" 58.

56. José Freaza, a Peronist legislator, cited in Schmidt, "Do You Have an Opy?" 63.

57. Donna Lee Van Cott, "Latin America: Constitutional Reform and Ethnic Right," *Parliamentary Affairs* 53, no. 1 (2000): 41–54; Carlos Reboratti, personal communication.

58. Mario Boleda, "El Proceso Emigratorio Misionero En Las Últimas Tres Décadas," *Desarrollo Económico* 23, no. 90 (1983): 287–98; Maeder, *Misiones*.

59. Jaquet, *Los Combates por la Invención de Misiones*; Anssi Paasi, "Boundaries as Social Processes: Territoriality in the World of Flows," in *Boundaries, Territory and Postmodernity*, ed. David Newman (London: F. Cass, 1999).

60. John Child, "Geopolitical Thinking in Latin America," *Latin American Research Review* 14, no. 2 (1979): 89–111; Juan E. Guglialmelli, "Argentina Frente Al 'Operativo Misiones' Del Brasil," *Estrategia* 19–20 (1972–1973): 19–20.

61. Ferradás, *Power in the Southern Cone Borderlands*.

62. Reboratti, personal communication.

63. R. C. Rey Balmaceda, *Límites y Fronteras de la República Argentina: Epítome Geográfico* (Buenos Aires: OIKOS, 1979), 343.

64. Carlos Reboratti, "El Encanto de la Oscuridad. Notas Acerca de la Geopolítica en la Argentina," *Desarrollo Económico* 23, no. 89 (1983): 137–44.

65. Carmen A. Ferradás, "How a Green Wilderness Became a Trade Wilderness: The Story of a Southern Cone Frontier," *PoLAR* 21, no. 2 (1998): 11–25; Carmen A. Ferradás, "Environment, Security, and Terrorism in the Trinational Frontier of the Southern Cone," *Identities: Global Studies in Culture and Power* 11 (2004): 417–42; Grimson, "El Puente Que Separó Dos Orillas"; Lidia Schiavoni, *Pesadas Cargas, Frágiles Pasos: Transacciones Comerciales En Un Mercado De Frontera* (Asunción: CPES, 1993).

66. Grimson, "El Puente Que Separó Dos Orillas."

67. Schiavoni, *Pesadas Cargas, Frágiles Pasos.*

68. Schiavoni, *Pesadas Cargas, Frágiles Pasos.*

69. Schiavoni, *Pesadas Cargas, Frágiles Pasos*, 36.

70. Grimson, "El Puente Que Separó Dos Orillas"; Ferradás, "Environment, Security, and Terrorism in the Trinational Frontier of the Southern Cone," 418.

71. Grimson, "El Puente Que Separó Dos Orillas." Grimson suggests that the bridge did not unite as much as its planners hoped; it, and Mercosur generally, provoked new insistence on difference and redefinition and entrenchment of identity on both sides.

72. Ferradás, "How a Green Wilderness Became a Trade Wilderness."

73. Ferradás, "Environment, Security, and Terrorism in the Trinational Frontier of the Southern Cone."

74. Larry Rohter, "Terrorists Are Sought in Latin Smugglers' Haven," *New York Times*, 27 September 2001, A3.

75. Greg Grandin, "The Wide War: How Donald Rumsfeld Discovered the Wild West in Latin America," *TomDispatch.com*, 7 May 2006, http://www.tomdispatch.com/post/82089/grandin_on_rumsfeld_s_latin_american_wild_west_show (8 August 2008); Timothy L. O'Brien, "South American Area Is Cited as Haven of Terrorist Training," *New York Times*, 10 October 2003, A28; Rohter, "Terrorists Are Sought in Latin Smugglers' Haven"; Douglas Waller, "A Terror Threat from the South," *Time Magazine*, 10 December 2001, 25.

76. Ferradás, "Environment, Security, and Terrorism in the Trinational Frontier of the Southern Cone"; Grandin, "The Wide War."

77. This argument is inspired by the work of Erik Swyngedouw, Saskia Sassen, and Robert C. Smith. See Erik Swyngedouw, "Neither Global nor Local: 'Glocalization' and the Politics of Scale," in *Spaces of Globalization: Reasserting the Power of the Local*, ed. Kevin R. Cox (New York: Guilford, 1997); Saskia Sassen, *Globalization and Its Discontents* (New York: New Press, 1998); Robert C. Smith, *Mexican New York: Transnational Lives of New Immigrants* (Berkeley: University of California Press, 2006).

78. Ferradás, "Environment, Security, and Terrorism in the Trinational Frontier of the Southern Cone."

79. Grimson, "El Puente Que Separó Dos Orillas."

80. The author wishes to thank Carlos Reboratti, Neela Nandyal, and the editors of this volume for their generous and helpful comments on previous versions of this

manuscript. Thanks also to Sergio Luis Paez, Susana Curto, and Alfredo Bolsi for facilitating this research.

Chapter 11: Point Roberts, Washington: Boundary Problems of an American Exclave

1. Richard L. Merritt, "Noncontiguity and Political Integration," in *Linkage Politics*, ed. James N. Rosenau (New York: Free Press, 1969), 237–72; G. W. S. Robinson, "Exclaves," *Annals of the Association of American Geographers* 49, no. 3 (1959): 283–95; Roger E. Kasperson and Julian V. Minghi, eds., *The Structure of Political Geography* (Chicago: Aldine, 1969), 152–55.

2. Kasperson and Minghi, *The Structure*, 78, 208.

3. Whatcom County Planning Commission, *The Plight of Point Roberts: A Brief to the Area Redevelopment Administration* (Bellingham, Wash.: 1965).

4. Julian V. Minghi, *Some Aspects of the Impact of an International Boundary on Spatial Patterns: An Analysis of the Pacific Coast Lowland Region of the Canada-United States Boundary* (Seattle: PhD dissertation, University of Washington, 1962), 114–29; Julian V. Minghi, "Point Roberts, Washington—The Problem of an American Exclave," *Association of Pacific Coast Geographers Yearbook* 24 (1962): 29–34.

5. Julian V. Minghi, "Teaching Political Geography," *Journal of Geography* 65, no. 8 (1966): 362–70; Julian V. Minghi, "Point Roberts: Activity Five," in *Geography in an Urban Age*, Political Geography, Teacher's Guide, ed. Association of American Geographers (New York: Macmillan, 1970), 47–63; Julian V. Minghi, "Point Roberts," in *Geography in an Urban Age*, Political Geography, Student Materials, ed. Association of American Geographers (New York: Macmillan, 1970), 49–50.

6. Julian V. Minghi and Dennis Rumley, "Integration and Systems Stress in an International Enclave Community: Point Roberts, Washington," in *Peoples of the Living Land: Geography of Cultural Diversity in British Columbia*, ed. Julian V. Minghi (Vancouver: Tantalus Research, 1972), 213–28.

7. International Joint Commission, United States and Canada, *Public Hearing on Point Roberts, Washington* (Point Roberts, Wash.: December 18, 1971).

8. Richard E. Clark, *Point Roberts, USA: The History of a Canadian Enclave* (Bellingham, Wash.: Textype Publishing, 1980).

9. Julian V. Minghi, "The Evolution of a Border Region: The Pacific Coast Section of the Canada-United States Boundary," *Scottish Geographical Magazine* 80, no. 1 (1964): 37–52.

10. Drew D. Pettus, "The Problem of Administering Point Roberts, Washington," a study presented to Lloyd Meeds, Congressman for the Second Congressional District, Washington, D.C., 31 December 1969.

11. Pettus, "The Problem of Administering."

12. International Joint Commission, *Public Hearing*, 4–5.

13. Minghi and Rumley, "Integration and Systems Stress."

14. Merritt, "Noncontiguity and Political Integration"; Robinson, "Exclaves."

15. Meg Olson, "More Local Border Control Wanted," *The All Point Bulletin*, March 2008, http://www.allpointbulletin.com/archives/2008/apb_mar08/front_page2.html (30 July 2008).

16. Meg Olson, "NEXUS Refusals Inspire Locals to Call for Changes," *The All Point Bulletin*, May 2008, http://www.allpointbulletin.com/archives/2008/apb_may08/front_page3.html (30 July 2008).

17. "3-Day Limit on Mail Boxes Imposed," *All Point Bulletin*, March 2008, http://www.allpointbulletin.com/archives/2008/apb_mar08/front_page7.html (30 July 2008).

18. "Letters to the Editor," *All Point Bulletin*, March 2008, http://www.allpoint bulletin.com/archives/2008/apb_mar08/editor_letters.html (30 July 2008).

19. Meg Olson, "Neither Rain, nor Snow, nor Border Shall Stop, Oops, Think Again," *All Point Bulletin*, May 2008, http://www.allpointbulletin.com/archives/2008/apb_may08/front_page4.html (30 July 2008).

20. Peter Hamilton, "Wild at the Point," *All Point Bulletin*, June 2008, http://www.allpointbulletin.com/archives/2008/apb_june08/front_page10.html (30 July 2008).

21. Richard E. Clark, *Social Change in an American Exclave Community: A Social-Historical Description of Point Roberts, Washington* (Bellingham, Wash.: master's thesis, Western Washington State College, 1970).

22. Meg Olson, "Border Talk Major Concern at Voters AGM," *All Point Bulletin*, April 2008, http://www.allpointbulletin.com/archives/2008/apb_april08/front_page3.html (30 July 2008)

Chapter 12: Conclusion: Borders in a Changing Global Context

1. Larry Collins and Dominique Lapierre, *O Jerusalem* (New York: Simon & Schuster, 1972), 83.

2. Robert Sack, *Human Territoriality: Its Theory and History* (Cambridge: Cambridge University Press, 1986), 5.

3. James Anderson and Liam O'Dowd, "Borders, Border Regions and Territoriality: Contradictory Meanings, Changing Significance," *Regional Studies* 33, no. 7 (1999): 594.

4. See John Agnew, "The Territorial Trap: The Geographical Assumptions of International Relations Theory," *Review of International Political Economy* 1, no. 1 (1994): 53–80; John Agnew, *Globalization and Sovereignty* (Lanham, Md.: Rowman & Littlefield, 2009), 22.

5. John Agnew, *Geopolitics: Re-Visioning World Politics* (London: Routledge, 1998), 49.

6. Anthony Smith, *Nationalism in the Twentieth Century* (Oxford: Martin Robertson, 1979), 191.

7. Smith, *Nationalism*, 51.

8. David Delaney, *Territory: A Short Introduction* (London: Blackwell, 2005), 64; Alexander C. Diener and Joshua Hagen, "Theorizing Borders in a 'Borderless World': Globalization, Territory and Scale," *Geography Compass* 3, no. 3 (2009): 1196–1216.

9. John Herz, "The Rise and Demise of the Territorial State," *World Politics* 9, no. 4 (1957): 473–93.

10. Samuel Huntington, *The Clash of Civilizations* (New York: Touchstone, 1997).

11. Anderson and O'Dowd, "Borders," 595–96.

12. David Newman, "The Lines That Continue to Separate Us: Borders in Our 'Borderless' World," *Progress in Human Geography* 30, no. 2 (2006): 146.

Glossary

administration   The implementation of policy by representatives of a particular governing body.

aristocracy   A traditional class distinction, often associated with powerful landowners in a feudal society.

authoritarian   A form of rule that vests all political power in the state and is normally characterized by general disregard for the constraints of human rights and popular opinion.

autonomy   The political circumstance when a territory has some form of self-government but not full sovereignty. Autonomy may take economic, political, and/or cultural form.

border   A line used to divide one jurisdiction from another.

borderlands   Regions proximate to either side of a border. Borderlands may also be interpreted as the spaces of hybridity created by the proximity of two or more distinct cultures, economic systems, or political entities.

boundary   The limits of a territory; the boundary of a state defines the scope of its sovereignty.

boundary disputes

    allocational   Relating to the administration of boundaries, allocational disputes revolve around the division of resources within a border region.

    definitional   Such disputes relate to definition of a boundary, for example, if a river is used as a physiographic boundary but the river changes course.

locational Such disputes relate to arguments over the delimitation and/or demarcation of a boundary. Many historical boundaries were drawn in reference to hilltops, trees, and large boulders. The passage of time has often altered the landscape and thus markers may no longer be apparent. GPS technology is making this type of dispute far less common.

operational Disputes of this nature relate to administration of the boundary. States have very different ideas as to how a boundary should function. One state may desire a porous, free-flowing boundary, while its neighbor may want a rigid barrier.

territorial Disputes of this nature relate to broader claims to specific territorial entitities or entire regions. Classic examples relate to islands.

boundary making The process of establishing the formal borders between different jurisdictions; boundary making usually occurs in four phases:

1. **definition** This first phase involves description of the boundary and the territory through which it runs. This phase is often formalized in treaties.

2. **delimitation** This second phase involves cartographers using maps and satellite imagery to plot the boundary. The use of global positioning systems (GPS) is making this process much more exact.

3. **demarcation** The third phase involves marking the boundary using objects such as poles, stones, fences, and walls. Once again, GPS technology is increasing the accuracy and sustainability of this process.

4. **administration** This final phase involves the establishment of procedures to maintain the boundary markers, manage transboundary movement of people and goods, and set protocols for borderland activity (notification of military exercises, natural hazard cooperation, etc.).

bureaucracy A system for managing a country, company, or organization that involves the employment of a large number of people in an official status. Such a system often entails the establishment of rules, which are often associated with institutionalized impediments to the accomplishment of goals by those forced to deal therewith.

capital city The official site of the main elements of the state's government, administration, and decision making.

civil society Originally devised as a concept to represent society outside the activities of the state, civil society has come to represent the sum of all the voluntary associations through which a social system operates.

classification of boundaries

artificial A boundary that has been demarcated without concern for physical features of the landscape:

antecedent A boundary drawn prior to intensive land use and settlement.

consequent A boundary drawn to reflect patterns (linguistic, cultural, economic, or political) in an existing landscape.

natural A boundary that is demarcated in accordance with some physical feature of the landscape (e.g., river, mountain, etc.).

pioneer A boundary drawn through "unoccupied" territory.

relict A boundary that no longer divides different jurisdictions, although its former role may still be visible on the landscape.

subsequent A boundary drawn after the establishment of cultural land-scapes and settlement patterns.

superimposed A boundary that has been imposed by an outside source upon an existing cultural or settlement pattern.

colonialism The occupation of territory beyond the commonly accepted jurisdiction of a given state for the purposes of settlement and economic exploitation. The term is generally associated with the overseas expansion of European state sovereignty over much of Africa, Asia, and the Americas beginning around 1500.

colony A territory commonly recognized to be under the sovereignty of a foreign power.

core area of states An area where a state originates and around which it has gradually built up its territory.

corridor A section of territory assigned to the jurisdiction of a given state to provide access to a separate portion of that state or to a particular geo-graphic feature (e.g., river, railroad, highway, ocean, lake).

country *See* state.

county A district or territorial division deriving power from the provincial level of political administration within a sovereign state.

criteria for boundaries

   cultural/political A boundary drawn to create culturally uniform territo-rial units.

   geometric A boundary that consists of straight lines and/or arcs with little or no regard to the physical or cultural landscapes.

   physiographic A boundary drawn parallel to a prominent physical fea-ture of a given landscape.

decolonization Most often relating to the achievement of political indepen-dence, decolonization is the process by which power is transferred from a colonial political entity to the people of the colony. The term generally refers to the independence of many former colonies in Africa and Asia after 1945.

diaspora Persons claiming the same ethnic or national identity living out-side the borders of their historic homeland. The term was historically as-sociated with Jews and Armenians as victims of forced migration but has become more commonly applied to a variety of groups living beyond their national territories and does not necessarily connote a desire to "return" migrate.

elite A group within a given society wielding disproportionate influence over politics, economics, or society.

empire A political organization that subordinates several parts to one authority normally located in a central region of the greater jurisdictional space.

enclave A portion of one state's territory completely surrounded by the territory of another state. One state's enclave is often another state's exclave. The only exceptions would be enclaves that do not belong to another state (e.g., San Marino inside Italy).

exclave A territory belonging to one state that is not contiguous with the rest of the state. Most exclaves are also enclaves inside another state. The only exceptions would be exclaves that are not completely surrounded by another state (e.g., Cueta, the Spanish exclave on the coast of Morocco).

federation A state-level political system that facilitates the sharing of power between two levels of government: a central or "federal" government and a tier of provincial governments.

feudalism A societal system in which peasants or serfs provided agricultural labor to landlords in return for military protection. These landlords, usually lesser nobles, pledged loyalty and military service to a king or emperor in exchange for their recognition of the lesser noble's land titles. This patently hierarchical system preceded capitalism in Europe.

forced migration The process of compelling people to relocate their permanent residences for political purposes. This can take various forms, including controlled population transfers with planned resettlement programs and spontaneous flight catalyzed by fear of physical harm.

frontier The ill-defined zone of overlap or transition between political, cultural, or economic systems. Frontiers were historically common prior to the rise of the nation-state system and the pervasive demarcation of borders.

fundamentalism An attitude or set of beliefs stressing the defense of traditional ideals against the advance of modernity.

globalization A process resulting in the increasing impact of global systems on daily human activity as well as the perpetuation of transnational relations across traditional territorial divides. Though a contentious term, it has become associated with challenges to the primacy of the state in political, economic, and social processes.

government The system used to control or manage a country, city, or group of people.

hegemony A political state of being whereby the will of a particular state or class group is so dominant that voluntary compliance by other actors in that system occurs.

homeland A potion of the earth's surface rendered significant by its association with group history, identity, and usually the ultimate goal of sovereignty. Nationalism is commonly employed to convert a given territory into a homeland.

hybridity A state of being that combines the cultural and often political ideals of two or more groups. Hybridity is considered an increasingly prominent condition in the globalized world, where transnationalism enables people to be "both/and" rather than "either/or."

imperialism Historically, this term has applied to a system in which a country rules other countries. Often force was used to obtain and maintain power. More recently, the term has is applied to the de facto rather than de jure exercise of one country's power or influence over others, especially in political and economic matters.

international governmental organizations (IGO) Administrative bodies sanctioned with power by a conglomerate of states. The United Nations, the World Bank, the International Monetary Fund, and NATO are examples of such bodies.

irredentism Claims levied by one state on the territory of another. Such claims generally derive from the historical movement of borders and are often supported by the existence of diasporic or minority groups.

jurisdiction The territory within which the authority of a particular person, group, or institutional entity legally pervades.

legal categories of boundaries
    de facto A boundary that is disputed by one or more adjacent states but continues to function in relation to the power of one state.
    de jure A boundary that has been recognized by international legal bodies.
    fictitious A boundary that exists on maps but not in the real world.

migration Permanent or semipermanent change of residence by an individual or group of people.

minorities A group of persons in a society who view themselves as separate from the rest of society on ethnic, linguistic, or religious grounds.

nation A group of persons who collectively designate themselves as a single, distinct group based upon historical and cultural criteria, possessing a political agenda with the ultimate goal of achieving territorial sovereignty.

nation-state A sociopolitical ideal wherein all inhabitants of a given state belong to one nation.

nationalism An ideology and political practice that assumes all nations should have their own state, a nation-state, in their own territory, the national homeland.

nongovernmental organization (NGO) Actors within the international system whose power and purpose is not directly linked to a particular state. NGOs often function in philanthropic efforts. They should not be confused with IGOs. Members of NGOs are usually individuals, while states usually constitute the membership of IGOs.

partition The process of dividing a state into two or more jurisdictional territories.

place In geography, place is often counterposed to space as indicating a more humanized locality through which humans live their lives.

population transfer The forced relocation of people under the direction of an authoritative body.

protectorate A small state under the direct political and usually economic control of a foreign power.

province An administrative district or division deriving power from the state in which it exists.

scale A reference to the multiple levels of representation, experience, and organization of geographical events and processes.

secession The act of separating a territory from a state. The territory may become independent or join another state.

sovereignty As the legal foundation of an interstate system, sovereignty represents the unique right of physical coercion within territory. Sovereignty is not just proclaimed; it has to be recognized by other members of the interstate system, i.e., other states that recognize a particular government has the exclusive right to exercise its authority within a specific territory.

state A government recognized as possessing sovereignty over a territory and its people. States are the primary political units of the modern world and together constitute the interstate system.

supranational institutions *See* international governmental organizations and nongovernmental organization.

territoriality Behavior that uses bounded space to control activities.

territory A general term used to describe a portion of space occupied by a person, groups, local economy, or state.

Thirty Years War This conflict occurred between 1618 and 1648 and involved nearly all European powers. It marked the decline of Hapsburg power, the ascendance of France as the foremost continental power, and the confirmation of Dutch sovereignty. Along with the Protestant Reformation, it is often seen as marking the turning point from medieval, feudal Europe to the gradual emergence of the modern nation-state system.

transnationalism A process by which cross-border links between people and institutions challenge the sovereignty of states and the nation-state system.

Treaty of Westphalia Brought to an end the Thirty Years War in 1648. It is commonly regarded as the cornerstone agreement of modern international law.

Bibliography

Ackleson, Jason. "Constructing Security on the U.S.-Mexico Border." *Political Geography* 24, no. 2 (2004): 165–84.

Agnew, John. "The Territorial Trap: The Geographical Assumptions of International Relations Theory." *Review of International Political Economy* 1, no. 1 (1994): 53–80.

———. *Geopolitics: Re-Visioning World Politics.* London: Routledge, 1998.

Agnew, John, and Stuart Corbridge. *Mastering Space: Hegemony, Territory and International Political Economy.* London: Routledge, 1995.

Ahmed, Rafiuddin. *The Bengal Muslims, 1871–1906: A Quest for Identity.* Delhi: Oxford University Press, 1981.

———. *Understanding the Bengal Muslims: Interpretative Essays.* New Delhi: Oxford University Press, 2001.

Alamanov, C. K. *Kyrgyztandyn Mamlakettik Chegarasynyn Kalyntanyshy (The Formation of Kyrgyzstan's State Boundary).* Bishkek: Friedrich Ebert Siftung, 2005.

All Point Bulletin, March 2008–June 2008, http://www.allpointbulletin.com/archives/archives.html (30 July 2008).

Anderson, Benedict. *Imagined Communities: Reflections on the Origin and Spread of Nationalism.* London: Verso, 1983.

Anderson, James, and Liam O'Dowd. "Borders, Border Regions and Territoriality: Contradictory Meanings, Changing Significance." *Regional Studies* 33, no. 7 (1999): 593–604.

Anderson, Joan, and Egbert Wever. "Borders, Border Regions and Economic Integration: One World, Ready or Not." *Journal of Borderland Studies* 18, no. 1 (2004): 27–38.

Anderson, Malcolm. *Frontiers: Territory and State Formation in the Modern World.* Cambridge: Polity Press, 1996.

Andreas, Peter, and Thomas Biersteker. *The Rebordering of North America: Integration and Exclusion in a New Security Context*. New York: Routledge, 2003.

Asimov, M., ed. *Tadzhikskaia Sovetskaia Sotsialisticheskaia Respublika*. Dushanbe: Glavnaia Nauchnaia Redaktsiia Tadzhikskoi Sovetskoi Entsiklopedii, 1984.

Babakulov, Ulugbek. "Kyrgyz-Uzbek Border Tensions." *Reporting Central Asia*. London: Institute for War and Peace Reporting, 2002. http://www.iwpr.net (16 June 2002).

Bagiński, Henryk. *Poland's Freedom of the Sea*, 4th ed. Kirkcaldy, U.K.: Allen Lithographic, 1944.

Balmaceda, R. C. Rey. *Límites y Fronteras de la República Argentina: Epítome Geográfico*. Buenos Aires: OIKOS, 1979.

"Bangladesh, India Joint Team Assesses Possible Enclave Exchange." *Prothom Alo*, 30 May 2007.

Barrow, Ian. *Making History, Drawing Territory: British Mapping in India c. 1756–1905*. New Delhi: Oxford University Press, 2003.

Bartolomé, Leopoldo J. *Los Colonos de Apóstoles: Estrategias Adaptativas y Etnicidad en Una Colonia Eslava en Misiones*. Posadas, Argentina: Universidad Nacional de Misiones, 2000.

Barton, William. *India's North-West Frontier*. London: John Murray, 1939.

Bassin, Mark. "Imperialism and the Nation-State in Friedrich Ratzel's Political Geography." *Progress in Human Geography* 11, no. 4 (1987): 473–95.

Batten, Bruce. "Frontiers and Boundaries in Pre-Modern Japan." *Journal of Historical Geography* 25, no. 2 (1999): 166–82.

Beattie, David. *Liechtenstein: A Modern History*. London: I. B. Tauris, 2004.

Bennigsen, Alexandre, and Marie Broxup. *The Islamic Threat to the Soviet State*. London: Croom Helm, 1983.

Berdahl, Daphne. *Where the World Ended: Re-Unification and Identity in the German Borderland*. Berkeley: University of California Press, 1999.

Bergne, Paul. *The Birth of Tajikistan*. London: I. B. Tauris, 2007.

Bhattacharyya, Pranab Kumar. *The Kingdom of Kamata Koch Behar in Historical Perspective*. Calcutta: Ratna Prakashan, 2000.

Biger, G. *The Boundaries of Modern Palestine, 1840–1947*. London: Routledge, 2004.

———. "The Boundaries of Israel—Palestine, Past, Present and Future: A Critical Geographical View." *Israel Studies* 13, no. 1 (2008): 68–93.

Bilainkin, George. *Within Two Years! Being the Narrative of a Journey to the Polish Corridor, the Tinder Box of Europe*. London: Marston, 1934.

Bilgrami, Asghar H. *Afghanistan and British India: 1793–1907*. New Delhi: Sterling Publishers, 1972.

Blake, Gerald. "State Limits in the Early Twenty-First Century: Observations on Form and Function." *Geopolitics* 5, no. 1 (2000): 1–18.

Blanke, Richard. *Orphans of Versailles: The Germans in Western Poland 1918–1939*. Lexington: University Press of Kentucky, 1993.

Boggs, Samuel. *International Boundaries: A Study of Boundary Functions and Problems*. New York: Columbia University Press, 1940.

Boleda, Mario. "El Proceso Emigratorio Misionero En Las Últimas Tres Décadas." *Desarrollo Económico* 23, no. 90 (1983): 287–98.

Bolsi, Alfredo S. C. *Misiones: Una Aproximación Geográfica al Problema de la Yerba Mate y Sus Efectos en la Ocupación del Espacio y el Poblamiento.* Resistencia, Argentina: Instituto de Historia de la Facultad de Humanidades de la Universidad Nacional del Nordeste, 1986.

Brawer, M. *The Borders of Israel* (in Hebrew). Yavneh Press, 1987.

———. "The Making of an Israeli-Palestinian Boundary." Pp. 473–92 in *The Razor's Edge: International Boundaries and Political Geography*, edited by C. Schofield, D. Newman, A. Drysdale, and J. Brown. London: Kluwer Law International, 2002.

Browning, Christopher, and Pertti Joenniemi. "Contending Discourses of Marginality: The Case of Kaliningrad." *Geopolitics* 9, no. 3 (2004): 699–730.

Bruce, Richard Isaac. *The Forward Policy and Its Results or Thirty-Five Years' Work amongst the Tribes on Our North-Western Frontier of India.* London: Longmans, Green, 1900.

Buchanan, Allen, and Margaret Moore, eds. *States, Nations and Borders: The Ethics of Making Boundaries.* Cambridge: Cambridge University Press, 2003.

Burnett, Victoria. "Morocco Angry at Royal Visit to Enclaves." *New York Times*, 6 November 2007, A14.

Buursink, Jan. "The Binational Reality of Border-Crossing Cities." *GeoJournal* 54, no. 1 (2001): 7–19.

Cámara de Senadores de la Nación. *Diario de Sesiones*, Vol. I. Buenos Aires: 1881.

Cambas, Aníbal. *Historia Política e Institucional de Misiones: Los Derechos Misioneros ante la Historia y ante la Ley.* Posadas, Argentina: Ediciones S.A.D.E.M., 1984 [1945].

Castells, Manuel. *The Rise of the Network Society.* Malden, Mass.: Blackwell Publishers, 1996.

Census of India. Delhi: Manager of Publications, 1941.

Chaliand, Gerard. *The Kurdish Tragedy.* London: Zed Books, 1992.

Chatterjee, Shiba Prasad. *The Partition of Bengal: A Geographical Study with Maps and Diagrams.* Calcutta: D. R. Mitra Press, 1947.

Child, John. "Geopolitical Thinking in Latin America." *Latin American Research Review* 14, no. 2 (1979): 89–111.

Churchill, Rogers Platt. *The Anglo-Russian Convention of 1907.* Cedar Rapids: Torch Press, 1939.

CIA. *The World Factbook.* "Liechtenstein." 31 December 2001, https://www.cia.gov/library/publications/the-world-factbook/geos/ls.html#Econ (11 March 2008).

Cienciala, Anna. "The Battle of Danzig and the Polish Corridor at the Paris Peace Conference of 1919." Pp. 71–94 in *The Reconstruction of Poland, 1914–1923*, edited by Paul Latawski. New York: St. Martin's Press, 1992.

Clark, Christopher. *Iron Kingdom: The Rise and Fall of Prussia, 1600–1947.* Cambridge, Mass.: Belknap Press of Harvard University Press, 2006.

Clark, Richard E. *Social Change in an American Exclave Community: A Social-Historical Description of Point Roberts, Washington.* Bellingham, Wash.: Master's thesis, Western Washington State College, 1970.

———. *Point Roberts, USA: The History of a Canadian Enclave.* Bellingham, Wash.: Textype Publishing, 1980.

Cohen, Roger. "A Wartime Scenario, Starring the Swiss." *International Herald Tribune,* 9 March 2007, http://www.iht.com/protected/articles/2007/03/09/news/globalist.php (11 March 2008).

Colás, Alejandro. *Empire.* Cambridge: Polity Press, 2007.

Coleman, Nick. "Tajik Leader, Aga Khan Open Afghanistan Bridge." *Agence France-Presse* 31 October 2006, as reported in *Ismaili Mail,* http://ismailimail.wordpress.com/2006/10/31/tajik-leader-aga-khan-open-afghanistan-bridge/ (8 January 2008).

Collins, Larry, and Dominique Lapierre. *O Jerusalem.* New York: Simon & Schuster, 1972.

"A Conflict Inevitable." *New York Times,* 24 April 1885, 1.

Conquest, Robert. *Stalin: Breaker of Nations.* London: Phoenix, 1991.

Council of Europe: European Commission against Racism and Intolerance. *Second Report on Liechtenstein, Adopted 28 June 2002,* 15 April 2003, http://www.coe.int/t/e/human_rights/ecri/1-ecri/2-country-by-country_approach/Liechtenstein/Liechtenstein_CBC_2en.asp (11 March 2008).

Craib, Raymond B. *Cartographic Mexico: A History of State Fixations and Fugitive Landscapes.* Durham, N.C.: Duke University Press, 2004.

Culcasi, Karen. "Cartographically Constructing Kurdistan within Geopolitical and Orientalist Discourses." *Political Geography* 25, no. 6 (2006): 680–706.

Curta, Florin, ed. *Borders, Barriers, and Ethnogenesis: Frontiers in Late Antiquity and the Middle Ages.* Turnhout, Belgium: Berpols, 2005.

Curzon, George. *The Pamirs and the Source of the Oxus.* London: The Royal Geographic Society, 1896.

———. *Frontiers.* Oxford: Clarendon Press, 1907.

Dahlman, Carl. "The Political Geography of Kurdistan." *Eurasian Geography and Economics* 43, no. 4 (2002): 271–99.

Dalton, Hugh. *Towards the Peace of Nations: A Study of International Politics.* London: George Routledge, 1928.

Davies, C. Collin. *The Problem of the North-West Frontier, 1890–1908.* Cambridge: Cambridge University Press, 1932.

Davies, Norman. *God's Playground: A History of Poland,* Vols. I and II. New York: Columbia University Press, 1982.

Davis, H. W. C. *The Great Game in Asia (1800–1844).* London: Humphrey Milford, Oxford University Press, 1927.

Delaney, David. *Territory: A Short Introduction.* London: Blackwell, 2005.

Diener, Alexander C., and Joshua Hagen. "Theorizing Borders in a 'Borderless World': Globalization, Territory and Scale." *Geography Compass* 3, no. 3 (2009): 1196–1216.

Dilks, David. *Curzon in India in Two Volumes.* New York: Taplinger, 1969.

Dirks, Nicholas. "Guiltless Spoliation, Picturesque Beauty, Colonial Knowledge, and Colin Mackenzie's Survey of India." Pp. 211–32 in *Perceptions of South Asia's Visual*

Past, edited by Catherine Asher and Thomas Metcalf. New Delhi: American Institute of Indian Studies, 1994.

Dobson, Christopher, John Miller, and Ronald Payne. *The Cruelest Night*. Boston: Little, Brown, 1979.

Documents on Germany 1944–1961. U.S. Government Printing Office, 1961.

Donald, Robert. *The Polish Corridor and the Consequences*. London: Thornton Butterworth, 1929.

Drechsler, Horst. *Let Us Die Fighting: The Struggle of the Herero and Nama against German Imperialism (1884–1915)*. London: Zed Press, 1980.

Dupree, Louis. *Afghanistan*. Oxford: Oxford University Press, 1997.

Ebel, Kathryn. "Representations of the Frontier in Ottoman Town Views of the Sixteenth Century." *Imago Mundi* 60, no. 1 (2008): 1–22.

Edney, Matthew. *Mapping an Empire: The Geographical Construction of British India 1765–1843*. Chicago: University of Chicago Press, 1997.

Edsall, Robert M. "Iconic Maps in American Political Discourse." *Cartographica* 42, no. 4 (2007): 335–47.

Edwards, H. Sutherland. *Russian Projects against India: From the Czar Peter to General Skobeleff*. London: Remington & Co. Publishers, 1885.

"Effect on the Money Markets." *New York Times*, 9 April 1885, 1.

Eidt, Robert C. *Pioneer Settlement in Northeast Argentina*. Madison: University of Wisconsin Press, 1971.

Englebert, Pierre. *Should I Stay or Should I Go? Compliance and Defiance in National Integration in Barotseland and Casamance*, unpublished manuscript, December 2004, http://www.politics.pomona.edu/penglebert/Compliance%20and%20Defiance-afrika%20spectrum.pdf 50 (11 March 2008).

Escolar, Marcelo, Silvina Quintero Palacios, and Carlos E. Reboratti. "Geographical Identity and Patriotic Representation in Argentina." Pp. 346–366 in *Geography and National Identity*, edited by David J. M. Hooson. Cambridge: Blackwell, 1994.

Eskander, Saad. "Britain's Policy in Southern Kurdistan: The Formation and the Termination of the First Kurdish Government, 1918–1919." *British Journal of Middle Eastern Studies* 27, no. 2 (2000): 139–63.

The Essential Facts about the League of Nations. Geneva: Secretariat, Information Section, 1938.

Evans, George de Lacy. *On the Designs of Russia*. London: John Murray, 1828.

———. *On the Practicability of an Invasion of British India*. London: J. M. Richardson, 1829.

Evans, Richard. *The Third Reich in Power*. New York: Penguin, 2005.

Falah, G. "The Green Line Revisited: October 2000." Pp. 493–512 in *The Razor's Edge: International Boundaries and Political Geography*, edited by C. Schofield, D. Newman, A. Drysdale, and J. Brown. London: Kluwer Law International, 2002.

———. "Dynamics and Patterns of the Shrinking of Arab Lands in Palestine." *Political Geography* 22, no. 2 (2003): 179–209.

Falah, G., and D. Newman. "The Spatial Manifestation of Threat: Israelis and Palestinians Seek a 'Good' Border." *Political Geography* 14, no. 8 (1995): 689–706.

Farinelli, F. "Friedrich Ratzel and the Nature of (Political) Geography." *Political Geography* 19, no. 8 (2000): 943–55.

Fawcett, C. B. *Frontiers: A Study in Political Geography.* Oxford: Clarendon Press, 1918.

Felmy, Sabine, and Hermann Kreutzmann. "Wakhan Woluswali in Badakhshan: Observations and Reflections from Afghanistan's Periphery." *Erdkunde* 58, no. 2 (2004): 97–117.

Ferradás, Carmen A. *Power in the Southern Cone Borderlands: An Anthropology of Development Practice.* Westport: Bergin & Garvey, 1998.

———. "How a Green Wilderness Became a Trade Wilderness: The Story of a Southern Cone Frontier." *PoLAR* 21, no. 2 (1998): 11–25.

———. "Environment, Security, and Terrorism in the Trinational Frontier of the Southern Cone." *Identities: Global Studies in Culture and Power* 11 (2004): 417–42.

Fisch, Maria. *The Caprivi Strip during the German Colonial Period, 1890–1914 [with a Chapter on the Boundary Dispute up to the Present].* Windhoek: Out of Africa Publishers, 1999.

———. *The Secessionist Movement in the Caprivi: A Historical Perspective.* Windhoek: Namibia Scientific Society, 1999.

Fitzherbert, Anthony, and Charudutt Mishra. *Afghanistan Wakhan Mission Technical Report.* Geneva: United Nations Environmental Programme, Food and Agriculture Organization, 2003.

Fleck, Fiona. "Prince to People: I'll Sell Up to Bill Gates." *Telegraph.co.uk,* 19 June 2001, http://www.telegraph.co.uk/news/main.jhtml?xml=/news/2001/02/11/wlich11.xml (11 March 2008).

Flint, Colin, ed. *The Geography of War and Peace: From Death Camps to Diplomats.* Oxford: Oxford University Press, 2005.

Foreign Policy Service. "German-Polish Relations: Danzig–the Polish 'Corridor'–East Prussia–Upper Silesia." *Information Service* 3, no. 12 (1927): 169–84.

Fraser-Tytler, William K. *Afghanistan: A Study of Political Developments in Central and Southern Asia.* London: Oxford University Press, 1967.

Frechtling, Louis E. "Anglo-Russian Rivalry in Eastern Turkistan, 1863–1881." *Journal of the Royal Central Asian Society* 26, no. 3 (1939): 471–89.

Fuchs, Werner, and Robert Sherwood Allan. *Poland's Policy of Expansion as Revealed by Polish Testimonies.* Berlin: Deutscher Ostmarken-Verein, 1932.

Fürst, Johann. *Der Widersinn des polnischen Korridors.* Berlin: Deutsche Rundschau, 1926.

Fyodorov, Gennady M. "The Social and Economic Development of Kaliningrad." Pp. 32–56 in *Kaliningrad: The European Amber Region,* edited by Pertti Joenniemi and Jan Prawitz. Aldershot, U.K.: Ashgate, 1998.

Gallero de Urfer, María Cecilia. *La Inmigración y Colonización Alemana en Misiones.* Buenos Aires: Academia Nacional de la Historia, 2003.

Ganguly, Sumit. *Conflict Unending: India and Pakistan Tensions Since 1947.* New York: Columbia University Press, 2002.

Geithner, Konrad, et al. *Lichtenstein 1212–1995*. Vaduz: Stadtverwaltung Lichtenstein, 1996.

Gerner, Deborah J., and Jillian Schwedler. "Trends and Prospects." Pp. 425–37 in *Understanding the Contemporary Middle East*, edited by Deborah J. Gerner and Jillian Schwedler. Boulder, Colo.: Lynne Reinner Publishers, 2004.

Gilbert, M. *Atlas of the Arab-Israeli Conflict*. London: Routledge, 2002.

Glassner, Martin Ira, and Chuck Fahrer. *Political Geography*. 3rd ed. New York: Wiley, 2004.

Gold, Peter. *Europe or Africa? A Contemporary Study of the Spanish North African Enclaves of Ceuta and Melilla*. Liverpool: Liverpool University Press, 2000.

Goldberg, Jeffrey. "After Iraq." *The Atlantic* (January/February 2008): 69–79.

Goodes World Atlas. 2nd ed. Skokie, Ill.: Rand McNally, 2005.

Gordillo, Gastón. *Landscapes of Devils: Tensions of Place and Memory in the Argentinean Chaco*. Durham, N.C.: Duke University Press, 2004.

Gordon, Raymond G., Jr., ed. *Ethnologue: Languages of the World*. 15th ed. Dallas: SIL International, 2005, http://www.ethnologue.com/ (11 March 2008).

Gorosito, AnaMaria. *Censo Indígena Provincial 1979*. Posadas, Argentina: Dirección de Asuntos Aborígenes y Universidad Nacional de Misiones, 1981.

Grandin, Greg. "The Wide War: How Donald Rumsfeld Discovered the Wild West in Latin America." *TomDispatch.com*, 7 May 2006, http://www.tomdispatch.com/post/82089/grandin_on_rumsfeld_s_latin_american_wild_west_show (8 August 2008).

Greene, Barbara. *Liechtenstein: Valley of Peace*. Vaduz: Liechtenstein-Verlag, 1967.

Gregory, Timothy. *A History of Byzantium*. Malden, Mass.: Blackwell, 2005.

Grimson, Alejandro. "El Puente Que Separó Dos Orillas. Notas Para Una Crítica Del Esencialismo De La Hermandad." Pp. 201–31 in *Fronteras, Naciones e Identidades: La Periferia Como Centro*, edited by Alejandro Grimson. Buenos Aires: Ediciones Ciccus/La Crujía, 2000.

Grousset, René. *The Empire of the Steppes: A History of Central Asia*. New Brunswick, N.J.: Rutgers University Press, 1970.

Guéhenno, Jean-Marie. *The End of the Nation-State*. Minneapolis: University of Minnesota Press, 1995.

Guglialmelli, Juan E. "Argentina Frente Al 'Operativo Misiones' Del Brasil." *Estrategia*, no. 19–20 (1972–1973): 19–20.

Gunter, Michael. "A De Facto Kurdish State in Northern Iraq." *Third World Quarterly* 14, no. 2 (1993): 295–319.

Guttzeit, Emil J. *Ostpreussen in 1440 Bildern—Geschichtliche Darstellung*. Leer, Germany: Gerhard Rautenberg, n.d.

Habberton, William. *Anglo-Russian Relations concerning Afghanistan 1837–1907*. Urbana, Ill.: University of Illinois, 1937.

Hamilton, Lindsay. "Whoops! Swiss Accidentally Invade Liechtenstein." *ABC News*, 3 March 2007, http://abcnews.go.com/International/story?id=2921407&page=1 (11 March 2008).

Hartshorne, Richard. "Suggestions on the Terminology of Political Boundaries." *Annals of the Association of American Geographers* 26, no. 1 (1936): 56–57.

———. "A Survey of the Boundary Problems of Europe." Pp. 163–213 in *Geographic Aspects of International Relations*, edited by Charles Colby. Chicago: University of Chicago Press, 1938.

Haskins, Charles Homer, and Robert Howard Lord. *Some Problems of the Peace Conference*. Cambridge, Mass.: Harvard University Press, 1922.

Hauner, Milan. *India in Axis Strategy: Germany, Japan and Indian Nationalists in the Second World War*. Stuttgart: Klett-Cotta, 1981.

Heffernan, Michael. "History, Geography and the French National Space: The Question of Alsace-Lorraine, 1914–18." *Space & Polity* 5, no. 1 (2001): 27–48.

Heiss, Friedrich. *Deutschland und der Korridor*. Berlin: Volk und Reich, 1939.

Helmreich, Paul. *From Paris to Sevres: The Partition of the Ottoman Empire at the Peace Conference of 1919–1920*. Columbus: Ohio State University Press, 1974.

Hernández, Rafael. *Cartas Misioneras*. Buenos Aires: Editorial Universitaria de Buenos Aires, 1973 [1887].

Herold, Christopher. *Bonaparte in Egypt*. New York: Harper & Row, 1962.

Herz, John. "The Rise and Demise of the Territorial State." *World Politics* 9, no. 4 (1957): 473–93.

Herzliyah Conference, *Demarcating an Israel-Palestine Boundary: Principles and Professional Considerations*. Working Group of Geographers, EUROBorder Conf Project, January 2006.

"Hindus Protest Transfer." *Washington Post*, 27 June 1992, A14.

Hirsch, Francine. *Empire of Nations: Ethnographic Knowledge and the Making of the Soviet Union*. London: Cornell University Press, 2005.

Hobsbawm, E. J., and T. O. Ranger. *The Invention of Tradition*. Cambridge: Cambridge University Press, 1983.

Holdrich, Thomas. *Political Frontiers and Boundary Making*. London: MacMillan, 1916.

Holtom, Paul. "Detached Regions and Their Role in Return to Empire: The Cases of East Prussia and Kaliningrad." Pp. 219–51 in *Baltic Democracy at the Crossroads*, edited by Sten Berlund and Kjetil Duvold. Kristiansand, Norway: HøyskoleForlaget, 2003.

———. "The Kaliningrad Test in Russian-EU Relations." *Perspectives on European Politics and Society* 6, no. 1 (2005): 31–54.

Hopkirk, Peter. *The Great Game: The Struggle for Empire in Central Asia*. New York: Kodansha International, 1992.

Hue, Fernand. *Les Russes et les Anglais dans L'Afghanistan*. Paris: E. Dentu, Libraire-Éditeur, 1885.

Humlum, Johannes. *La géographie de l'Afghanistan*. Copenhagen: Gyldendal, 1959.

Huntington, Samuel. *The Clash of Civilizations*. New York: Touchstone, 1997.

Huttenbach, Henry R. "The Origins of Russian Imperialism." Pp. 18–44 in *Russian Imperialism from Ivan the Great to the Revolution*, edited by Taras Hunczak. New Brunswick, N.J.: Rutgers University Press, 1974.

IFES (International Foundation for Election Systems). "Election Guide: Liechtenstein Referendum, Results for Provision 1, Constitutional Referendum—Princely Initiative." 14 March 2003, http://www.electionguide.org/results.php?ID=326 (11 March 2008).

"The Impending Conflict." *New York Times*, 17 April 1885, 1.

"India and Bangladesh; No Light for the Corridor." *Economist*, 13 June 1992, 33.

"Indian Enclave People Want to Become Bangladeshi." *Independent*, 28 April 2003, A1.

An Indian Officer, *Russia's March towards India*. London: Sampson Low, Marston & Company, 1894.

"Indo-Bangla Officials Visit Enclaves." *Statesman*, 30 May 2007, A3.

Ingram, Edward. *In Defense of British India: Great Britain in the Middle East, 1775–1842*. London: Frank Cass, 1984.

International Joint Commission, United States and Canada. *Public Hearing on Point Roberts, Washington*. Point Roberts, Wash.: 1971.

Israel Information Center. *Saving Lives: Israel's Security Fence*. Jerusalem: Ministry of Foreign Affairs, 2003.

Izady, Mehrdad. *A Concise Handbook: The Kurds*. Washington, D.C.: Taylor & Francis, 1992.

Jackson, W. A. Douglas. "Whither Political Geography?" *Annals of the Association of American Geographers* 48, no. 2 (1958): 178–83.

Jahan, Rounaq. *Pakistan: Failure in National Integration*. New York: Colombia University Press, 1972.

Jansen, Norbert, ed. *Beiträge zur liechtensteinischen Identität*. Liechtensteiner Politische Schriften, Band 34. Schaan, Liechtenstein: Verlag der Liechtensteiner Akademischen Gesellschaft, 2001.

Jaquet, Héctor Eduardo. *Los Combates por la Invención de Misiones*. Posadas, Argentina: Universidad Nacional de Misiones, 2005.

Jelavich, Barbara. *A Century of Russian Foreign Policy 1814–1914*. Philadelphia: Lippincott, 1964.

Johanson, Märta. *Self-Determination and Borders: The Obligation to Show Consideration for the Interests of Others*. Åbo, Finland: Åbo Akademi University Press, 2004.

Jones, Reece. "Whose Homeland? Territoriality and Religious Nationalism in Pre-Partition Bengal." *South Asia Research* 26, no. 2 (2006): 115–31.

———. "Sacred Cows and Thumping Drums: Claiming Territory as 'Zones of Tradition' in British India." *Area* 39, no. 1 (2007): 55–65.

———. "Searching for the Greatest Bengali: The BBC and Shifting Identity Categories in South Asia." *National Identities* 10, no. 2 (2008): 149–65.

Jones, Stephen. "Boundary Concepts in the Setting of Place and Time." *Annals of the Association of American Geographers* 49, no. 3 (1959): 241–55.

———. "The Description of International Boundaries." *Annals of the Association of American Geographers* 33, no. 2 (1943): 99–117.

Jordine, Melissa. *The Dispute over Gibraltar*. New York: Chelsea House, 2007.

Kabir, Ekram. *Border Fencing: A Major Irritant in Indo-Bangla Relations.* Dhaka: News Network, 2005.

Kahler, Miles, and Barbara Walter, ed. *Territoriality and Conflict in an Era of Globalization.* Cambridge: Cambridge University Press, 2006.

Kaiser, Peter. *Geschichte des Fürstenthums Liechtenstein.* Chur, Switzerland: Grubenmann, 1847; reprinted Nendeln, Liechtenstein: Krauss, 1974.

Kaplan, David, and Jouni Häkli, eds. *Boundaries and Place: European Borderlands in Geographical Context.* Lanham, Md.: Rowman & Littlefield, 2002.

Kashani-Sabet, Firoozeh. *Frontier Fictions: Shaping the Iranian Nation, 1804–1946.* Princeton, N.J.: Princeton University Press, 1999.

Kasperson, Roger E., and Julian V. Minghi, eds. *The Structure of Political Geography.* Chicago: Aldine, 1969.

"Katta fitnaning bir xalqasi." *Halq So'zi* 179, no. 2217, 9 September 1999, 1.

Kellerman, A. *Society and Settlement: Jewish Land of Israel in the Twentieth Century.* Albany: State University of New York Press, 1993.

Kendal, "The Kurds under the Ottoman Empire." Pp. 11–37 in *A People without a Country,* edited by Gerard Chaliand. New York: Olive Branch Publishing, 1993.

Kershner, I. *Barrier: The Seam of the Israeli-Palestinian Conflict.* New York: Palgrave Macmillan, 2005.

Kessler, Oliver, and Jan Helmig, "Of Systems, Boundaries, and Regionalisation." *Geopolitics* 12, no. 4 (2007): 570–85.

Khanna, Parag. "Waving Goodbye to Hegemony." *New York Times Magazine,* section MM, 27 January 2008, 34.

Kimmerling, B. *Zionism and Territory.* Berkeley: University of California Press, 1983.

Knappe, Elke. "Der ländliche Raum des Gebietes Kaliningrad: Der Transformationsprozess in der Viehwirtschaft." *Europa Regional* 4, no. 3 (1996): 24–30.

Knight, Edward F. *Where Three Empires Meet: A Narrative of Recent Travel in Kashmir, Western Tibet, Gilgit, and the Adjoining Countries.* London: Longmans, Green, and Co., 1897.

Koichiev, Arslan. "Ethno-Territorial Claims in the Ferghana Valley during the Process of National Delimitation, 1924–7." Pp. 45–56 in *Central Asia: Aspects of Transition,* edited by Tom Everett-Heath. London: RoutledgeCurzon, 2003.

Kolossov, Vladimir. "Border Studies: Changing Perspectives and Theoretical Approaches." *Geopolitics* 10, no. 4 (2005): 606–32.

Krader, Lawrence. *Peoples of Central Asia.* Bloomington: Indiana University Publications, 1966.

Kreutzmann, Hermann. "Ethnic Minorities and Marginality in the Pamirian Knot: Survival of Wakhi and Kirghiz in a Harsh Environment and Global Contexts." *The Geographical Journal* 169, no. 3 (2003): 215–35.

———. "The Significance of Geopolitical Issues for Development of Mountainous Areas of Central Asia." Paper presented at the Strategies for Development and Food Security in Mountainous Areas of Central Asia International Workshop. 2005, http://www.akdn.org/publications/2005_akf_mountains_paper2_english.pdf (23 February 2008).

Krickus, Richard. *The Kaliningrad Question.* Lanham, Md.: Rowman & Littlefield, 2002.

Kristof, Ladis. "The Nature of Frontiers and Boundaries." *Annals of the Association of American Geographers* 49, no. 3 (1959): 269–82.

Kushnirsky, Fyodor. "Post Soviet Attempts to Establish Free Economic Zones." *Post Soviet Geography and Economics* 38, no. 3 (1997): 144–62.

Kuus, Merje. "Something Old, Something New: Eastness in European Union Enlargement." *Journal of International Relations and Development* 10, no. 2 (2007): 150–67.

Kuznetsova, O. V., and V. A. Mau. *Kaliningradskaya oblast: ot "nepotoplyaemogo avianostsa" k "nepotop-lyaemomu sborochnomu tsehu" (Kaliningrad Oblast: From the "Unsinkable Aircraft Carrier" to the "Unsinkable Assembly Shop")*. Moscow: Russia in United Europe Committee, 2002.

"Kyrgyz Opposition Holds 'Public Trial' of Leaders for Violent Clash." *RFE/RL Newsline* 12, no. 53, Part I. Prague: Radio Free Europe/Radio Liberty, 18 March 2008.

"Kyrgyz Report Progress in Border Talks with Uzbekistan." *RFE/RL Newsline* 10, no. 219, Part I. Prague: Radio Free Europe/Radio Liberty, 29 November 2006.

"Landlocked People's Plight." *Statesman*, 13 April 2006, A1.

Le Goff, Jacques. *The Birth of Europe*, translated by Janet Lloyd. Malden, Mass.: Blackwell, 2005.

Legal Assistance Centre. *NAMLEX: Index to the Laws of Namibia, 2004 Update* (Windhoek), 1–4, http://www.lac.org.na/Pdf/namlex2004.pdf (11 March 2008).

Legvold, R. "Great Power Stakes in Central Asia." Pp. 1–38 in *Thinking Strategically: The Major Powers, Kazakhstan, and the Central Asian Security Nexus*, edited by R. Legvold. Cambridge, Mass.: American Academy of Arts and Sciences, 2003.

Lengyel, Emil. *The Cauldron Boils*. London: Dial Press, 1932.

Léon Lecestre, ed. *Lettres Inédites de Napoléon Ier*. Paris: E. Plon, Nourrit et Cie, Imprimeurs-Éditeurs, 1897.

"Liechtenstein: How Does Liechtenstein Envision Its Future?" *Mondag*, 27 February 2008, http://www.mondaq.com/article.asp?articleid=57740 (11 March 2008).

Lovell, Julia. *The Great Wall: China against the World 1000 BC–AD 2000*. New York: Grove Press, 2006.

Luknitsky, Pavel N. *Soviet Tajikistan*. Moscow: Foreign Languages Publishing House, 1954.

Lunden, Thomas. *On the Boundary: About Humans at the End of Territory*. Stockholm: Södertörns Högskola, 2004.

Lutman, Roman. *The Truth about the "Corridor": Polish Pomerania: Ten Points*. Toruń, Poland: Baltic Institute, 1933.

Lyall, Sarah. "Vaduz Journal; For Rent One Principality. Prince Not Included." *New York Times*, 25 March 2003, http://query.nytimes.com/gst/fullpage.html?res=9A01E6D91530F936A15750C0A9659C8B63 (11 March 2008).

MacGregor, C. M. *The Defence of India: A Strategical Study*. Simla, India: Government Central Branch Press, 1884.

Machray, Robert. *East Prussia: Menace to Poland and Peace*. Chicago: American Polish Council, 1943.

MacMillan, Margaret. *Peacemakers: The Paris Peace Conference of 1919 and Its Attempt to End War*. London: John Murray, 2001.

MacNeill, John. *The Progress and Present Position of Russia in the East.* London: RoutledgeCurzon, 2004 [1854].

MacPhail, Robert. "King Stirs Up Hornets' Nest with Trip to Disputed Towns." *The Times,* 5 November 2007, 37.

Maeder, Ernesto J. A. *Misiones: Historia de la Tierra Prometida.* Buenos Aires: Eudeba, 2004.

Makovsky, D. *A Defensible Fence: Fighting Terror and Enabling a Two State Solution.* Washington, D.C.: Washington Institute for Near East Policy, 2004.

Malleson, George B. *The Russo-Afghan Question and the Invasion of India.* London: George Routledge and Sons, 1885.

Manzi, Francisco. *Impresiones De Viaje: Breves Apuntes Sobre El Territorio De Misiones.* Corrientes, Argentina: La Popular, 1910.

Margalot, José A. *Geografía De Misiones.* Buenos Aires: Cultural Argentina, 1971.

Marks, Sally. *The Illusion of Peace: International Relations in Europe, 1918–1933.* New York: Palgrave Macmillan, 2003.

Martin, Graham. "The Principality of Liechtenstein—A Living Fossil from the Time of the Holy Roman Empire." *German Life and Letters* 42, no. 1 (1988): 72–90.

Marvin, Charles. *Russia's Power of Seizing Herat, and Concentrating an Army There to Threaten India.* London: W. H. Allen & Co., 1884.

Matthiesen, Ulf, and Hans-Joachim Bürkner. "Antagonistic Structures in Border Areas: Local Milieux and Local Politics in the Polish-German Twin City Gubin/ Guben." *GeoJournal* 54, no. 1 (2001): 43–50.

Maunsell, F. R. "Kurdistan." *Geographical Journal* 3, no. 2 (1894): 81–92.

Maxwell, Neville. "How the Sino-Russian Boundary Conflict Was Finally Settled: From Nerchinsk 1689 to Vladivostok 2005 via Zhenbao Island 1969." *Critical Asian Studies* 39, no. 2 (2007): 229–53.

McDowall, David. "The Kurdish Question: A Historical Review." Pp. 10–32 in *The Kurds: A Contemporary Overview,* edited by Philip Kreyenbroek and Stephan Sperl. New York: Routledge, 1992.

———. *A Modern History of the Kurds.* New York: I. B. Tauris, 2000.

McHugo, J. "Resolution 242: A Legal Reappraisal of the Right Wing Israeli Interpretation of the Withdrawal Phrase with Reference to the Conflict between Israel and the Palestinians." *ICLQ* 51 (2002): 851–82.

Meliá, Bartomeu. *El Guaraní—Conquistado y Reducido: Ensayos de Etnohistoria.* Asunción: Centro de Estudios Antropológicos, Universidad Católica, 1986.

Menon, K. S. *The "Russian Bogey" and British Aggression in India and Beyond.* Calcutta: Eastern Trading Company, 1957.

Menon, Ritu, and Kamla Bhasin. *Borders and Boundaries: Women in India's Partition.* New Brunswick, N.J.: Rutgers University Press, 1998.

Megoran, Nick. "The Critical Geopolitics of the Uzbekistan-Kyrgyzstan Ferghana Valley Boundary Dispute, 1999–2000." *Political Geography* 23, no. 6 (2004): 731–64.

———. "For Ethnography in Political Geography: Experiencing and Re-imagining Ferghana Valley Boundary Closures." *Political Geography* 25, no. 6 (2006): 622–40.

Merritt, Richard L. "Noncontiguity and Political Integration." Pp. 237–72 in *Linkage Politics,* edited by James N. Rosenau. New York: Free Press, 1969.

Bibliography 249

Meyer, Karl E., and Shareen Blair Brysac. *Tournament of Shadows: The Great Game and the Race for Empire in Central Asia.* Washington, D.C.: Counterpoint, 1999.

Minghi, Julian V. *Some Aspects of the Impact of an International Boundary on Spatial Patterns: An Analysis of the Pacific Coast Lowland Region of the Canada-United States Boundary.* Seattle: PhD dissertation, University of Washington, 1962.

———. "Point Roberts, Washington—The Problem of an American Exclave." *Association of Pacific Coast Geographers Yearbook* 24 (1962): 29–34.

———. "Boundary Studies in Political Geography." *Annals of the Association of American Geographers* 53, no. 3 (1963): 407–28.

———. "The Evolution of a Border Region: The Pacific Coast Section of the Canada-United States Boundary." *Scottish Geographical Magazine* 80, no. 1 (1964): 37–52.

———. "Teaching Political Geography." *Journal of Geography* 65, no. 8 (1966): 362–70.

———. "Point Roberts." Pp. 49–50 in *Geography in an Urban Age*, Political Geography, Student Materials, edited by Association of American Geographers. New York: Macmillan, 1970.

———. "Point Roberts." Pp. 47–63 in *Geography in an Urban Age*, Political Geography, Teacher's Guide, edited by Association of American Geographers. New York: Macmillan, 1970.

Minghi, Julian V., and Dennis Rumley. "Integration and Systems Stress in an International Enclave Community: Point Roberts, Washington." Pp. 213–28 in *Peoples of the Living Land: Geography of Cultural Diversity in British Columbia*, edited by Julian V. Minghi. Vancouver: Tantalus Research, 1972.

Misiunas, Romuald J. "Rootless Russia: Kaliningrad—Status and Identity." *Diplomacy and Statecraft* 15, no. 2 (2004): 385–411.

Mitchell, Stephen. *A History of the Later Roman Empire.* Malden, Mass.: Blackwell, 2007.

Moisio, Sami. "Redrawing the Map of Europe: Spatial Formation of the EU's Eastern Dimension." *Geography Compass* 1, no. 1 (2007): 82–102.

Mommsen, Hans. *The Rise and Fall of Weimar Democracy.* Chapel Hill: University of North Carolina Press, 1996.

Morgan, Delmar. "Progress of Russian Explorations in Turkistan." *Proceedings of the Royal Geographical Society of London* 14, no. 3 (1870): 229–35.

Morgan, Gerald. *Anglo-Russian Rivalry in Central Asia: 1810–1895.* London: Frank Cass, 1981.

Morris, B. *The Birth of the Palestinian Refugee Problem, 1947–1949.* Cambridge: Cambridge University Press, 1989.

———. *Israel's Border Wars 1949–1956: Arab Infiltration, Israeli Retaliation, and the Countdown to the Suez War.* Oxford: Clarendon Press, 1993.

———. *The Birth of the Palestinian Refugee Problem Revisited.* Cambridge: Cambridge University Press, 2004.

"Moving toward Herat." *New York Times*, 14 April 1885, 1.

Murphy, Alexander. "The Sovereign State System as Political-Territorial Ideal: Historical and Contemporary Considerations." Pp. 81–120 in *State Sovereignty as*

Social Construct, edited by T. J. Biersteker and C. Weber. Cambridge: Cambridge University Press, 1996.

"Narkobiznes—terrorning moliyaviy rahnamosi." *Halq So'zi* 190, no. 2228, 24 September 1999, 1.

Natali, Denise. *The Kurds and the State: Evolving National Identity in Iraq, Turkey, and Iran*. Syracuse, N.Y.: Syracuse University Press, 2005.

National Geographic Atlas of the Middle East. Washington, D.C.: National Geographic Society, 2003.

Newman, David. "The Role of Civilian and Military Presence as Strategies of Territorial Control: The Arab-Israel Conflict." *Political Geography Quarterly* 8, no. 3 (1989): 215–27.

———. "The Functional Presence of an 'Erased' Boundary: The Re-emergence of the "Green Line."'" Pp. 71–98 in *World Boundaries: The Middle East and North Africa*, edited by C. H. Schofield and R. N. Schofield. London: Routledge, 1993.

———. *Boundaries in Flux: The Green Line Boundary between Israel and the West Bank—Past, Present and Future.* Monograph Series, *Boundary and Territory Briefings*, no. 7, International Boundaries Research Unit. Durham, U.K.: University of Durham, 1995.

———. "Borders and Bordering: Towards an Interdisciplinary Dialogue." *European Journal of Social Theory* 9, no. 2 (1996): 171–86.

———. "The Territorial Politics of Exurbanisation: Reflections on Thirty Years of Jewish Settlement in the West Bank." *Israel Affairs* 3, no. 1 (1996): 61–85.

———. "Creating the Fences of Territorial Separation: The Discourse of Israeli-Palestinian Conflict Resolution." *Geopolitics and International Boundaries* 2, no. 2 (1998): 1–35.

———. "The Geopolitics of Peacemaking in Israel-Palestine." *Political Geography* 21, no. 5 (2002): 629–46.

———. "Boundaries." Pp. 123–37 in *A Companion to Political Geography*, edited by John Agnew, Katharyne Mitchell, and Gerard Toal. Oxford: Blackwell, 2003.

———. "From 'hitnachalut' to 'hitnatkut': The Impact of Gush Emunim and the Settlement Movement on Israeli Society." *Israel Studies* 10, no. 3 (2005): 192–224.

———. "Colonization as Suburbanization: The Politics of the Land Market at the Frontier." Pp. 113–20 in *City of Collision*, edited by P. Misselwitz et al. Basel, Switzerland: Birkhäuser Publishers, 2006.

———. "The Lines That Continue to Separate Us: Borders in our 'Borderless' World." *Progress in Human Geography* 30, no. 2 (2006): 143–61.

———. "A Green Line in the Sand." *New York Times*, 9 January 2007, 17.

Newman, David, and Anssi Paasi. "Fences and Neighbours in the Postmodern World: Boundary Narratives in Political Geography." *Progress in Human Geography* 22, no. 2 (1998): 186–207.

Newman, E. W. Polson. *Britain and the Baltic.* London: Methuen, 1930.

Newton, Ronald C. *The "Nazi Menace" in Argentina, 1931–1947.* Stanford, Calif.: Stanford University Press, 1992.

Nisan, Mordechai. *Minorities in the Middle East: A History of Struggle and Self Expression.* Jefferson, N.C.: McFarland & Company, 1991.

Northrop, Douglas. *Veiled Empire: Gender and Power in Stalinist Central Asia.* New York: Cornell University Press, 2004.

Ó Tuathail, Gearóid. *Critical Geopolitics: The Politics of Writing Global Space.* London: Routledge, 1996.

———. "Borderless Worlds? Problematising Discourses of Deterritorialisation." *Geopolitics* 4, no. 2 (1999): 139–54.

O'Brien, Richard. *Global Financial Integration: The End of Geography.* New York: Council of Foreign Relations Press, 1992.

O'Brien, Timothy L. "South American Area Is Cited as Haven of Terrorist Training." *New York Times,* 10 October 2003, A28.

O'Leary, Carole. "The Kurds of Iraq: Recent History, Future Prospects." *Middle East Review of International Affairs* 6, no. 4 (2002): 17–29.

O'Shea, Maria. "Between the Map and the Reality: Some Fundamental Myths of Kurdish Nationalism." *Peuples Mediterraneens* no. 68–69 (1994): 165–83.

———. *Trapped between the Map and Reality.* New York: Routledge, 2004.

Ohmae, Kenichi. *The Borderless World: Power and Strategy in the Interlinked Economy.* New York: HarperBusiness, 1990.

———. *The End of the Nation State: The Rise of the Regional Economies.* New York: Free Press, 1995.

Olcott, Martha Brill. "Ceremony and Substance: The Illusion of Unity in Central Asia." Pp. 17–46 in *Central Asia and the World: Kazakhstan, Uzbekistan, Tajikistan, Kyrgyzstan, and Turkmenistan,* edited by Michael Mandelbaum. New York: Council on Foreign Relations, 1994.

Oliver, Mark, and agencies. "Liechtenstein: No Retaliation for Swiss 'Invasion.'" *Guardian,* 2 March 2007, http://www.guardian.co.uk/world/2007/mar/02/markoliver (11 March 2008).

Olson, Robert. *The Emergence of Kurdish Nationalism and the Sheikh Said Rebellion, 1880–1925.* Austin, Tex.: University of Texas Press, 1989.

Olson, Robert, ed. *The Kurdish National Movement in the 1990s: Its Impact on Turkey and the Middle East.* Lexington: The University Press of Kentucky, 1996.

Osborn, Andrew. "Russia Opens Sea Route to Kaliningrad to Break 'Blockade.'" *The Independent,* 12 September 2006, 19.

Özoglu, Hakan. "'Nationalism' and Kurdish Notables in the Late Ottoman Republican Era." *International Journal of Middle East Studies* 33, no. 3 (2001): 383–409.

———. *Kurdish Notables and the Ottoman State: Evolving Identities, Competing Loyalties, and Shifting Boundaries.* Albany: State University of New York, 2004.

Paasi, Anssi. "Boundaries as Social Processes: Territoriality in the World of Flows." *Geopolitics* 3, no. 1 (1998): 69–88.

———. "Boundaries as Social Processes: Territoriality in the World of Flows." Pp. 69–88 in *Boundaries, Territory and Postmodernity,* edited by David Newman. London: Frank Cass, 1999.

Palestinian Environmental NGOs Network (PENGON). *The Wall in Palestine.* Jerusalem, 2003.

Pasha, Sherif. "Memorandum on the Claims of the Kurdish People, Paris, March 22, 1919." *International Journal of Kurdish Studies* 15, no. 1–2 (2001): 131–36.

Perdue, Peter C. "Where Do Incorrect Political Ideas Come From? Writing the History of the Qing Empire and the Chinese Nation." Pp. 174–99 in *The Teleology of the Modern Nation-State: Japan and China*, edited by Joshua A. Fogel. Philadelphia: University of Pennsylvania Press, 2005.

Peters, Ralph. "Blood Borders: How a Better Middle East Would Look." *Armed Forces Journal* (2006): 1–3.

Pettus, Drew D. "The Problem of Administering Point Roberts, Washington." Study presented to Lloyd Meeds, Congressman for the Second Congressional District, Washington, D.C., 31 December 1969.

Peyret, Alejo. *Cartas Sobre Misiones.* Buenos Aires: Imprenta de la Tribuna Nacional, 1881.

Pfanner, Eric, and Mark Landler. "Tax Inquiry? Principality Is Offended." *New York Times*, 20 February 2008, http://www.nytimes.com/2008/02/20/business/worldbusiness20 evasion.html?ex=1361163600&en=0e347c04aa77d059&ei=5088&partner=rssnyt &emc=rss (11 March 2008).

Pohl, Walter, Ian Wood, and Helmut Reimitz, eds. *The Transformation of Frontiers from Late Antiquity to the Carolingians.* Boston: Brill, 2001.

Polat, Necati. *Boundary Issues in Central Asia.* Ardsley, N.Y.: Transnational Publishers, 2002.

"A Poll Meaningless For Some Indians." *Statesman*, 1 October 1999, A1.

Portugali, J. "Nomad Labour: Theory and Practice in the Israeli-Palestinian Case." *Transactions of the Institute of British Geographers* 14, no. 2 (1989): 207–20.

Pounds, Norman J. G. "The Origins of the Idea of Natural Frontiers in France." *Annals of the Association of American Geographers* 41, no. 2 (1951): 146–57.

———. "France and 'Les Limites Naturelles' from the Seventeenth to the Twentieth Centuries." *Annals of the Association of American Geographers* 44, no. 1 (1954): 51–62.

———. "A Free and Secure Access to the Sea." *Annals of the Association of American Geographers* 49, no. 3 (1959): 256–68.

———. *Political Geography.* New York: McGraw-Hill, 1963.

Prescott, J. R. V. *The Geography of Frontiers and Boundaries.* London: Hutchinson University Library, 1965.

Proeller, A. *The Polish Corridor, East Prussia and the Peace.* London: Williams and Norgate, 1929.

Programa Misiones Jesuiticas. "Misiones Jesuitico Guaranies." n.d.

Prozorov, Sergei. "The Narratives of Exclusion and Self-Exclusion in the Russian Conflict Discourse on EU-Russian Relations." *Political Geography* 26, no. 3 (2007): 309–29.

Radcliffe, Sarah A. "Frontiers and Popular Nationhood: Geographies of Identity in the 1995 Ecuador-Peru Border Dispute." *Political Geography* 17, no. 3 (1998): 273–93.

Raton, Pierre. *Liechtenstein: History and Institutions of the Principality.* Vaduz: Liechtenstein-Verlag, 1970.

Reboratti, Carlos. "Migraciones y Frontera Agraria: Argentina y Brasil en la Cuenca del Alto Paraná-Uruguay." *Desarrollo Económico* 19, no. 74 (1979): 189–209.

———. "El Encanto de la Oscuridad. Notas Acerca de la Geopolítica en la Argentina." *Desarrollo Económico* 23, no. 89 (1983): 137–44.

Redford, Kent H. "The Ecologically Noble Savage." *Cultural Survival Quarterly* 15, no. 1 (1991): 46–48.

Ree, Jonathan. "Internationality." *Radical Philosophy* 60 (1992): 1–13.

Reeves, Madeleine. "Travels in the Margins of the State: Everyday Geography in the Ferghana Valley Borderlands." Pp. 281–300 in *Everyday Life in Central Asia: Past and Present,* edited by Jeff Sahadeo and Russell Zanca. Bloomington: Indiana University Press, 2007.

Reichman, Shalom. "Policy Reduces the World to Essentials: A Reflection on the Jewish Settlement Process in the West Bank since 1967." Pp 83–96 in *Planning in Turbulence,* edited by D. Morley and A. Shachar. Jerusalem: Magnes Press, 1987.

Roberts, J. Timmons, and Nikki Demetria Thanos. *Trouble in Paradise: Globalization and Environmental Crises in Latin America.* New York: Routledge, 2003.

Robinson, G. W. S. "Exclaves." *Annals of the Association of American Geographers* 49, no. 3 (1959): 283–95.

Rodenbough, Theo F. *Afghanistan and the Anglo-Russian Dispute.* New York: G. P. Putnam's Sons, 1885.

Rohter, Larry. "Terrorists Are Sought in Latin Smugglers' Haven." *New York Times,* 27 September 2001, A3.

Rowe, William C. *On the Edge of Empires: The Hisor Valley of Tajikistan.* Austin: PhD dissertation, University of Texas at Austin, 2002.

Roy, Olivier. "Is the Conflict in Tajikistan a Model for Conflicts throughout Central Asia?" Pp. 132–47 in *Tajikistan: The Trials of Independence,* edited by Mohammad-Reza Djalili, Frédéric Grare, and Shirin Akiner. New York: St. Martin's Press, 1997.

Sack, Robert. *Human Territoriality: Its Theory and History.* Cambridge: Cambridge University Press, 1986.

Sahlins, Peter. *Boundaries: The Making of France and Spain in the Pyrenees.* Berkeley: University of California Press, 1989.

———. "Natural Frontiers Revisited: France's Boundaries Since the Seventeenth Century." *American Historical Review* 95, no. 5 (1990): 1423–52.

Sarkar, D. "Indian Chitmahals Are a Haven for Terrorists." *Times of India,* 16 January 2001, A1.

Sassen, Saskia. *Globalization and Its Discontents.* New York: New Press, 1998.

"Saving a Banking Boom from Berlin." *Time,* 28 February 2008, http://www.time.com/time/world/article/0,8599.1717950,00.html (11 March 2008).

Sawyer, Suzana. *Crude Chronicles: Indigenous Politics, Multinational Oil, and Neoliberalism in Ecuador.* Durham, N.C.: Duke University Press, 2004.

Schama, Simon. *A History of Britain: At the Edge of the World? 3000 BC–AD 1603.* New York: Hyperion, 2000.

Schechtman, Joseph B. *Post War Population Transfers in Europe.* Philadelphia: University of Pennsylvania Press, 1962.

Schiavoni, Lidia. *Pesadas Cargas, Frágiles Pasos: Transacciones Comerciales En Un Mercado De Frontera.* Asunción: CPES, 1993.

Schmidt, Alex. *The Preposterous Corridor: Polish Testimony against Germany's Mutilation.* Berlin: Edwin Runge, 1933.

Schmidt, Donatella. "Do You Have an Opy? Politics and Identity among the Mbya-Guarani of Argentina and Eastern Paraguay." Bloomington: PhD dissertation, Indiana University, 1991.

Schofield, Olive, and Gerald Blake, eds. *The Razor's Edge: International Boundaries and Political Geography.* New York: Kluver Law International, 2002.

Seed, Patricia. *Ceremonies of Possession in Europe's Conquest of the New World, 1492–1640.* New York: Cambridge University Press, 1995.

Seger, Otto. *A Survey of Liechtenstein History.* Vaduz: Press and Information Office of the Principality of Liechtenstein, 1984.

Semyonov, M., and N. Lewin-Epstein. *Hewers of Wood and Drawers of Water: Noncitizen Arabs in the Israeli Labor Market.* Ithaca, N.Y.: Cornell University Press, 1987.

Sengupta, Nitish. *History of the Bengali Speaking People.* New Delhi: UBS Publishers, 2001.

Sever, Adrian. *Documents and Speeches on the Indian Princely States.* Delhi: B. R. Publishing, 1985.

Shahrani, M. Nazif. *The Kirghiz and Wakhi of Afghanistan: Adaptation to Closed Frontiers and War.* Seattle: University of Washington Press, 1979.

———. "Afghanistan's Kirghiz in Turkey." *Cultural Survival Quarterly* 8, no. 1 (1984): 31–34.

Sharp, Tony. "The Russian Annexation of the Königsberg Area 1941–1945." *Survey* 23, no. 4 (1977–78): 156–62.

Shor, Jean, and Franc Shor. "Argentina: Young Giant of the Far South." *National Geographic* 113, no. 3 (1958): 297–352.

Shumway, Nicolas. *The Invention of Argentina.* Berkeley: University of California Press, 1991.

Skrine, Francis Henry, and Edward Denison Ross. *The Heart of Asia.* New York: Arno Press, 1973.

Slater, Candace. *Entangled Edens: Visions of the Amazon.* Berkeley: University of California Press, 2002.

Slawski, Stanislaw. *Poland's Access to the Sea and the Claims of East Prussia.* London: Eyre and Spottiswoode, 1925.

Smith, Anthony. *Nationalism in the Twentieth Century.* Oxford: Martin Robertson, 1979.

Smith, Graham. "The Soviet State and Nationalities Policy." Pp. 2–22 in *The Nationalities Question in the Post-Soviet States,* edited by Graham Smith. London: Longman, 1996.

Smith, Robert C. *Mexican New York: Transnational Lives of New Immigrants.* Berkeley: University of California Press, 2006.

Smogorzewski, Casimir. *Poland, Germany and the Corridor.* London: Williams & Norgate, 1930.

———. *East Prussia Must Disappear.* London: Free Europe, 1944.

Soucek, Svat. *A History of Inner Asia*. Cambridge: Cambridge University Press, 2000.

Sparrow, Glen. "San Diego-Tijuana: Not Quite a Binational City or Region." *GeoJournal* 54, no. 1 (2001): 73–83.

Spencer, Philip, and Howard Wollman. *Nationalism: A Critical Introduction*. London: Sage, 2002.

Srokowski, Stanisław. *East Prussia*. Toruń, Poland: Baltic Institute, 1934.

Stalin, Joseph. "The Nation." Pp. 18–21 in *Nationalism*, edited by John Hutchinson and Anthony Smith. Oxford: Oxford University Press, 1994.

Stamm, Peter. "Swiss Miss." *New York Times*, 10 March 2007, http://www.nytimes .com/2007/03/10/opinion/10stamm.html (11 March 2008).

Stanley, William R. "Russia's Kaliningrad." *The Pennsylvania Geographer* 39, no. 1 (2001): 18–37.

Stein, M. Aurel. *Ruins of Desert Cathay: Personal Narrative of Explorations in Central Asia and Westernmost China*. London: Macmillan and Co., 1912.

———. "Innermost Asia: Its Geography as a Factor of History." *Geographical Journal* 65, no. 5 (1925): 377–402.

———. *Innermost Asia: Detailed Report of Explorations in Central Asia, Kan-su and Eastern Iran*. Oxford: Clarendon Press, 1928.

Stone, Shepard. "German-Polish Disputes: Danzig, the Polish Corridor and East Prussia." *Foreign Policy Reports* 9, no. 9 (1933): 94–104.

Strasburger, Henry. *German Designs on Pomerania: An Analysis of Germany's Revisionistic Policy*. Toruń, Poland: Baltic Institute, 1933.

Stumm, Hugo. *Russia in Central Asia: Historical Sketch of Russia's Progress in the East up to 1873, and of the Incidents Which Led to the Campaign against Khiva*. London: Harrison and Sons, 1885.

Swyngedouw, Erik. "Neither Global nor Local: 'Glocalization' and the Politics of Scale." Pp. 137–66 in *Spaces of Globalization: Reasserting the Power of the Local*, edited by Kevin R. Cox. New York: Guilford, 1997.

Sykes, Mark. "The Kurdish Tribes of the Ottoman Empire." *Journal of the Royal Anthropological Institute of Great Britain and Ireland* 38 (1908): 451–86.

Sykes, Percy. *A History of Afghanistan, Volume II*. London: Macmillan & Co., 1940.

Tadjbakhsh, Shahrbanou. "Causes and Consequences of the Civil War." *Central Asia Monitor* no. 1 (1993): 10–14.

Tan, T. Y., and Gayendra Kudaisya. *The Aftermath of Partition in South Asia*. New York: Routledge, 2000.

Taylor, Peter. "The State as Container: Territoriality in the Modern World-System." *Progress in Human Geography* 18, no. 2 (1994): 151–62.

Tétreault, Mary Ann. "International Relations." Pp. 131–68 in *Understanding the Contemporary Middle East*, edited by Deborah J. Gerner and Jillian Schwedler. Boulder, Colo.: Lynne Reinner Publishers, 2004.

Thelan, David. "Rethinking History and the Nation-State: Mexico and the United States." *Journal of American History* 86, no. 2 (1999): 439–52.

Thomson, H. C. *The Chitral Campaign: A Narrative of Events in Chitral, Swat, and Bajour.* London: William Heinemann, 1895.

Thöni, Julien. *The Tajik Conflict: The Dialectic between Internal Fragmentation and External Vulnerability, 1991–1994.* Geneva: Programme for Strategic and International Security Studies, Occasional Paper No. 3, 1994.

Tilley, Virginia. *Seeing Indians: A Study of Race, Nation, and Power in El Salvador.* Albuquerque: University of New Mexico Press, 2005.

Todd, Malcolm. *The Early Germans.* Malden, Mass.: Blackwell, 2004.

Vali, Abbas. "The Kurds and their 'Others': Fragmented Identity and Fragmented Politics." *Comparative Studies of South Asia, Africa and the Middle East* 18, no. 2 (1998): 82–95.

Vambéry, Arminius. *The Coming Struggle for India: Being an Account of the Encroachments of Russia in Central Asia, and of the Difficulties Sure to Arise Therefrom to England.* London: Cassell & Company, 1885.

Van Bruinessen, Martin. *Agha, Shaikh, and State: The Social and Political Structures of Kurdistan.* London: Zed Books, 1992.

Van Cott, Donna Lee. "Latin America: Constitutional Reform and Ethnic Right." *Parliamentary Affairs* 53, no. 1 (2000): 41–54.

van Houtum, Henk, and Ton van Naerssen. "Bordering, Ordering, and Othering." *Tijdschrift voor Economische en Sociale Geografie* 93, no. 2 (2002): 125–36.

van Houtum, Henk, Olivier Kramsch, and Wolfgang Zierhofer, eds. *B/ordering Space.* Aldershot, U.K.: Ashgate, 2005.

Van Schendel, Willem. "Stateless in South Asia: The Making of the India-Bangladesh Enclaves." *Journal of Asian Studies* 61, no. 1 (2002): 115–47.

———. *The Bengal Borderlands: Beyond State and Nation in South Asia.* London: Anthem Press, 2005.

Verrier, Anthony. *Francis Younghusband and the Great Game.* London: Jonathan Cape, 1991.

Vesilind, Priit. "Kaliningrad: Coping with a German Past and a Russian Future." *National Geographic* 191, no. 3 (1997): 110–23.

Vinokurov, Evgeny. *The Theory of Exclaves.* Lanham, Md.: Lexington Books, 2007.

von Borcke, Astrid. *Der tadschikische Bürgerkrieg: Lokale Tragödie oder geopolitische Herausforderung?* Köln: Bundesinstitut für ostwissenschaftliche und internatonale Studien, 1995.

Vyas, Ram Prasad. *British Policy towards Princely States of India.* Jodhpur: Twenty-First Century Publishers, 1990.

Wakhan Development Project. "Wakhan District." 2002, http://www.wakhandev.org .uk/ (23 February 2008).

Waller, Douglas. "A Terror Threat from the South." *Time,* 10 December 2001, 25.

Weidlich, Bridget. "Caprivi Strip Proclaimed Park." *The Namibian* (Windhoek), 23 November 2007, http://allafrica.com/stories/printable/200711230655.html (11 March 2008).

Weizman, E. *Hollow Land: Israel's Architecture of Occupation.* London: Verso Publishers, 2007.

Wellman, Christian. "Recognising Borders: Coping with Historically Contested Territory." Pp. 273–96 in *The Kaliningrad Challenge*, edited by Hanne-Margret Birckenbach and Christian Wellmann. Münster, Germany: Lit Verlag, 2003.

Wells, H. G. *The Shape of Things to Come: The Ultimate Revolution*. London: Hutchinson, 1933.

Whatcom County Planning Commission. *The Plight of Point Roberts: A Brief to the Area Redevelopment Administration*. Bellingham, Wash.: 1965.

Wheeler, Geoffrey. *The Modern History of Soviet Central Asia*. New York: Praeger, 1964.

White, George. *Nation, State, and Territory: Origins, Evolutions, and Relationships*, Vol. I. Lanham, Md.: Rowman & Littlefield, 2004.

Whittaker, Christopher. *Frontiers of the Roman Empire: A Social and Economic Study*. Baltimore: John Hopkins University Press, 1994.

Whyte, Brendan. *Waiting for the Esquimo: An Historical and Documentary Study of the Cooch Behar Enclaves of India and Bangladesh*. Melbourne: University of Melbourne, 2002.

Williams, Derek. *The Reach of Rome: A History of the Roman Imperial Frontier 1st–5th Centuries AD*. New York: St. Martin's Press, 1997.

Williams, Mary Wilhelmine. "The Treaty of Tordesillas and the Argentine-Brazilian Boundary Settlement." *Hispanic American Historical Review* 5, no. 1 (1922): 3–23.

Wilson, Thomas, and Hastings Donnan, eds. *Border Identities: Nation and State at International Frontiers*. Cambridge: Cambridge University Press, 1998.

Wilson, Woodrow. "Address to a Joint Session of Congress on the Conditions of Peace, January 8th, 1918." *The American Presidency Project*, http://www.presidency.ucsb.edu/ws/index.php?pid=65405 (1 June 2007).

Winichakul, Thongchai. *Siam Mapped: A History of the Geo-Body of a Nation*. Honolulu: University of Hawai'i Press, 1994.

Wood, John. *A Journey to the Source of the River Oxus*. London: John Murray, 1872.

World Bank. "GNI per Capita 2006, Atlas Method and PPP," http://siteresources.worldbank.org/DATASTATISTICS/Resources/GNIPC.pdf (11 March 2008).

Yapp, M. E. *Strategies of British India: Britain, Iran and Afghanistan 1798–1850*. Oxford: Clarendon Press, 1980.

Younghusband, Francis E. *The Heart of a Continent: A Narrative of Travels in Manchuria, across the Gobi Desert, through the Himalayas, the Pamirs, and Chitral, 1884–1894*. London: John Murray, 1896.

———. *The Northern Frontier of Kashmir*. Delhi: Oriental Publishers, 1973 [1890].

Zeballos, Estanislao S. *Argument for the Argentine Republic upon the Question with Brazil in Regard to the Territory of Misiones*. Washington, D.C.: Gibson Bros., 1894.

Zehn Thesen ueber Pommerellen. Toruń, Poland: Baltic Institute, 1933.

Zelle, Arnold. *50 Korridorthesen: Abrechnung mit Polen*. Berlin: Volk und Reich, 1939.

Zertal, I., and A. Eldar. *Lords of the Land: The War over Israel's Settlements in the Occupied Territories, 1967–2007*. New York: Nation Books, 2007.

Zimonian, Haig. "Liechtenstein Offers to Push Bank Reform." *Financial Times*, 5 March 2008, http://www.ft.com/cms/s/0/c52b3b8c-ea3d-11dc-b3c9-0000779fd2ac .html (11 March 2008).

Zverev, Yury. "Kaliningrad: Problems and Paths of Development." *Problems of Post Communism* 54, no. 2 (2007): 9–25.

Index

About the Contributors

Eric D. Carter is an assistant professor at Grinnell College (Iowa), where he teaches courses in geography, anthropology, and global development studies. His research interests include disease ecology; development in peripheral regions of modernizing states; and the nexus of state-sponsored science, regional development, and nationalist discourse, mainly in Latin America. He has published research on the historical geography of malaria control in Argentina in such journals as *Geoforum*, the *Journal of Historical Geography*, and the *Journal of the History of Medicine*.

Karen Culcasi is Assistant Professor of Geography in the Department of Geology and Geography at West Virginia University. Employing a critical geopolitical lens, Karen's research examines both Western and Arab geographical imaginings of the Middle East. Her recent publications include articles in *Political Geography*, *Aether: The Journal of Media Geography*, and several entries in volume six of the *History of Cartography*.

Alexander C. Diener is Associate Professor of Geography at Pepperdine University. He is the author of *One Homeland or Two?: Nationalization and Transnationalization of Mongolia's Kazakhs* (2009) and *Homeland Conceptions and Ethnic Integration among Kazakhstan's Germans and Koreans* (2004). His research and teaching interests include borders, migration, nationalism, transnationalism, and the moral consequences of territorialization. His area studies specialty is Central Eurasia and Mongolia.

Joshua Hagen is Associate Professor of Geography at Marshall University. In addition to international borders and border theory, he has broad research interests spanning architecture, urban design, and political authority; cultural politics of place names; geographies of tourism and heritage; geographies of national identity and territoriality; and historic preservation and places of memory. His research has been published in several prominent academic journals, including the *Annals of the Association of American Geographers, Political Geography, Cultural Geographies, Journal of Historical Geography,* and *Journal of Urban History.*

Reece Jones is Assistant Professor of Geography at the University of Hawai'i at Mñoa. His research investigates the political geography of globalization, particularly as it relates to political borders and the boundaries of group identity categories. He has most recently published articles in the journals *Progress in Human Geography* and *Transactions of the Institute of British Geographers.*

Robert Lloyd is Associate Professor of International Relations at Pepperdine University and directs its International Studies program. He has published numerous scholarly articles on international conflict management and negotiation, democratization, and Africa. Recent publications include several edited volume chapters and an article in *Current History: A Journal of Contemporary World Affairs.* Prior to Pepperdine, he worked for five years in Kenya, South Africa, and Mozambique with a nongovernmental organization. Dr. Lloyd has been an election observer in Mozambique, Liberia, and Nigeria.

Nick Megoran is a Lecturer in Political Geography at Newcastle University, School of Geography, Politics, and Sociology. His research interests relate to political geography of Central Asia; the legacy of Halford Mackinder; and Christianity and US/UK foreign policy. He has published in a number of prominent journals, including *Environment and Planning D: Society and Space, Political Geography, Antipode,* and *Geopolitics.* He is also the author of *The War on Terror: How Should Christians Respond?* (2007).

Julian V. Minghi is Distinguished Professor Emeritus in Geography at the University of South Carolina. His major research interests are in political geography with a special emphasis on boundaries and borderlands. He was awarded a Canada Council research grant (1969–1970), held a research grant from the National Geographic Society (1980), and was a senior Fulbright research scholar (1993–1994). Books include (with Roger Kasperson) *The Structure of Political Geography* (1969) and several others, including *The Geography of Border Landscapes* (with Dennis Rumley) in 1991. He has also contributed more than sixty chapters in edited books and articles in scholarly journals on a wide variety of topics, but with emphasis on borderland problems in Europe and North America over the past five decades.

David Newman is Professor of Political Geography and Geopolitics at Ben Gurion University in Israel. He is currently the co-editor of the quarterly journal *Geopolitics*. His research interests focus on the territorial dimensions of ethnic conflict and the conceptualization of borders in the contemporary world, with an empirical focus on the Israel-Palestine arena. He is also interested in issues relating to politics and science. His recent publications on borders include articles in the *European Journal of Social Theory, Progress in Human Geography,* and a chapter in *Ashgate's Research Companion to Border Studies.*

Robert Ostergren is Professor of Geography at the University of Wisconsin, Madison. He is co-author of *The Europeans: A Geography of People, Environment and Culture,* and does research on place identity, regionalism, migration, and iconic landscapes and architecture in Europe, particularly in Scandinavia and Germany. His current project explores the political uses of place and architecture during the National Socialist period in Germany. He is also known for his work on nineteenth-century European immigration to and settlement in North America, which includes the award-winning book, *A Community Transplanted: The Trans-Atlantic Experience of a Swedish Immigrant Community in the Upper Middle West, 1835–1915,* as well as the edited volume *Wisconsin German Land and Life.*

William C. Rowe is Assistant Professor of Geography at Louisiana State University. He has contributed essays to *World Regional Geography: A Development Approach* (2010) and *Geographies of Muslim Identities: Diaspora, Gender and Belonging* (2007). His research and teaching interests include cultural/political ecology, geography of religion, and economic geography. His area studies specialty is the Persian- and Arabic-speaking areas of Central Asia, the Middle East, and North Africa.